The Family and Public Policy

Frank F. Furstenberg, Jr., and Andrew J. Cherlin
General Editors

Valuing Children

RETHINKING THE ECONOMICS OF THE FAMILY

NANCY FOLBRE

HARVARD UNIVERSITY PRESS

Cambridge, Massachusetts, and London, England   2008

Library of Congress Cataloging-in-Publication Data

Folbre, Nancy.
Valuing children : rethinking the economics of the family / Nancy Folbre.
p. cm.—(The family and public policy)
Includes bibliographical references and index.
ISBN-13: 978-0-674-02632-2 (alk. paper)
ISBN-10: 0-674-02632-2 (alk. paper)
1. Family—Economic aspects—United States.   2. Child rearing—Economic
aspects—United States.   3. Households—Economic aspects—United States.
4. Family allowances—United States.   I. Title.

HQ536.F65   2008
306.850973—dc22   2007018581

Contents

Acknowledgments

This book survived a long childhood and difficult adolescence thanks to support from a large community of students, friends, and colleagues. Tamara Ohler and Jayoung Yoon both coauthored chapters and helped shape the book as a whole. Jonathan Teller-Elsberg, Pamela Davidson, and Kade Finoff provided invaluable research assistance. The MacArthur Foundation Research Network on the Family and the Economy provided generous financial and intellectual resources.

Over the course of six years, my cochair, Robert Pollak, as well as members of the MacArthur network—Jeanne Brooks-Gunn, Lindsay Chase-Lansdale, Cecilia Conrad, Greg Duncan, Paula England, Irv Garfinkel, Shelly Lundberg, Sara McLanahan, Ronald Mincy, Timothy Smeeding, and Robert Willis—developed my capabilities and expanded my horizons. They responded to early versions of the arguments developed here with a patient and intelligent skepticism that often inspired me to reconsider and revise. In addition to helping the network run smoothly, Joanne Spitz provided detailed editorial feedback on several chapters.

Paula England, my coauthor on many related projects, helped conceive this book and constantly urged it forward. Julie Nelson played a kindred role, pushing me to think harder about the nexus between love and money. Other members of the International Association for Feminist Economics worked fearlessly and effectively to create a network of support for new approaches to the study of gender and family. Students in my graduate seminar, Political Economy of Race and Gender, helped me grapple with complicated and often disparate ideas.

Several visits at the Research School of Social Sciences at Australian National University as a visiting fellow and, later, adjunct faculty member allowed me to take advantage of great minds on another continent. Michael Bittman taught me to appreciate and analyze time-use data. Robert Goodin generously applied the many virtues of political philosophy and offered prompt and helpful comments on every version of the manuscript I dared to send him. Robert Haveman and Barbara Wolfe, frequent visitors to the Research School, gave me the benefit of their expertise. Discussions with Bruce Bradbury, Geoffrey Brennan, Jack Caldwell, Lyn Craig, and Peter McDonald gave me new perspectives on both theory and policy.

Two conferences organized in conjunction with Irv Garfinkel, Sara McLanahan, and Timothy Smeeding, one at Australian National University, the other at Princeton University, proved especially useful. My participation in a National Academy of Sciences panel on the valuation of nonmarket work yielded many indirect benefits, particularly specific exchanges with Katharine Abraham, Barbara Fraumeni, Dan Hamermesh, Chris Mackie, and Robert Michael. A visit to Notre Dame in March 2005 to give several public lectures helped me improve several chapters with useful feedback from David Betson, Jennifer Warlick, and Martin Wolfson. Mildred Warner encouraged me to present portions of two chapters at a conference on regional economics and child care that improved my understanding of macroeconomic issues. My collaboration with David Bollier, Jim Boyce, and Michael Conroy in the Forum on Social Wealth created many valuable spillovers that I have tried to capture here.

For help and encouragement in the final stages I am especially grateful to Andrew Cherlin, Frank Furstenberg, and three anonymous reviewers. Janet Gornick provided useful feedback on close-to-final versions of several chapters. Revisions were completed during a year as Visiting Fellow at the Russell Sage Foundation, an extraordinarily supportive environment. Caroline Carr provided both logistical assistance and comic relief. Ann Twombly applied eagle eyes and a sharp pencil in the final draft. Michael Aronson managed the editorial process with thoughtful and therapeutic grace. Thanks to all for adding value to the ideas developed here.

Valuing Children

Introduction

We produce things in order to care for ourselves and our families. We sometimes forget that the process of caring is also a process of production. Indeed, our language often implies that the purpose of raising and educating children is simply to produce more things. We "invest in human capital" to increase our gross domestic product. But the purpose of gross domestic product, after all, is to make lives better now and for generations to come. Children look ahead. They tug us away from our immediate self-interest toward a longer-run concern for the future of something bigger and more difficult to define.

Child rearing fits uncomfortably within our economic system. Parents provide services of great value directly to their children and indirectly to those who benefit from their children's future contributions. Yet parents receive little or no economic reward. Mothers tend to pay a higher price for children than fathers do. Partly as a result, they typically earn less than men and remain more vulnerable to poverty. Children do not choose their parents or their communities. Consequently, their freedom to choose other things, such as a good education, is limited. Equal opportunity for adults can often be satisfied by the lack of barriers, the absence of discrimination. Children require the full development of their capabilities to take advantage of the opportunities they will face as adults.

Most people don't think about children in economic terms. Their mental image of the economy features individuals pursuing their self-interest within a market, buying and selling commodities that carry an explicit price tag. Parenting sits outside that picture because it is an activity that people pursue for love rather than for money. But love for others can be just as powerful an economic motive as self-interest. And whatever its underlying motives, work that takes place outside the marketplace represents a very important part of our economy. The value of the money, time, and care that parents devote to children is substantial. And children are not the only ones who benefit. Children grow up to become the workers, caregivers, and taxpayers on whom our economy depends.

Economists have begun to devote more attention to the family. But progress in this area remains uneven and unsatisfactory. Mainstream microeconomics describes child rearing as a process of consumption aimed to maximize family happiness. For parents, apparently, virtue should be its own reward. National income accounts rely on measures of market income that exclude the value of nonmarket work. The resulting distortions in our yardstick of economic growth are widely acknowledged in theory but blithely disregarded in practice.

Economists who are worried about inequality focus primarily on wages, profits, and other sources of money income. They seldom note that responsibility for the care of dependents lowers the disposable income of parents. Virtually all empirical studies of income distribution that compare households of different demographic composition assume that young children can be provided for more cheaply than adults—an assumption that ignores the value of the time devoted to their care. Would any young mother agree that it is cheaper to live alone with an infant who requires constant care than with another adult?

People generally try to do what they think will make them happy. Beyond this truism, economic theory offers little by way of a theoretical framework for analyzing what we spend on children. Existing studies of age-targeted private and public expenditures in the contemporary United States offer a patchwork of disparate numbers. Some studies of family expenditures look at cash spending, whereas others look at hours of time. Some assign a dollar value to time based on the cost of buying replacements in the market, some according to the opportunity cost or wages forgone. Estimates of public support for child rearing often look only at means-tested transfers, ignoring the value of tax benefits. Budget studies typically offer measures of aggregate spending, but public spending on education and health services benefits some children far more than others.

This book develops a new way of thinking about spending on chil-

dren. It takes an institutional approach, arguing that individual decisions are constrained and coordinated by contractual arrangements that
channel the flow of resources between parents and children, men and
women, parents and nonparents. Capitalist economic development de-
stabilizes traditional patriarchal arrangements, and the combined forces
of technological, social, and demographic changes lead to increased
public spending on education and old-age security. Forms of distributional conflict based on class and race or ethnicity, as well as gender and
age, shape the allocation of resources to the young.

This book paints a broad picture of private and public transfers to
children in the United States at the beginning of the twenty-first century.
It shows how children affect adult standards of living, what parents
spend on average in both money and time, and what public programs
do and don't deliver. It emphasizes the need to develop new sources of
data and better accounting systems for monitoring expenditures on children. It also encourages efforts to envision a more equitable and efficient institutional framework for child rearing—a new and improved
social-family contract.

Why should we care about spending on children? How much money
and time do families devote to children? How much money do taxpayers spend on children? These three questions, which represent the focal
points of the three sections of this book, lead to a final question: who
should pay for the kids?

Why Should We Care about Spending on Children?

Is spending on children best characterized as an investment, an exchange, and obligation, a gift, or all of the above? Many economists describe child rearing as an investment: individuals choose to become parents because they believe that children, like pets or consumer durables,
will yield a flow of future happiness. Parental altruism is, paradoxically,
selfish, offering parents precious satisfaction. But the parental investment model, however apt, is incomplete. We expect parents to care for
children whether they are feeling happy about them or not. And unlike
pets and consumer durables, children cannot be freely bought and sold.

Children represent social as well as parental investments. In addition
to the happiness we hope they will provide their parents (and themselves), they provide benefits to their future fellow workers and taxpayers. The contributions they make to the economy can easily exceed the
cost of the resources devoted to raising them. Those who enjoy those

contributions are not necessarily those who paid the costs. Children may not be born with a price tag attached, but they impose very real costs on their caregivers. We can estimate these costs in much the same way that we value environmental services such as clean air or a stable climate: by asking what we would have to pay for a substitute for parental services if they were withdrawn.

Children are more than mere investments. None of us has a moral obligation to bring children into this world. But once they are here, we share certain obligations to them. The way we specify these obligations defines an implicit social-family contract, a set of rules, norms, and expectations about the opportunities children should have to develop their capabilities. This implicit social-family contract is seldom openly debated, but it is constantly under negotiation. Many disagreements about public policy can be boiled down to questions about who should pay for the kids—whose kids and how much and for how long. It might be easier to agree on good answers to these questions if we had a better picture of what is actually being spent.

Chapter 1 challenges the conventional textbook emphasis on the circular flow of market exchanges between households and markets, calling for more appreciation of the flow of nonmarket services that are not motivated by immediate self-interest. Child rearing involves transfers of resources within and among households and between households and the state. Individuals seldom have much control over these transfers, which are determined largely by institutional rules and social norms.

Yet individuals often choose to become parents. Even when births are unplanned, individuals have some power to choose their level of commitment to their children. Chapter 2 asks how we should conceptualize these choices. While acknowledging the contributions of Gary Becker and other proponents of the "new home economics," it challenges the assumption that families make rational, unanimous, and efficient choices regarding investments in children. Though parents try to do what they think is best, they often end up making imperfect choices that have uncertain outcomes. Their behavior is better described as a commitment than an investment—a commitment with intrinsic value that can, nonetheless, prove quite costly.

How Much Money and Time Do Parents Devote to Children?

If parents used perfect knowledge of the future to make perfect decisions regarding children, there would be little reason to study parental spending. But parents often have no idea how much money or time their children will require, and they can never be completely confident of each other's future contributions. These uncertainties are compounded by other dimensions of economic and political change. Who knows what child care, much less college, will cost a few years down the road? Increases in the costs and risks of rearing children have contributed to fertility decline and increases in childlessness in the United States, as well as most other affluent nations. Inequality among children remains high, and our success at educating the younger generation remains uneven. A closer look at family expenditures on children helps explain these trends.

Most estimates of the proportion of family budgets devoted to children focus on relative amounts of money spent on food and clothing for persons of different ages, ignoring the value of time devoted to children's care. But there are only twenty-four hours in a day. Time devoted to the care of children must be withdrawn from other activities, such as housework, paid work, sleep, and leisure.

Chapter 3 explains debates over children and standards of living, challenging the U.S. poverty line and other equivalence scales that assume that children cost relatively little. This assumption often creates the misleading impression that a family consisting of a mother and a young child is better off economically than a two-adult family with the same income. Chapter 4 reviews studies of parental expenditures on children under age eighteen provided by the U.S. Department of Agriculture, and it argues that they provide only a lower-bound, or minimum, estimate of what parents actually spend while their children are under eighteen. It looks in more detail at spending on child care, an increasingly important component of overall spending.

Chapter 5 brings spending on children outside the household into the picture. Since a large percentage of children in this country today live apart from at least one parent, rules of child custody, visitation, and support have significant effects on them. Spending on children who attend college has also grown, and many affluent parents leave their children and grandchildren with substantial bequests.

Chapter 6 moves beyond a consideration of cash expenditures to account for family time. A number of studies track the hours that parents and others devote to children, and analysis of time diaries collected by the Child Development Supplement of the Panel Survey of Income Dynamics (PSID-CDS) in 1997 provides additional detail. Chapter 7 explains how these inputs of family time can be assigned a monetary value on the basis of a specific counterfactual question: If parents were to withdraw their services, what would it cost society to provide replacement services with a similar ratio of adults to children? By this measure, the value of parental time far exceeds the value of cash expenditures on children.

How Much Money Do Taxpayers Spend on Children?

Family spending is supplemented by a complex array of public subsidies for parents and direct expenditures on children's education and health care. Chapter 8 details the relative contribution of social insurance and tax policies in 2000. Surprisingly, the overall level of tax subsidy through deductions and credits is comparable to the level of family allowances provided by many European countries. But the United States stands out internationally in its lack of public support for paid family leave from work. Furthermore, its parental subsidies treat some parents far less generously than others. "Nontraditional" families—those with single parents or with two parents both working long hours in paid employment—get the short end of the stick.

Chapter 9 focuses on public investments in children's health and education, placing these in the context of federal and state budgets. Here, too, significant inequalities are apparent. Though poor children benefit from transfers through means-tested programs such as Medicaid, affluent children often enjoy tax-subsidized health benefits via their parents' employers. Wealthy school districts typically have better schools than poor districts. Children from low-income families are less likely than their affluent counterparts to graduate from high school and go on to college. As a result, they seldom benefit from public subsidies for higher education. In short, public policies fall far short of the promise of equal opportunity.

Who Should Pay for the Kids?

Investments in children offer a high payoff to society as a whole. Increased public investments in early-childhood education and after-school and summer programs would offer especially important benefits to low-income families and their children. Family time is an important "input" into children, and child "outputs" cannot be reduced to measures such as performance on standardized tests or the value of children's future earnings. We should recognize—and emphasize—the intrinsic value of developing children's capabilities.

Chapter 10 explains why parents, voters, and policy makers need to stand back and think more broadly about our social-family contract. Because children are social goods that benefit the economy as a whole, familial commitments to children deserve consistent and equitable public support. We need to develop a better system of national income accounting that includes the "human capital sector" of the economy as part of a larger set of nonmarket accounts. A more accurate picture of the intergenerational transfers that take place through both the family and the government could improve public debates over social policy.

Principles of fairness and reciprocity—as well as efficiency—should guide discussion of what we owe our children, and what they owe us in return. Current policies have not done enough to help parents meet the growing costs of child rearing. Indeed, they have, in a sense, exploited parents by taxing the younger generation to help finance the spending of the older generation with little regard for who devoted time and money to raising those taxpayers. Current democratic rules lead to the underrepresentation of all children's interests, particularly those living in low-income families. We should all help pay for the kids because as they grow up, we grow old. We care for them partly out of the hope that they will care for us, whether for love or money or both.

PART ONE

Conceptualizing the Costs of Children

CHAPTER ONE

Children and the Economy

Most economic theory describes the production of commodities by means of commodities as a circular flow. Purchased inputs, including labor, are combined to produce outputs that can be sold. Dollars go in and dollars come out. But not all the inputs and outputs come with price tags attached. Somewhere along the way, babies are conceived, nurtured, educated, and launched into adulthood in a process that requires considerable time and effort as well as money. The production of people by means of people (and commodities) is a part of the circular flow sometimes called *social reproduction*.[1] What we call it is less important than how we picture its relationship to the economy as a whole.

National income accounts are designed to reveal inputs into the sale of all goods and services within the country. The value of final output, termed gross domestic product (GDP), provides benchmarks for economic well-being and growth. The children who grow up to become workers and taxpayers are important inputs into this output. But we can also turn the accounting system around and think of goods that are bought and sold as inputs into the development of human capabilities. The conventional picture of the circular flow of exchanges between households and businesses can be expanded to reveal the movement of economic resources among men and women, to children, and back again.

We tend to think of child rearing in terms of mothers, fathers, and children. The big picture of the circular flow reminds us of more complex dynamics. Households are connected to businesses and government in ways that affect—and are affected by—child rearing. In most industrialized countries today, the government taxes the working-age population to finance spending on the elderly population. Parents contribute more than nonparents to the next generation, yet their claims on the public purse are not much greater. Mothers contribute more to child rearing than fathers do, yet they are more vulnerable to poverty in old age. Families of color in the United States raise more children than white families, but the elderly population is disproportionately white. Poverty among families with children is significantly higher than poverty among the elderly.

Conventional macroeconomic theory treats households as consumption units. Businesses are the only true production units. Government simply redistributes resources. This book focuses on the production of human capabilities. From this perspective, households are primarily producers, not consumers. Governments make an important secondary contribution through the provision of education, health, and social insurance. Businesses also provide many important inputs. As this book will show, however, the value of market exchanges is small compared to the price that would have to be paid for nonmarket services if substitutes for them were purchased in the market.

This chapter calls attention to the flow of resources between adults and children, situating the market economy within a larger picture and developing an important analogy between the contributions of families and those of the natural environment. It provides a brief overview of historical changes in the structure of intergenerational commitments, emphasizing the growing importance of state spending on children and the elderly. It also frames an important question: What would happen to our market economy if individuals became less willing to devote love, energy, time, and money to the task of raising the next generation?

Circular Flows

Introductory economics textbooks typically picture a circular flow of exchanges among households, businesses, and government (Figure 1.1). Households supply labor to firms and receive income in return. They use this income to buy the goods and services that businesses produce. This conventional diagram focuses attention on the black arrows that represent market exchange. Households supply labor to firms and use their income to buy the goods and services that firms produce. Businesses purchase goods and services, but since these are intermediate purchases, they are represented in the value of the goods and services sold to consumers. Households and businesses pay taxes and receive services. The final purchased value of all goods and services produced within our national boundaries represents the gross domestic product of the United States.

In Figure 1.1, all the arrows are drawn at about the same width; but if their width reflected the size of the resource flows they represent, some would be much bigger than others, and some would be swelling over time, while others would be shrinking. Government transfers to households, such as Social Security payments or public assistance, don't represent purchases of goods or services, so the arrow representing these transfers in Figure 1.1 is gray rather than black. Government transfers show up indirectly in the GDP because they increase the funds available to households for consumption expenditures. But transfers and transactions *within* the three sectors remain invisible.

Our national income accounts track household expenditures in general, but not the expenditures that parents devote to children or spouses to one another. Many adults share their earnings with one another and their children, but this transfer of money remains invisible. If parents buy child-care services in the market, this increases the GDP. If they pro-

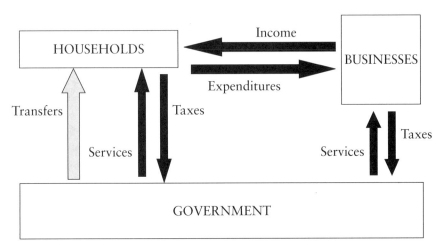

Figure 1.1 Conventional model of circular flow

vide child-care services in the home, this does not increase the GDP. If a couple pays someone to clean their house, this shows up in the GDP; their own activities cleaning their own house do not.

Many transactions also take place inside individual businesses. But the difference between the goods and services that firms buy and the value of the product they sell, their "value added," shows up in the GDP. In a sense, many households also sell a product—labor services. After all, households create and maintain the workers who are employed in business and government. But they do not receive any accounting credit for their "value added." Household services are treated much like the services of Mother Nature—appreciated but not counted.

The size of what might be termed the Total Economy far exceeds that of the Market Economy.[2] The time that household members devote to care, as well as the money they share with one another, remains invisible to our market-based accounting system. Yet these flows of time and money are not just quantitatively large. They have changed considerably over time, with important implications for the size of the arrows in the picture.[3] Over the last one hundred years, women's participation in the labor market has grown because their time devoted to the household has declined. Similarly, government has grown in size partly because of transfers of money and time to children and the elderly that would otherwise have taken place within households. Our accounting system highlights the growth of market work and the welfare state, but it leaves intrafamily transfers and nonmarket work in the shadows.

Time devoted to cooking, cleaning, shopping, and other household activities, as well as time devoted to the direct care of children, the sick or disabled, and the elderly, represents productive activity because it provides benefits to others. The new time-use surveys that are being administered by many national governments are analogous to the radio telescopes that expanded the scope of astronomy beyond the spectrum of visible light.[4] A nationally representative sample of time-budget diaries for U.S. residents shows that in 2003, individuals fifteen years or older spent about the same amount of time in nonmarket work (household activities, purchasing goods and services, caring for and helping household and nonhousehold members, and educational activities) as they did in market work—about four hours a day on average for each.[5]

Over the last century, many of the transfers that once took place within the family economy were relocated to government. The growth of educational and Medicaid spending on the young, combined with Social Security and Medicare spending on the elderly, helps explain steep increases in government budgets in the latter half of the twentieth century. If these programs had not been in place, the transfers within the household would have increased, as working families devoted more of their earnings to provision for children and grandparents. Family income would have been distributed away from the working-age population toward dependents. The rise of the welfare state represents, in part, a redistribution or socialization of spending on dependents.

Inside the Household Box

Economists have not traditionally paid much attention to what goes on inside the household box. Labor is considered one of the most important factors of production in a modern capitalist economy. But labor, like land, is generally treated as a "nonproduced commodity." When economists emphasize investments in human capital, they are usually referring to formal education, not the family care that actually produces the little bodies and brains and readies them for school.[6] Those few introductory textbooks that refer to child rearing treat it as a form of consumption rather than production.

The money and time that household and family members devote to one another provides great satisfaction and happiness. In this sense, these expenditures resemble consumption. But family care also creates something of value to others. Whatever motives parents have, their commitments to children help create the next generation of workers and taxpayers.

Unlike the purchase of consumer durables or the care of pets, child rearing entails a circular flow of resources both within the household box and within the economy as a whole. Parents care for their children and hope to receive at least some care in return as they age. Parents rear children who often grow up to become parents. Wage earners share their earnings with caregivers. These intrafamily exchanges are crucial to the production and maintenance of the labor power that households provide to employers in the business sector. Likewise, they help create the labor power and taxes provided to the government sector.

Figure 1.2 pictures resource flows within the household among working-age men and women, the elderly, and children. Flows of money and time are represented by the gray arrows. These arrows are pictured as though they are all two-way and similar in size. In reality, the flows tend to move predominantly in one direction. Most parents devote more time and money to children than they ever get in return. Most mothers devote more time to children than most fathers do. Most men spend

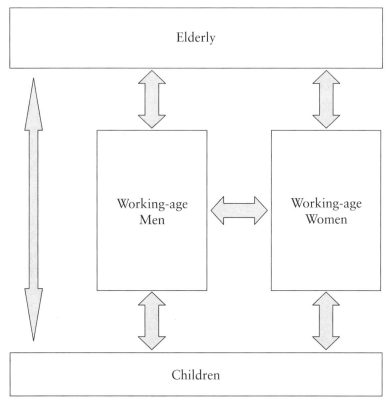

Figure 1.2 Flows of money and time within the household box

more time in wage employment than nonmarket work. When they live with family members, they tend to devote more money than time to the circular flow within households. Parts II and III of this book will summarize what we know about the average size of the net flows that these arrows represent.

Fertility Decline

The importance of flows of money and time within the family becomes increasingly apparent as they change over time. If parents were unable or unwilling to raise children, the households that buy and sell services in the marketplace would eventually dwindle and disappear. Women must bear an average of slightly more than two children to ensure that two adults reach maturity to replace their mother and father. Fertility rates in most industrialized countries—and many developing countries such as South Korea and China—are now below this replacement level of 2.1 children per woman.[7] U.S. fertility remains slightly above replacement primarily because recent immigrants, especially Hispanics, bear more children than the native-born population. Still, fertility has gone down over the long run, and the percentage of women who remain childless by age forty now approaches 20 percent.[8]

Fertility decline represents a change in the circular flow of resources within families. Children symbolically repay their parents by spending money and time on children of their own. The terms of this repayment are modified when the next generation has fewer children (or none at all). The terms are also modified when there is a shift in the distribution of spending on children between mothers and fathers. In the United States, as in many other countries, the percentage of children being reared by mothers alone has increased considerably over time.

Fertility decline contributes to economic growth partly because of the way national income is defined. Reallocation of effort from reproduction to production boosts market output because most reproductive work takes place outside the market economy. A woman who earns a wage or turns a profit increases the GDP, whereas one who devotes all her energy to caring for children at home remains off the books. But not all the benefits of fertility decline are produced by accounting definitions. Small families make it easier to devote more resources to each child, which represents a shift from quantity to quality. Also, childless individuals can afford to pay higher taxes to finance schools that improve the productivity of the younger generation, which then pays higher taxes when it grows up to help support those individuals in their old age through Social Security and Medicare.

On the other hand, fertility decline can lead to economic stress. Holding immigration constant, a reduction in the relative size of the youngest cohort eventually reduces the size of the working-age population. While the burden of caring for children diminishes, the burden of caring for the elderly grows. The supply of labor available to business and government declines. The shifting age structure poses a particularly serious challenge to countries like the United States that have made strong public commitments to the standard of living of the older generation. We deduct Social Security taxes from the earnings of the working-age population to help finance benefits for the population of retirement age. All else being equal, a decline in the number of workers relative to retirees will require higher taxes. Such concerns have led journalists, as well as social scientists, to express concerns about the economic effect of fertility decline.[9] Accurate evaluation of this effect requires a closer look at transfers among households, businesses, and government.

Inside the Government Box

Economists usually explain the growth of government spending as a response to problems in the market economy. Governments produce goods and services that the market cannot provide, such as legal infrastructure, national defense, and regulation. The so-called welfare state compensates for market-related problems such as unemployment and poverty. But many of the largest components of welfare-state spending, such as education for the young and income support and health insurance for the elderly, are substitutes for transfers that would otherwise have taken place within families.[10] Though working-age adults now pay more in taxes, they pay less than they probably would have otherwise to educate and care for their dependents (both young and old) and purchase insurance for themselves. The relative size of government increases when it socializes the flows that once took place within families.

Employers and workers pay taxes to help finance public education and other programs that benefit children. Children grow up, become employers and workers, and pay taxes themselves. Whether they simply repay what was spent on them or pay more or less than that depends on the structure of taxes and transfers as well as the relative size of different age cohorts. Both our Social Security and Medicare systems and our method of financing national debt establish public claims on the income of future adult citizens.[11] Although economists disagree over exactly how these intergenerational transfers should be measured, most agree that the current generation of working adults has an economic stake in the productive capabilities of the younger generation.[12]

Outside the Boxes

Not all flows of money and time are captured by arrows connecting distinct groups within distinct boxes. Some spill over, often with unintended effects on others. Consider a beekeeper, an orchard owner, and a college professor who is taking a walk in the woods. The beekeeper benefits from the proximity of a nearby apple orchard, which provides pollen and nectar for her bees. The orchard owner benefits from the pollination that bees provide. On the other hand, the college professor risks a bee sting.

A more modern example of flows outside the boxes lies in the transfer of free knowledge resources on the Web. Much of what is available there comes neither from market exchange nor from reciprocal transfers. It is nonrival in consumption: what you download from the Web does not reduce what I download. It also represents a "cook-pot economy," in which many individuals contribute to a rich stew that nourishes a larger group.[13] The right combination of ingredients, allowed to simmer, creates value much greater than the mere sum of its parts.

Informal exchanges and transfers within the household can be pictured as a circular flow among individuals. Yet household activities overflow into other sectors through more indirect cook-pot effects. The creation and maintenance of human capabilities that take place within households benefit the economy as a whole. On the other hand, all forms of production can contribute to environmental degradation, a negative spillover.

Economists often term spillovers "externalities" because they are external to individual transactions. This term is misleading because it implies a small quantity escaping a larger container. But the size of economic flows between sectors that do not go through the market is quite large, analogous more to an ocean than to spills from a pitcher or leakages from a pipe. No one owns the ocean, and nations have a hard time regulating pollution and overexploitation of it. Yet the ocean constitutes a large part of our global economy. Likewise, no one owns a community, and community members often find it difficult to control what happens on the streets, the amount of noise, or the general level of trust. Yet communities are also part of our economy.

One way to revisualize the circular flow is to imagine the boxes representing households, businesses, and government as islands floating in an ocean that represents a stock of physical, natural, and social resources that are not individually owned—"the commons." In Figure 1.3, this external commons is represented by the gray background of the large circle, connected by the white flows that represent spillovers from each of the three boxes. These arrows, like the others, flow both ways—resources are drawn in from the commons and spill over as well. The light gray arrows within the household sector are like rivers on an island. The black arrows connecting the islands, as well as the dark gray arrow representing government transfers, are like pipes whose flow is metered, directly measured in monetary units.

This figure offers a more realistic picture than the traditional circular flow depicted in Figure 1.1, although it requires more effort to quantify. Many of the arrows represent flows that we have not yet learned to measure accurately, much less convert to a common denominator such as dollars. This picture builds on standard environmental economics by emphasizing the importance of nonmarket flows within households and

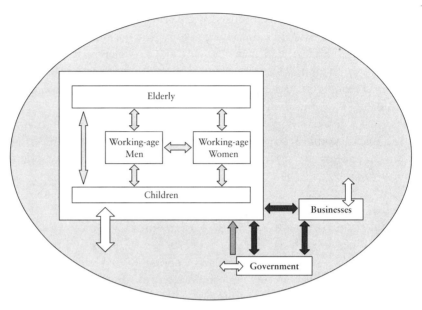

Figure 1.3 Circular flows within a larger environment with spillovers

their similarity to ecological services. Often prices can be assigned to nonmarket transfers only by posing a counterfactual question: If bees disappear, how much will the next best method of pollination cost? If wild fish populations decline below harvestable levels, how much would it cost to raise them in captivity? Similarly, we can ask how much it would cost to replace the money and time that parents provide their children.

The following chapters fill in more information about the size of the arrows most directly relevant to children in the United States. But the size of flows of money and time does not tell us much about their interactions. To explore these, we need to ask how the actors within our economic system—both groups and individuals—are affected by the size and shape of economic commitments to the next generation.

Intergenerational Transfers

Neoclassical economists generally focus on the individual choices of an able-bodied adult, rather like Robinson Crusoe on a desert island seeking to meet his own basic needs.[14] The decision to raise a child is treated as a matter of personal preference, a source of personal satisfaction.

Though it is important to acknowledge individual preferences and explain individual decisions, it is also important to recognize that parents in countries such as the United States do not live on a desert island. They live on a set of islands full of preexisting circular flows running through metaphorical rivers and pipes, emptying into the surrounding ocean and subject to rain, drought, and thunderstorms. A hydraulic infrastructure—constructed from cultural norms, political rules, and patterns of wealth ownership—imposes significant constraints on the decisions individuals make.

The relative size of the arrows reflecting transfers of money and time to children seems to have varied through history, reflecting differences in what nineteenth-century political economists such as Karl Marx called modes of production. Most human societies can be roughly sorted into three types: small-scale, hunter-gatherer societies, more centralized, patriarchal, agrarian societies based on land ownership, and capitalist or state socialist industrial societies based on wage employment. These societies are characterized by very different contractual arrangements governing intergenerational transfers.

Transfers Based on Age

Parents obviously spend a substantial amount of money and time raising children. The extent to which they are repaid by transfers in old age either from children or from the younger generation as a whole varies systematically across societies. Evidence suggests that the net flow of money and time from parents to children was positive in many hunter-gatherer societies.[15] Children often had to be physically carried as tribes moved in search of food. Adults contributed substantial resources to children and grandchildren, who often did not become self-supporting until they gained skills that took a long time to acquire. Because parents received little or no payback, the cost of raising children was relatively high. Group sanctions that encouraged forms of abstinence that lowered birth rates and infanticide were not uncommon.

In agricultural societies, child rearing could be combined with other activities, and children could begin performing productive work at a relatively early age. Paternal control over private property provided leverage over adult children: gifts and bequests could be made contingent on obedience and provision of support to elders.[16] As a result, parents who survived to old age probably recouped some of the costs of raising children. Though the net flow of resources to children may have remained positive, economic incentives contributed to high fertility.

In industrial societies characterized by wage employment and increased geographic mobility, parents have lost much of their ability to capture benefits from adult children. Young adults enjoy more economic independence. As education has become increasingly important, many of the costs of providing it have been assumed by government. Not incidentally, governments also have begun to socialize at least some of the benefits of this investment by taxing the working-age population to provide public pensions for the older generation.[17]

Demographic changes associated with economic development have reinforced these trends. Marriages have become less stable, and intra-family transfers to the elderly have diminished. Increases in life expectancy have magnified the burden of provision for the elderly, and fertility decline has reduced the size of the working-age population compared to the older generation. Among the relatively advanced countries belonging to the Organization for Economic Cooperation and Development, age-related transfers loom large in national budgets, and transfers to the elderly average about twice those to children.[18] In the United States, as elsewhere, a "pay-as-you-go" pension system reallocates taxes paid by the working age population to the elderly population. Guaranteed medical benefits to the elderly through Medicare also represent a large public liability.

Most citizens of this country who have worked for pay or married a wage earner are eligible for Social Security and Medicare. Low earners in general enjoy higher benefits relative to their contributions than high earners, though as Chapter 8 will show, much depends on family structure and life expectancy. Children derive special advantages from Social Security's survivors' and disability benefits, which insure them against the risk that a parent will die or become disabled. But the time and effort that parents put into raising children do not improve their own income security in old age—indeed, they often have just the opposite effect.

Transfers Based on Gender

Nonmarket dimensions of the circular flow have particularly momentous implications for women, who typically devote more time to child rearing than men do and are more likely to become single parents. Efforts to understand and explain gender inequality typically focus too narrowly on the relative wages of men and women. The extent of public support for child rearing and provision for old age strongly affects women's standards of living.

Historical research suggests strong linkages between intergenerational and intergender resource flows.[19] In many hunter-gatherer societies with relatively low fertility, women enjoyed substantial autonomy and independence. In many agrarian societies based on private property, by contrast, patriarchal property rights gave elder males considerable control over wives as well as children. Men could shift many of the costs of high fertility to women by requiring them to work long hours. Though husbands and wives typically shared a similar bundle of consumption goods, "a woman's work was never done." Restrictions on women's access to activities outside the home helped guarantee that they would offer a large supply of caring labor to children and other dependents.[20]

Wage employment and industrial development—as well as the geographic mobility that accompanied European expansion into the New World—brought new opportunities for women and children outside the patriarchal household. Increased demand for education, as well as a higher opportunity cost to keeping women at home, raised the cost of children even as their economic benefits declined. Fertility began a downward trend in both Europe and the United States long before the advent of modern contraceptives.[21]

In advanced industrial economies, women enjoy historically unprecedented rights, but they nonetheless pay a high price for motherhood. The increased probability of both divorce and nonmarital births weakens maternal claims on paternal income. Even within married-couple families, mothers tend to devote far more time to children than fathers do. Though public support for child rearing in the form of paid parental leave and subsidized child care has increased over time, it covers only a small share of the lifetime cost of raising children.

Women in the United States have a longer life expectancy than men, which may enable them to collect longer lifetime benefits from Social Security and Medicare. On the other hand, the average benefits they receive are lower, and because so many elderly women care for their husbands before they outlive them, they are far more likely to require direct care. More than 80 percent of the indigent elderly living in nursing homes in this country today are women.[22]

Transfers Based on Class, Race, and Ethnicity

Age and gender are not the only dimensions of social identity that affect the distribution of the costs of social reproduction. In the United States today, low-income families tend to raise more children than the affluent. Immigrants and people of color tend to raise more children than whites. Government transfers to poor families with children through programs such as Temporary Assistance to Needy Families (TANF) and the Earned Income Tax Credit (EITC) are substantial, but as Chapter 8 will show they are not much greater per child than government transfers to affluent families through tax exemptions and credits.

Since most educational spending is financed by local property taxes, rich families tend to send their children to rich schools. Family background has a significant influence on the probability of a child's attending college. And though most children in the United States today will grow into substantial tax obligations to repay our national debt, those growing up in affluent families are likely to receive substantial bequests from their parents that will help compensate for those taxes.

Subsidizing the Market

Children grow up to become workers as well as taxpayers, and the older generation is not the only group that benefits from their existence. Imagine an economy in which all paid work is performed by battery-powered androids programmed to obey orders, work hard, and never harm a human. Assume that these androids take twenty-two years to produce. Once they reach this age, they require nothing more than a new battery every week, until they reach the age of sixty-five, when they recycle their useful body parts and then turn themselves off.

In this economy, the cost of an android would be at least as high as the cost of producing it, which could be amortized over its working life. In order to actually perform work, however, the androids require batteries, analogous to the wages that must be paid to obtain the services of a human worker. A slightly more complicated scenario could allow for differences in wages: Android engineers might instill androids with a desire to compete with other androids to gain extra batteries (higher pay) that they could use to play computer games when they are not working for their human bosses.

Android owners would enjoy a surplus or profit equal to the value of the goods and services produced by the android, minus the costs of purchasing and operating the android (and any other costs). In long-run competitive equilibrium, profits would be driven to zero, and the cost of the android would equal the net present discounted value of the income it yields. Whether they reach this theoretical equilibrium or not, employers would generally be required to pay the full costs of producing an android.

In our wage-based economy, by contrast, parents voluntarily assume most of the costs of producing human workers. Employers pay only for the batteries represented by wages. Parents and nonparents alike are paid what they are able to command in the labor market, which is based on the supply and demand for their market-related skills. In the real world, of course, employers pay taxes that may help finance education, and they also raise children of their own. Still, businesses often hire workers produced by families and schools in other countries, either through immigration or location of production facilities overseas. By doing so, they largely escape responsibility for the costs of producing the workers they employ.

Parental commitments effectively lower wages below what would be required if wage earners had to repay their parents for the costs of producing them. In many economic circumstances, this has the effect of increasing profits. In the stylized competitive general equilibrium of neoclassical theory, lower wages lead to lower prices. In this case, the benefits are realized by all consumers of commodities, whether they have raised children or not.

Developing Accounts

The pictures of circular flow developed in this chapter provide a way of describing—and posing questions about—flows of money and time between adults and children. Some of the most interesting questions relate to current debates about intergenerational transfers, gender justice, and equal opportunity for children. These debates will not be resolved in this book. But they will be enriched by more careful attention to the flow of resources that do not carry an explicit market price.

The circular flow of resources to children raises questions of efficiency as well as fairness. Is there some way of modifying this flow in ways that could make us all better off? It would be easier to answer this question if we knew more about the relationship between inputs and outputs in the production of human capabilities. Economists have studied the quantitative relationship between changes in some inputs—such as maternal education or early-childhood education—and changes in some outputs—such as children's later test scores or success in school. We know far less about the relationship between total expenditures on a child and total benefits, or the way that these costs and benefits are distributed among distinct social groups, such as mothers and fathers, parents and nonparents, rich and poor.

The only way to puzzle out this macroeconomic picture is to develop better ways of measuring the inputs and outputs, costs and benefits, that we consider most important. The circular flow of resources moves through an infrastructure of social institutions. When parents rear children, the costs they incur are heavily influenced by cultural norms, legal rules, employment practices, and government policies. Individual decisions take place within an institutional context that deserves careful consideration.

CHAPTER TWO

Commitments and Capabilities

Individuals are not swept helplessly along by the circular flows and institutional rules of the economic system. They are decision makers who often have opportunities to alter their trajectory and to modify existing rules. A macroeconomic picture, however useful, raises microeconomic questions. How can we best describe the decisions families make to devote resources to children?

Neoclassical economists like Gary Becker offer an exceptionally clear answer to this question.[1] They describe rational economic agents who seek to maximize their own happiness through decisions to allocate time and money. They argue that families know exactly what they want and how to get it, without any explicit efforts to coordinate with others. In this conceptual world, families behave exactly the same way as individuals buying and selling in a competitive market. Decisions to raise children represent decisions to invest in a form of capital, like consumer durables, that yields a future flow of valuable services.

Some families may behave this way some of the time, especially if their adult members majored in economics. Yet few families are perfectly rational, well-informed units. Most experience regular disagreements and resort to imperfect choices in a world of uncertain outcomes. Neoclassical economic reasoning offers some important insights, but it does not provide an adequate framework for analyzing family decisions regarding children.

This chapter outlines an alternative approach, drawing from the insights of institutional and behavioral economics to conceptualize commitments to the development of human capabilities.[2] Commitments resemble investments in some respects, requiring, for instance, expenditures of time and money. But commitments have moral as well as practical dimensions and are typically culturally rather than individually defined. The cultural norms that help motivate our commitments to family members have large spillover effects on others. Though these norms represent what we might consider "noneconomic" factors, they are often influenced by economic pressures. For instance, as the cost of conforming to traditional norms of motherhood goes up, the likelihood of conformity to them tends to decline.

Imperfect Choices, Uncertain Outcomes

> I suggest the simple but fundamental proposition that
> the replacement of a continually aging citizenry by new
> recruits is much too important to the entire body politic
> to tolerate untrammeled individual choice to hold sway.

—NORMAN RYDER, "A New Approach to the Economic Theory of
Fertility Behavior: A Comment"

People often don't know what will make them happy, change their minds about what they want, and face an uncertain world with help from their family, their friends, and their government. Even when parents try to make economically rational decisions, information about future consequences is hard to come by. Even if children are like consumer durables in some respects, potential buyers cannot thumb through the pages of *Consumer Reports* to find information on their performance standards or repair records. Each child is unpredictably unique. As Audre Lorde puts it, children "bedevil us by becoming themselves."[3]

It seems unlikely that prospective parents correctly estimate how much they will spend on children over a lifetime. Magazines and newspapers occasionally run feature articles on the subject precisely because the estimates they provide are startling to most readers. Students in introductory economics classes gain a new appreciation of their parents (as well as some apprehension about becoming parents in the near future) when they learn that two-parent families with two children devote, on average, about 40 percent of their annual expenditures to those children until they reach eighteen, and they often continue paying the same share or even more to cover college expenses (see Chapters 4 and 5).

Even if potential parents have the information they need, they don't always act in rational or predictable ways. Love is not a mathematically specified constant but a complicated emotion that ebbs, flows, and changes over time.[4] Human beings may have evolved emotional responses over which they have little cognitive control because this helps solve commitment problems and improve trust. Sexual intercourse is high on the list of areas of human decision making likely to depart from rational calculation.[5] About one-half of all pregnancies in the United States are unplanned, and about one-half of these end in abortion.[6]

Once born, children exert a powerful emotional pull on their parents, especially their mothers. Surveys designed to determine whether births are wanted or unwanted show that parents are often reluctant to choose between these two extremes. Their tendency to explain that they wanted to have a child but "not at that particular point in time" or "under different conditions" reflects a kind of "continuum of wantedness."[7] Consumers can declare bankruptcy and liquidate their assets. Parents can also declare bankruptcy. They cannot, however, liquidate their children, any more than they can trade them in for a new model.

Some individuals may know exactly what they want and how to get it. But it is often hard for individuals to find the right balance between their own desires and those of the people they care for. Familial altruism is intense but sometimes variable and uneven. The high rate of entrances into and exits from family relationships—not to mention the large percentage of children being raised by mothers alone—undermines the assumption that families can be treated as dynasties with perfect knowledge of the future.

Family members often disagree about priorities. However altruistic parents are, they generally prefer to spend less on children than children wish for.[8] Many empirical studies show that income under the control of a wife is spent differently from income under the control of a husband. Men and women, parents and children, often bargain over the allocation of resources; their relative influence is determined by fallback positions either inside or outside the family.[9]

Family responses to changes in prices and incomes are complicated by changes in relationships among family members. Even if individual preferences remain stable over time, an increase in the relative bargaining power of the younger generation can increase the costs children impose on their parents. Likewise, an increase in the relative bargaining power of mothers can shift more of the cost of children onto fathers.

Acknowledgment of distributional conflict calls attention to nonmarket institutions such as laws and norms. It also raises questions about the genesis of individual preferences.

Preference Problems

Most economists take preferences as a given, without asking where they come from, why they might vary among individuals, or how they change over time. By contrast, evolutionary biologists emphasize parent-offspring conflict and differences in maternal and paternal interests. To the extent that preferences are shaped by culture and experience, we are all at the mercy of history as well as biology. Parents, like others in positions of authority, often influence the formation of their children's preferences.

In conventional economic models, parents value either their children's happiness or their children's consumption (presumed to be positively related to their happiness). But many parents have paternalistic preferences, and they are willing to make their children unhappy "for their own good." They may offer financial assistance for some things (such as schooling or the purchase of a home) but not for others (sports cars or expensive vacations).[10] Parents may also assess their children's well-being relative to their own, rather than setting an absolute target. For instance, they may spend more on their children to protect them from downward mobility, less if children already seem upwardly mobile.[11]

Neoclassical theory predicts that government spending on children will "crowd out" parental spending. If a family has already maximized its collective happiness, and a child receives extra resources from outside the family, the family will compensate by reallocating its own resources away from the child. But while parents want their children to be happy, they also have other goals. They want to make a difference in their children's lives—a form of altruism distinct from merely wanting to make someone happy.[12] As one father in a longitudinal study put it, "I see having a child as a chance to shape the life of another human being—someone who will be very important to me and who I can teach about my view of the world."[13] Such parents may respond to government transfers by spending more on their children rather than less.

The desire to raise children, however natural, is not explicitly embedded in our genes. For most of human history, the desire to engage in sexual intercourse led to conception and reproduction. Natural selection did not necessarily favor humans who had a desire to raise children. It favored those who engaged in forms of sexual intercourse that resulted in children who, once born, were successfully cared for. It also favored societies that developed institutional arrangements conducive to such care.[14] Both technological and social changes urge us to consider how our institutional supports for child rearing—as well as our individual decisions—should evolve.

Coordination Problems

Families often make informed choices. But outcomes depend partly on what other families choose. Strategic moves are often more complex than decisions to buy or sell in a competitive market. For instance, when family A chooses to pay for a child's college education, the payoff depends in part on whether families B through Z make similar decisions. A young adult without a college diploma may fare perfectly well in the labor market if few others have one. But if everyone else has a diploma, he or she goes to the back of the line.

Coordination problems are particularly serious where spillover effects are large. Parents surely derive great happiness from their investments in children. But children themselves are the primary beneficiaries, and other adults also benefit. Some spillovers affect preferences themselves. Most people would agree that successful parenting cultivates children's feelings of concern for others. Parenting itself contributes to the emotional well-being of adults and lowers their risk of involvement in dangerous and unhealthy activities.[15] Preferences offer benefits beyond the happiness they may or may not deliver to those who act upon them.

Consumers buying products often have clear information about prices, know what they want, and can anticipate what they will get. The same cannot be said of parents considering expenditures on children. Folk wisdom warns us not to throw the baby out with the bathwater. The baby, in this instance, represents the notion that families try to make good decisions. Surely they try. But families operate in an environment characterized by emotional variability, social uncertainty, and unintended consequences. We should throw out the assumption that they always make efficient decisions that maximize their—and our—collective happiness.

Commitments versus Investments

> *commitment.* . . . 2a. A pledge to do. b. Something
> pledged, especially an engagement by contract involving
> financial obligation. 3. The state of being bound emo-
> tionally or intellectually to a course of action or to an-
> other person or persons: a deep commitment to liberal
> policies; a profound commitment to the family.
>
> *investment.* . . . 3. Property or another possession ac-
>   quired for future financial return or benefit. 4. A
>   commitment, as of time or support.
>
> —AMERICAN HERITAGE DICTIONARY

As these dictionary definitions indicate, the meanings of commitment and investment are intertwined. But the small differences between them are telling. Their motivations differ: a commitment to someone is a pledge that remains binding even if an expected rate of return fails to materialize. Though a commitment to family members, like an investment, may be influenced by consideration of future benefits, it is less closely tied to rational calculation of the value of a flow of services. Personal commitment implies emotional ties. Commitments are reinforced by human tendencies to reward prosocial behavior and punish opportunism, even at some personal cost.[16] Individuals who make family commitments care about the motives of other actors, as well others' perceptions of their own motives.

Prisoners of Love

Most people talk about families using the language of commitment, and many parents describe the satisfactions of child rearing in moral terms. Amartya Sen describes commitment as a decision to do something despite the realization that it offers no personal benefits.[17] The feminist economist Julie Nelson applies this concept to childrearing when she writes: "If you get up in the middle of the night to feed a baby because you feel sorry for it, you are acting altruistically. If you get up when you would feel personally better off just putting your pillow over your head, you are acting responsibly. Since after the hundredth or so such occasion one is likely to feel more sorry for oneself than for the child, it is a good thing for children that most parents treat childrearing as a commitment."[18] Many parents express ambivalence about the pleasures of child rearing, even as they emphasize its intrinsic value. One of the few surveys asking mothers how they actually felt found about 20 percent reported that they received little pleasure from it—which, it is important to note, is not the same as saying they regretted having undertaken it.[19] A survey administered by the U.S. Census Bureau in 2000 found that 15 percent of parents reported that their child often or very often required more time than they expected, and 5 percent came right out and said that their children often or very often did things that really bothered them.[20]

The emotional connection that forms between parents and children has some foundation in biology. Mothers bond more quickly and more strongly with infants than fathers do. But emotional connection is also shaped by environment. Men as well as women experience physiological changes in response to the sound of a crying child. Primate mothers, including human mothers, are sometimes forced to make difficult choices about which offspring will survive, occasionally even resorting to infanticide.[21] As the primatologist Sarah Blaffer Hrdy writes, "There is no mammal in which maternal commitment does not emerge piecemeal and chronically sensitive to external cues. Nurturing has to be teased out, reinforced, maintained. Nurturing itself needs to be nurtured."[22]

In our culture, fathers seem particularly likely to default on parental commitments. A large percentage of children being raised by mothers alone enjoy little economic support from or social contact with their fathers.[23] But mothers also make decisions to part from their children; a not insignificant number of children live with fathers alone or with grandparents. Pregnant women may choose abortions not only to avoid unwanted pregnancy but also because they fear that if they bear a child, they will be unable either to part with the infant or to provide adequate care for it. When women become mothers against their will, they and their children experience increased vulnerability to both economic and psychological stress.

Emotional connection represents, to some extent, an endogenous preference, an acquired taste. Economists often describe endogenous preferences as *addiction*. Psychologists, more attuned to emotion, often use the term *attachment* and suggest that it is influenced by frequency of contact. People who care for children for a prolonged period tend to bond to them, and early involvement seems to increase fathers' commitments.[24] Stepfathers may bond less easily than biological fathers, but few studies of differences between these two groups adequately control for the difference in timing and duration of contact with children. Stepfathers probably require more time than biological fathers to form strong attachments.

The choices that shape commitments may include efforts to preemptively avoid situations in which emotional connection forms, or to exit relationships abruptly in order to disconnect emotionally. Such preemptive choices help explain why modern methods of contraception and abortion lead to increased childlessness as well as fertility decline. They also explain why many fathers avoid contact with their children once they no longer have an intimate relationship with the mother of those children. Preemption could also help explain why many social institutions seem designed to minimize contact between rich and poor. Individuals who find happiness in emotional connections may nonetheless fear the resulting reduction of individual autonomy. Attachment to others threatens a certain loss of control.

Calculating Commitments

Some commitments take place despite one's best intentions; others may be as carefully calculated as a professional investment portfolio. Most commitments probably fall somewhere in between, because they are encouraged by expectations of reciprocity. Few of us commit ourselves in advance to relationships that we think will make us unhappy. Indeed, unexpected increases in the cost of a commitment often motivate a decision to break it. Individuals frequently allow partners the benefit of the doubt, employing what game theorists call a strategy of "forgiving tit-for-tat."[25]

Investments are risky, but commitments to care for others are often uncertain—the magnitude of risk and the size of expected payoffs are difficult to assess. Children can be born disabled; spouses can develop debilitating diseases. Investments can range along a continuum from a dollar to the-sky's-the-limit. Commitments are discrete choices, and they typically require a large minimum, or threshold, to become credible. Diversification is possible but limited. One can choose to live with someone rather than to marry her, or to be a godmother or a parent figure rather than a parent. But one cannot always choose a specific level of emotional involvement.

Many financial investments are subject to monitoring and enforcement problems, commitments even more so. Strategic complexities abound. Individuals may be more likely to renege on their commitments if they believe someone else will fulfill them. Just as public support for children can lead parents to reduce private support, confidence in maternal commitments can make it easier for fathers to default. On the other hand, individuals may refuse to make commitments if the consequences are threatening and uncertain. Without assurances that get them over the hump or past the hurdle to reach the self-sustaining emotional engagement they need, they may avoid commitments altogether.

Intense personal or economic stress can have the effect of reducing emotional engagement, weakening commitments, even reducing an individual's abilities to make rational decisions. As John Stuart Mill observed over a century ago in his classic *Principles of Political Economy*, "Energy and self-dependence are liable to be impaired by the absence of help, as well as by its excess."[26] Families have breaking points. The stresses of dealing with a serious problem such as mental illness, violence, disabilities, or economic misfortune often lead to fracture. The rapid dismantling of social safety nets in the former Soviet Union and many Eastern European countries has been associated with plummeting marriage and birth rates.[27]

Emerging new family forms show surprising resilience. Divorce and single parenthood, once highly stigmatized, have become more common. Both parents and children have learned how to adapt to them. Yet we also see clear signs of family breakdown, such as the growth of no-parent families and the large percentage of children placed in foster care.[28] Economic stress undermines the values and preferences that sustain family commitments.

Culture and Commitments

Cultural norms often represent solutions to problems of uncertainty. The difficulties that individuals face making rational decisions regarding family commitments explain why they rely heavily on their perceptions of what others are doing. Many cultural norms seem to define economic hurdles for child rearing and marriage that limit individual ability simply to choose what price they will pay for these. Trends in child rearing and marriage seldom take a predictable linear form. Rather, periods of relative stability seem to alternate with periods of relatively rapid change.

Marriage is a commitment to give priority to one intimate relationship by promising not to enter another one. This commitment is made preemptively, before information about the quality of other possible relationships is complete. Likewise, child rearing is a commitment made despite the absence of complete information regarding future outcomes.

Normative pressures encourage and shape such commitments. Potential parents do not ask, "Can we afford a child?" in the abstract, but, rather, "Can we afford to raise a child in a way that satisfies the standards we set for ourselves and the child?"[29]

In both Spain and Italy, countries with strong profamily values, many young people postpone marriage and abjure parenthood. Fertility levels have fallen well below replacement levels.[30] Yet overall standards of living in these countries are far higher than they were when families typically raised five children. From a conventional neoclassical perspective, one could argue that potential parents have such a high demand for expenditures per child (or "child quality") that they cannot afford to have children. But why do such preferences emerge? It seems likely that cultural norms have raised the commitment hurdle for potential parents, leaving them reluctant to risk failure to provide a standard of living for children comparable to the one their parents provided them.

The long period required for children to attain educational credentials and obtain secure, well-paying jobs increases demands on parents. In the not-too-distant past, couples were expected to raise children as part of a larger cultural, often religious commitment. Children's future economic success may have factored into their decisions (particularly when families owned land or other resources), but it was probably a less prominent concern than it is today. As child-rearing decisions enter more fully into the realm of individual choice, the normative standards imposed on potential parents seem to ratchet up.

These normative standards vary for different groups within the population. In the United States, highly educated women tend to postpone child rearing and reach age forty with lower fertility rates than less well educated women. In June 2000 about 29 percent of women ages fifteen to forty-four who had completed high school but not college were childless, compared to 48 percent of those with a college degree.[31] One obvious reason is that the opportunity cost of time taken out of paid employment is higher for college-educated women—every hour that they reduce time in paid employment is more costly to them.[32]

But opportunity cost is relevant primarily because highly educated mothers tend to have high aspirations for their children and place a high value on the personal time they are able to devote to them. Though most people feel comfortable purchasing substitutes for the time they might devote to cooking or cleaning, child rearing has personal and emotional dimensions. What is the point of having children if you can't spend time engaging with them? All else being equal, education increases the amount of time parents devote to active child care.[33] Highly educated mothers and fathers often take it upon themselves to read aloud to their children, persuade them to love broccoli, and ferry them to ballet lessons and soccer games. The cultural value that we place on parental participation in child rearing (rather than just providing sperm or ova or gestating a fetus) is what makes parenthood particularly costly for women and men with a potential for high market earnings.

Parental commitments, once made, are not very sensitive to increased prices in the form of opportunity costs. This helps explain why individuals may choose not to make such commitments. Well-educated women now enjoy opportunities for professional careers that are personally rewarding as well as lucrative. Careers are not merely jobs, and they offer benefits far more compelling than mere income—the opportunity to develop new and interesting capabilities. Surveys suggest that educational attainment affects attitudes regarding the intrinsic importance of child rearing. In 1988 women who did not complete high school were about five times as likely as college-educated women to agree that "people who have never had children lead empty lives," and male high school dropouts were 2.5 times more likely to agree than male college graduates.[34] Preferences are changing, along with prices.

Bargaining over Commitments

Few individuals raise children entirely on their own. They join up with other adults to form families. However great their mutual affection and respect, they must also decide how to share their obligations. Economists generally assume that bargaining power is determined by fallback positions—the next-best alternative. Individuals must be at least as happy in a relationship as they would be outside it—else, why would they remain? In theory, bargaining should lead to efficient outcomes because individuals with perfect knowledge take advantage of any opportunities to make one person better off without making the other worse off.

But individual bargaining within the family is risky, because it sends signals about mutual affection and trust that can easily be misinterpreted. Successful negotiation of competing interests requires a high level of emotional skill. That many highly educated individuals spend money purchasing psychotherapy suggests that even they are not confident of their own happiness-maximizing capabilities. Couples therapy is designed to help individuals improve their emotional skills.[35]

Rather than threatening to exit a relationship if they don't get what they want, individuals may resort to a gentler fallback position defined by social norms, such as simply refusing to cooperate.[36] Even in this case, bargaining is likely to be complicated by "complex feelings of accountability, anxiety, insecurity, and entitlement."[37] Cultural norms of appropriate behavior for women and men also complicate the story. For instance, modest increases in women's relative contribution to household income seem to lead to reductions in the time they devote to housework. But if women's relative contributions are too large, they seem to do *more* housework, as if to compensate for their departure from traditional gender norms.[38]

As Shakespeare's *King Lear* dramatizes, bargaining between children and parents over control of property can also undermine commitments. Most parents in the United States today who leave bequests divide them equally among all their children.[39] This simple—and highly normative—rule of thumb avoids information problems (such as determining which child needs or provides the most help) and also discourages strategic maneuvering among children that, while individually rational, can undermine mutual affections.

Commitments, Norms, and Conventions

Rational economic man's emotional complexities help explain why cultural norms regarding family commitments are so important. But cultural norms are susceptible to economic pressures. Once in place, they may resist change. On the other hand, if nonconformity reaches a certain level, appropriately termed a "tipping point," norms may quickly unravel. Individual choices are often strongly affected by perceptions of what others are choosing. Women are far more likely to have a child out of wedlock if they perceive that others are doing so as well.[40]

Tipping models also help explain the tremendous significance of moral convictions. When even a small number of people commit to a certain course of action, signaling that their behavior does not depend on what others do (or on any shifts in relative prices or incomes), they provide an expectational anchor for the remainder of the population. Women who vow to demand individual rights even if they are punished, or men who vow not to marry women whose feet or genitals have been mutilated, alter the strategic decisions that others make.[41] On the other hand, strong moral positions articulated on both sides of a question, as in the current standoff in the United States on abortion—"right to life" versus "right to choose"—can have a politically polarizing effect that tends to slow normative change.

Capabilities, Not Capital

It may seem obvious that we should value children in and of themselves. But neoclassical economic theory describes children as units of human capital whose value is represented by a flow of future benefits. This description is inconsistent with the obligation that both parents and societies feel toward children, regardless of future payback. The human capital metaphor deemphasizes commitment. It also deflects attention from capabilities that cannot be easily described as the result of explicit investment decisions: genetic endowments, habits and preferences, emotional skills, and moral values. As Amartya Sen observes, "Human beings are not merely means of production (even though they excel in that capacity), but also the end of the exercise."[42]

Valuing Children

Human capital is typically measured in terms of the net present discounted value of future lifetime earnings.[43] Take Johnny or Jenny at age twenty-one, predict what his or her lifetime earnings will be, ask how much money you would have to put in the bank today at a 5 percent interest rate to generate that income, and subtract what was spent getting either of them to the start of a career. Their human capital is probably worth more than the value of your home. But notice that, by this measure, neither Van Gogh nor Mother Teresa was worth much, since neither enjoyed commercial success. Their lifetime earnings were close to zero. Also by this measure, a daughter is worth less than a son; her expected earnings are lower because of the time she will likely take out of paid employment to raise children.

Acknowledging some moral discomfort, most economists will emphasize that economic value is a narrower concept than social value. But the conventional measure of net present discounted value is only one of several ways of measuring *economic* value. Individuals can and often do make economic contributions that are not captured by their lifetime earnings. The nonmarket work they do (such as raising children) can be assigned an approximate dollar value. Further, individuals may generate benefits that spill over into the economy as a whole, into the larger circle pictured in Figure 1.3 in Chapter 1.

Neoclassical economics urges us to consider the happiness that children and those who care for them experience. But the only way to assign a monetary value to this happiness is to ask what individuals would pay for it.[44] We could ask what a potential child would be willing to pay for the privilege of being conceived, carried to term, and nurtured to adulthood. Outside science fiction, this question is nonsensical. Further, parental *willingness* to spend money on the health or happiness of an existing child is usually far greater than the parent's actual *ability* to pay. Few people would agree that rich children are worth more than poor children simply because their parents are able to spend more money on them.

Health and happiness are not the only goals that humans pursue. In the vivid imagery of the popular film *The Matrix*, some individuals are given the opportunity to choose between the mental sensation of happiness (an illusion created while sitting naked in a vat generating psychic energy for a neural network) and the prospect of painful, risky freedom. The heroes of the story choose the latter. Aristotle's vision of the intrinsic value of human capabilities is central to the Western intellectual tradition. Adam Smith himself insisted that men should not be valued, like some "chest of drawers," merely by their usefulness.[45] We should measure our economic success in terms of the development of human capabilities and expansion of human choices.[46]

Parents and Capabilities

The concept of capabilities is particularly appropriate to an analysis of parental commitments. As Diane Elson puts it, "The process of the reproduction and maintenance of human resources is different from any other kind of production because human resources are treated as having an intrinsic value, not merely an instrumental value."[47] Many people choose not merely to have a child but to become a parent. They make this commitment in part to alter themselves. Like choosing an occupation, becoming a parent represents an opportunity to develop one's capabilities and to alter one's preferences.

Investments in human capital yield payoffs that appear only inside the business or government boxes within the circular flow described in Chapter 1. Commitments to the development of human capabilities are more likely to yield payoffs that replenish and enrich shared assets and mutual expectations. Parents care about their children's happiness and their future income-earning abilities. But they also strive to increase their children's freedom to make their own decisions, even while trying to reward and reinforce good behavior. Parents care about the positive spillovers—the benefits to themselves and their children that cannot be captured by a purely market-based metric. Most societies, like families, define children's well-being in multidimensional terms, monitoring measures such as infant mortality, physical and mental health, educational attainment, and the risk of engaging in personally or socially destructive behavior.

Political philosophers often make a sharp distinction between equality of outcome and equality of opportunity. But equality of outcome for one generation shapes equality of opportunity for the next. Even those uninterested in the moral significance of this issue must acknowledge its implications for the development of human capabilities and efficiency of the economy as a whole. Inequalities of both outcome and opportunity have profound implications for children's motivations to develop their own capabilities.

Heterodox Economics and the Family

Understanding commitments to the development of human capabilities requires a broader perspective than analysis of investments in human capital. Chapter 1 emphasized the important role that spillovers play in the circular flow of the economy as a whole. This chapter emphasizes the importance of what might be termed social spillovers. Parental decisions are affected by their perceptions of what other parents are doing. Families coordinate their commitments through the development of cultural norms and moral principles. Individual preferences change over time, and the range of individual choice is limited. Like families, societies engage in bargaining that entails both conflict and cooperation. One of the many things they bargain over is which economic contributions should be measured and how they should be valued.

PART TWO

Private Spending on Children in the United States

CHAPTER THREE

Defining the Costs of Children

Economists have developed meters for measuring the flow of dollars within the market economy and constructing national income accounts. But these meters do not work very effectively for measuring the flow of resources within households, where direct transfers of money and time are more important than exchange. Children simultaneously represent an output of parental effort, an input into their consumption and happiness, and a cost that reduces parental consumption of other goods and services. Child rearing requires large commitments of time for supervisory as well as active care. These complications make it easy to underestimate the costs that children impose.

Consider two households with the same level of market income. One consists of two working-age adults, the other of a parent and a three-year-old child. Conventional economic measures portray the second household as better off, because it costs less to buy food and clothing for a child than for an adult. But small children require direct care and supervision, which is not free, even if it is provided outside the market. The time and effort that parents devote to children should not be taken for granted. Expenditures on children's food and clothing now represent a smaller share of all expenditures because child care, health care, and education make larger claims on family budgets.

Neoclassical economic theory focuses on subjective well-being. Institutional economics assesses standards of living in material rather than psychological terms, comparing resources to needs. Since national income accounts are based on material flows rather than measures of happiness, the institutionalist approach offers a more useful way of revising the macroeconomic picture. But even institutional economists have resisted consideration of the value of nonmarket work. Most comparisons of the standard of living of households of different composition rely on equivalence scales that make households with children seem better off than they are. Definitions of household resources, consumption, and needs should be expanded to include some consideration of the value of goods and services produced outside the market.

Happiness, Consumption, and Capabilities

How should we define household well-being? Neoclassical economists emphasize the happiness that is theoretically a function of the consumption of goods, services, and leisure.[1] Some institutional economists urge special attention to the satisfaction of basic needs, such as food and shelter.[2] Others insist on the importance of measuring specific human functionings and capabilities, such as health and educational attainment.[3] The Foundation for Child Development sponsors the publication of the "Index of Child and Youth Well-being" which relies on indicators in seven different domains, of which material well-being is only one.[4] Despite their differences, both neoclassical and institutionalist approaches require some assessment of the relative consumption needs of children.

Conventional neoclassical theory generally treats children as consumer goods that yield a flow of future happiness to their parents. By definition, their benefits must be at least equal to their cost (why else would a rational parent choose to raise them?). But as many neoclassical economists recognize, children themselves are also consumers, and they cannot choose their own parents. So-called conditional equivalence scales try to separate expenditures on children from expenditures on other sources of happiness.

Children as Consumer Goods

If children are like other consumer goods, then differences in the standard of living between families with children and those without do not matter any more than differences in the standard of living between families with golden retrievers and those without.[5] A family with annual spending of $10,000 devoted to food, clothing, shelter, and entertainment and $1,000 devoted to a golden retriever is no worse off than a family with annual spending of $11,000 on food, clothing, shelter, and entertainment. Likewise, a couple with the same total expenditures who devotes $5,000 to children is no worse off than a couple who devotes the same amount of money to scuba-diving vacations. These couples are simply making different consumption choices.

The notion that children provide a flow of services consumed by parents (thus providing benefits by definition equal to the costs) played a part in the early development of theories of equitable taxation. In a classic treatise of public finance published in 1938, Henry Simons wrote, "It would be hard to maintain that the raising of children is not a form of consumption on the part of parents, whether one believes in the subsidizing of such consumption or not."[6] The principle of horizontal equity stipulates that two families that share similar economic circumstances, differing only in their preferences, should pay the same percentage of their income in taxes.

If the presence of children is primarily an indicator of different preferences, rather than different economic circumstances, families with children do not deserve any special tax deductions or credits. Some important public policies reflect this assumption. For instance, the U.S. Board of Tax Appeals in 1939 held that child-care expenses should not be deductible as a work-related expense because they simply reflect a preference for a particular form of consumption.[7] Changes in tax law since then allow only a small proportion of actual child-care expenses to be deducted. Even so, policies that provide deductions or other benefits to parents are sometimes denounced for discriminating unfairly against nonparents.[8]

Similar reasoning is invoked by economists who insist that single mothers living in poverty are not as disadvantaged as they may seem. Mothers who freely choose the burden of custody must enjoy children more than fathers do. Their poverty simply reveals their willingness to pay for the consumption of child services, also known as the pleasures of motherhood.[9] If children are like pets, their presence is irrelevant to standards of welfare based on happiness: poverty lines should be the same whether mothers are raising children or not.[10]

Obviously, children are not pets, but human beings to whom we accord both rights and responsibilities. Parents choose to rear children but children do not choose to be born. Nor can they do much to influence their parents' decisions to raise additional children. Until they reach a certain age, they have little power to reveal their own preferences. But they presumably try to maximize their happiness as soon as they are able. Children are not merely consumed by parents, because they grow up to become consumers and producers in their own right.

Equivalent Levels of Happiness?

The notion that children could be reduced to consumer goods was challenged eloquently by the economist William Vickrey in 1947, in an explicit rebuttal of Henry Simons: "This reduction of children to a status comparable to that of a household pet is hardly acceptable. Almost everyone will concede that the community has a greater interest in the welfare of children than in the welfare of pets, even though there may be widespread disagreement as to the nature of that interest. A more satisfactory approach, on the whole, is to regard minors and other dependents as citizens in their own right."[11] Whether they maximize their own happiness or not, parents may have insufficient financial, cognitive, or emotional resources to guarantee the adequate development of their children's capabilities. Even if parents have sufficient resources, they may default on their responsibilities—for example, when a noncustodial parent fails to provide adequate child support. Government spending on children is substantial, as Chapters 8 and 9 will demonstrate. As a modern saying goes, "It may not take a village to raise a child, but these days it seems to take a village to pay for one."[12]

These conceptual problems, along with moral and practical concerns, help explain why many economists concede that children represent a cost to parents—that is, a reduction in their ability to consume goods and services.[13] A conditional equivalence scale is a scale conditioned on household structure: it asks, for instance, how much additional income a household with children requires to be as happy as a household without children, while ignoring the happiness that parents receive from children themselves. This approach assumes that the happiness that parents receive from children is separable from the happiness they receive from their consumption of other goods and services.

It is, however, impossible to directly measure the happiness of households with and without children (much less the happiness derived from everything except children). Therefore, some empirical proxy is required, typically a measure of material standards of living, such as the share of household budget devoted to necessities rather than luxuries. Such comparisons are based on arbitrary assumptions about the relationship between material standards of living and happiness. They also violate neoclassical admonitions against interpersonal comparisons of happiness.[14]

Economists who acknowledge the impossibility of comparing happiness across households sometimes take another tack, assuming instead that households or families equalize the happiness of all their members.[15] The happiness of one family member (a parent, for example) can then be taken as an indicator of the happiness of another (such as a child). The notion that everybody in a family is equally happy might be described as a happy assumption. It is not, however, a plausible one. It ignores two of the difficulties pointed out above: parents cannot compare their own happiness with that of their children, and children cannot always reveal their own preferences through informed choices. If families chose to equalize individual happiness, then the spoiled brats most difficult to please would receive the lion's share of all family resources.

Standards of Living, Consumption, and Income

Determining the material standard of living that households enjoy is easier than determining their subjective happiness, but it is still remarkably difficult. An emphasis on basic needs does not tell us whether child rearing represents a basic need.[16] An emphasis on human capabilities does not tell us how to balance the value of one capability (such as pursuing a career) against another (such as raising a child). Most assessments of standards of living focus on measures of consumption (based on market expenditures) relative to a set of presumed needs.

Household spending is a better measure of standard of living than income for several reasons.[17] Income fluctuates more than spending. Households may save money, or they may spend more than they earn, going into debt. Wealth (a stock) often has an effect on consumption that is independent of the flow of income over time. Wealth inequality is more extreme than income inequality in the United States, especially across racial and ethnic lines.[18]

The U.S. Consumer Expenditure Survey directly measures household spending. Knowing what households spend, however, does not provide a clear picture of what the individuals within them consume. People who live together can economize. Many goods and services are jointly, rather than individually, consumed. For instance, individuals in a household share the costs of shelter, utilities, and often meal preparation. But it is difficult to know how to distinguish improvements in efficiency from possible shifts in the distribution of consumption in the household. A low-income mother raising a child may not spend any more on shelter and food than another low-income woman who is living alone. But this does not mean the child is costless. The mother is probably reducing her own consumption of shelter and food in order to meet her child's needs.

The addition of another person may not change total expenditures at all (imagine someone sleeping on the couch and eating nothing but leftovers that nobody else wanted). But that person may lower the consumption of other household members by intruding on their privacy or reducing their control over the use of public goods. A television set benefits more than one person at once only if the other viewers are happy watching the same channel. The values of privacy and autonomy are harder to measure than out-of-pocket expenditures, but obviously many people cherish these deeply. In 2000 more than 25 percent of all U.S. households consisted of individuals living alone.[19]

One approach to measuring consumption is to compare the proportion of household budgets spent on "necessities," which reveals what they have left over for "luxuries." This line of reasoning was inspired by the nineteenth-century economist Ernst Engel, who found that the percentage of a household budget devoted to food tended to decline with family income. Many empirical studies of the cost of children (including some used by states in setting appropriate levels of child support for noncustodial parents) ask how much more income a household with children requires in order to spend the same percentage of its budget on food as a household without children.

Suppose that households without children with an income of $30,000 spend on average 30 percent of their income on food, and households with exactly the same income that include children spend on average about 40 percent of their income on food. Based on some simple assumptions, statistical analysis of the relationship among family composition, income, and expenditure can answer the hypothetical question: How much additional income would a family with children require in order to spend only 30 percent of its income on food?

Unfortunately, this approach is flawed by the unwarranted assumption that addition of a child (rather than an adult) to a household does not directly affect the proportion spent on food.[20] It is also flawed by the unwarranted assumption that food expenditure shares reflect a boundary between necessities and luxuries. In our day and age spending on food extends far beyond nutritional requirements and often leads to unhealthy levels of obesity. Types of food expenditure also vary. Poor families may spend proportionally more on groceries and fast food; affluent families spend proportionally more on expensive restaurant meals.

Similar problems afflict all approaches that use expenditures on a single category such as food to construct detailed equivalence scales.[21] One can ask how the presence of children affects the level of spending devoted to goods such as adult clothing or alcohol.[22] But spending on adult goods such as tobacco and alcohol is likely to reflect individual preferences (and health-related habits) rather than standards of living. Since most households spend a large portion of their budget on shared goods such as housing, consumer durables, and utilities, there is no direct trade-off between adult goods and children's goods.[23]

These problems are compounded by the direct and indirect effect that children have on adult behavior, including hours of paid employment. When women work outside the home, they spend considerably more on both food and clothing.[24] Control over sources of household income also matters: households with relatively high female earnings spend money differently from families with relatively low female earnings.[25] Men and women seem to have different preferences: households headed by women spend substantially more on clothing than households headed by men, all else being constant.[26] Families with sons spend money in different ways from families with daughters.[27]

Because technical efforts to measure equivalent levels of welfare and consumption in this way have run aground, most economists working on policy-related issues rely on measures of the ratio of household resources to household needs—measures that sidestep the issue of relative psychological welfare or happiness.

Equivalence Scales and Budget Standards

Many widely applied equivalence scales take the form of a simple mathematical formula or a set of budget standards used to adjust measures of income or consumption across households of different composition in ways that plausibly reflect their differing consumption needs. They are generally interpreted as a measure of material standards of living.[28] The resources available to a household are typically defined in terms of market income, and the needs of a household are typically defined in terms of expenditures necessary to purchase food, shelter, and other basic requirements.

Children's needs are almost always weighted less than those of adults.

Typical assumptions regarding economies of scale further discount the influence of children on adult standards of living. Most equivalence scales, including those implicit in U.S. poverty lines, understate the costs of children by assuming that neither child care nor college education represents a "need." Budget-based standards, predicated on what families would hypothetically spend for certain goods and services, can more easily take these additional costs into account, but they have not yet been very well developed in this country.

Relative Weights and Economies of Scale

Differences in consumption requirements that were based on age and gender played a central role in the early development of equivalence scales. Children are smaller than adults and need less food. Women are smaller, on average, than men, and also require fewer calories. These differences can be captured by application of a smaller weight on women and children than men as household consumers. For instance, if an infant consumes only 20 percent as much food as a fully grown adult, the household expenditures of one adult living with an infant can be divided by 1.2 instead of by 2 to arrive at an adjusted measure of per capita consumption. Similarly, if a woman consumes only 90 percent as much food as a man, the household expenditures of a man and woman living together can be divided by 1.9 instead of by 2.

Perhaps because food is easier to link to physiological requirements than most other aspects of household expenditure, it played a prominent role in the development of early equivalence scales. Most current efforts to define household needs (other than the U.S. poverty line, discussed below) look beyond food to components of spending such as housing, clothing, and health care. Children typically require less space and less clothing than adults, and health insurance can be purchased for them at a substantially lower cost than for adults (especially the elderly). Such differences provide an additional rationale for discounting their consumption needs. Though the tendency over time has been to increase relative weights on children they are still treated as less expensive than adults: a recent set of recommendations for revising the U.S. poverty line recommends weighting children at 70 percent of an adult.[29]

Economies of scale are improvements in the household's ability to convert expenditures into consumption resulting from increased household size.[30] They are typically attributed to the fact that many household goods such as living space, consumer durables, and utilities such as heat and light can be efficiently shared. But sharing entails a loss of privacy. In households, economies of scale often take the form of economies of affection. Most adults who share a home are either married or involved in an intimate relationship, and the children they live with are typically kin.

Economies of scale may also reflect the unmeasured benefits of nonmarket work. When breadwinner-homemaker families were typical, two could live more cheaply than one because a homemaker devoted considerable time and energy to converting purchased commodities into a standard of living—shopping, preparing meals, washing clothes, and tending to children. When two adults work full-time, they have less time to devote to nonmarket work. Furthermore, greater reliance on purchased goods and services reduces the effects of household economies of scale: neither restaurants nor child-care centers typically offer group discounts.

Assumptions regarding economies of scale have never been firmly based on empirical research, and most were adopted more than thirty years ago, when many households with children included a full-time housewife and mother. A common equivalence scale applied today assumes large economies of scale by dividing household income or consumption by the square root of the number of household members. In this case the income of a household with two adults is divided by the square root of 2 (or 1.4) instead of by 2. (Similarly, the income of a household with two adults and a child is divided by the square root of three, or 1.7, and a household with two adults and two children is divided by the square root of 4, or 2.) This scaling is simple to apply, and it does not explicitly weight women and children less than adult men. But it has the effect of making children seem quite inexpensive: the adjusted income of a household of two adults and two children is twice as high as if a per capita measure is used (because income is divided by 2 instead of by 4). Children are treated as though their needs are far lower than those of an adult.[31]

Dividing household consumption or income by the square root of household size may be appropriate for application to the countries of northwestern Europe in which child care is publicly provided and post-secondary education is offered at little charge. But if used to compare standards of living in countries that lack such public services, this equivalence scale overstates the relative standard of living of households that include children.

Poverty and Child Costs

The poverty lines that provide a reference point for many discussions of public policy in the United States suffer from distinct but related problems. The original benchmarks were set in the 1960s; they were based on a U.S. Department of Agriculture estimate of the basic caloric needs of adults and children, combined with the observation that most low-income families at that time spent about one-third of their budget on food. These lines simply multiply an estimate of the cost of meeting basic caloric requirements by three. Women were weighted less than men until 1981, when the threat of prosecution for sex discrimination led to equalization.[32]

Most researchers agree that reliance on estimates of necessary food expenditures as a benchmark for poverty is conceptually incorrect. Further, the assumption that food expenditures represent one-third of household budgets is antiquated: studies show that low-income households now spend a smaller proportion of their budgets on food and more on such necessities as rent, health care, and transportation. Among other distortions, this assumption leads to lower poverty thresholds for elderly persons because their caloric needs are lower than those of other adults; it ignores the greater need the elderly often have for health care.

Not surprisingly, U.S. poverty lines are quite low by international standards.[33] Like the more general equivalence scales above, they also understate the costs of children. When a child is added to a two-adult household, U.S. poverty thresholds imply that the child imposes only a 20 percent increase in the cost of meeting basic needs. When a child is added to a single-adult household, the thresholds imply only a 32 percent increase in the cost of meeting basic needs. Increments for additional children are based on apparently arbitrary assumptions.[34] For two-adult families, the second child's needs are weighted more heavily than those of the first; for single-adult families, the third child's needs are weighted most heavily.[35]

Dissatisfaction with the official poverty line motivated a panel of experts convened by the National Academy of Science (NAS) to suggest an alternative approach.[36] A new set of experimental poverty measures defines food, clothing, shelter and utilities as necessities and sets a threshold of need based on what most families spend. The minimum is set between 78 percent and 83 percent of the median expenditures on these items reported in the annual Consumer Expenditure Survey (CE). This threshold is multiplied by a number between 1.15 and 1.25 to account for other miscellaneous necessary expenditures.

The NAS approach subtracts many nondiscretionary expenditures, including taxes, from households' money and near-money income (such as food stamps) to arrive at a measure of disposable income available to meet the threshold described above. Expenditures on child care are considered nondiscretionary if they are a work-related cost—that is, if both parents living with the child are engaged in paid employment. Subtraction of these expenditures is capped at the level of the earnings of the lower-earning parent. Other work-related costs such as transportation are also subtracted, as are out-of-pocket expenditures on health.[37]

This approach represents a distinct improvement over the conventional poverty line and has been endorsed by most poverty researchers.[38] But though including expenditures on food, clothing, shelter, and necessities is better than relying entirely on expenditures on food as a marker of "necessities," it reflects a similarly antiquated emphasis on goods rather than services. Many expenditures on food (such as restaurant meals) and clothing (such as fashionable athletic shoes) represent luxuries, whereas most families regard expenditures on health and education services as necessities, especially for children.

Further, expenses for child care are not merely work-related expenses. Many recent studies emphasize the importance of early-childhood education for school readiness.[39] Many families hope to send their three- and four-year-olds to preschool whether or not mothers are working for pay. The experimental poverty measures also exclude consideration of other educational expenditures, whether for private schools, after-school tutoring or enrichment programs (such as sports and music), or postsecondary education. Poverty thresholds estimated on the basis of actual expenditures on child care and education would probably be higher, and they would increase the difference in thresholds for families with and without children.[40]

Budget Standards

One way of illustrating these conceptual issues is to examine directly the expenditures households would need to make to meet basic needs in different areas of the country. In an economy in which personal consumption (including that of food and clothing) extends well beyond the minimum requirements of physiological subsistence, the definition of need is inevitably contentious. Yet many communities reveal a strong desire to address the issue. As of May 2006, 140 communities had enacted local living-wage laws that set a higher minimum wage than the federal standard of $5.15 per hour for municipal employees or other subsets of workers, on the grounds that they should receive a wage sufficient to support themselves and their children at a decent level.[41] Levels are set by consideration of the relationship between locally prevailing wages and official poverty lines, usually specified as a simple threshold for workers with a typical family structure (that is, two parents working full-time and two children), an approach that avoids the equivalence scale issues described above.

To develop measures that do not rely on official poverty lines, some researchers use budget analysis to estimate family needs.[42] This exercise mimics the kind of reasoning families themselves apply when planning for the future. For instance, the U.S. Department of Agriculture estimates the cost of a basic food budget, and rents can be estimated using assumptions regarding the number of bedrooms required (such as a separate room for children, no more than two children in a single room), and a minimum standard of quality (considering the actual distribution of rents paid). The cost of basic necessities of transportation, health insurance, child care and clothing can also be estimated. Applying this approach, the economists Trudi Renwick and Barbara Bergmann find a much larger percentage of single mothers with children living below their minimum adequacy threshold than living below the official poverty line. Because they explicitly consider the need to pay for child care, these economists also report very different patterns of vulnerability between mothers working for pay and those caring for their own children full-time.[43]

The Economic Policy Institute takes a similar approach in a more recent study, focusing on housing, food, health insurance, and child-care costs in the late 1990s.[44] They calculate a minimum budget for a single parent with a four-year-old child that ranges from about $17,716 in Hattiesburg, Mississippi, $29,258 in Los Angeles–Long Beach, to $36,899 in New York City. They assume that the mother is working full-time and the four-year old receives full-time, center-based care.[45] Basic family budgets over a range of geographic locations yield an average needs threshold that is about twice the poverty line, and the percentage of families below these basic budgets is almost twice the percentage living in official poverty.

Diana Pearce and others have developed a series of minimal self-sufficiency standards for families in many communities within different states by several family types.[46] Self-sufficiency is defined in terms of the wages that full-time employed adults would need to earn to support their families at a minimum standard without assistance from the government or other sources (such as family or friends). The estimates are based on local estimates of actual costs such as fair market rents provided by the U.S. Department of Housing and Urban Development, typically set at the 40th percentile (meaning that 40 percent of the housing in a given area would be less expensive, and 60 percent would be more expensive).[47]

The budgets assume that all adults are employed full-time, that children under the age of two are placed in paid family care, and that preschoolers are placed in center-based care. Child-care costs are based on surveys of providers and set at the 75th percentile of prices charged. Standards also include consideration of expenditures on school-age children, ages six to twelve, and teenagers, thirteen years and older. Because these self-sufficiency standards are estimated for single adults as well as one- and two-adult households with one, two, or three children, they offer insights into the relative costs of meeting the basic needs of a child and an adult.

In general, the costs of meeting the basic needs of an infant or a preschooler relative to those a single adult range from about .75 to 1. The breakdown of the budgets shows that children have the greatest effect on child-care, housing, and health-care expenses. Overall, housing is the greatest expense, but child care for one infant almost always represents more than 60 percent of housing costs. The costs of accommodating an additional adult in the household are quite low (from .18 to .48 of a single adult) because it is presumed that the additional adult can share a room with the other adult, which leaves housing costs unchanged. These models assume that the addition of a second child has a smaller effect than the first child for the same reason.

The budget-standard approach to child care pays more attention to child-care costs than do the experimental poverty measures above, but it goes to the opposite extreme by assuming that all parents must pay for child care for young children. In fact, many low-income families simply cannot afford such purchases, and they rely on a patchwork of assistance from kin (especially grandmothers), friends, and split-shift working hours to care for children. In 1997 only about 40 percent of working families with income less than 200 percent of the federal poverty threshold with a child under thirteen reported child-care expenses.[48] On the other hand, a self-sufficiency standard is intended to capture what families need to spend in the absence of assistance from either the government or their extended kin. If many poor families received gifts of food from their relatives, would these be subtracted from their standard of need for food? Probably not.

Budget-standard approaches understate children's needs by ignoring the costs of college. Although college enrollment rises along with family income, virtually all high school seniors aspire to at least some post-secondary education.[49] The average annual cost of attending college in the academic year 1999–2000 was about $20,000 per year. Parents, on average, paid about 24 percent of this cost, or about $4,723 per year.[50] What if low-income parents aspired to pay only half the average amount? It would still amount to an additional $2,300 a year for about four years, a sizable increment. Many parents begin saving for college long before their children leave home, and a significant proportion of college students continue to live at home while attending college.

Budget analysis can usefully complement other efforts to develop better measures of family needs. But neither experimental poverty measures nor self-sufficiency standards tell us much about middle-income and affluent households with greater discretionary spending. For that reason, equivalence scales based on minimum thresholds should not be used to assess standards of living of the entire population. Furthermore, simply taking child-care expenses into account does not mitigate the larger failure—common to all the equivalence scales described above—to consider the effect of nonmarket work.

Nonmarket Work and Standards of Living

Benjamin Franklin's famous dictum that "time is money" is widely quoted but seldom consistently applied. Despite the rise of the new home economics, which emphasizes the significance of household production, most economists still use the word *work* to refer to paid work, the word *income* to refer to market income, and the word *consumption* to refer to consumption of purchased commodities. The result is a misleading picture of differences in standards of living among households of different composition.[51] The appendix to this chapter illustrates this point with numerical examples.

Time that individuals devote to nonmarket work such as child care, food preparation, home repairs, and gardening often results in the production of goods and services that would otherwise be purchased. Some measure of the value of this time should, in principle, be added to estimates of household income and consumption. At the same time, households with young children need more nonmarket work in the form of active child care and supervision, even if young children also spend many hours a week in paid child care. In other words, nonmarket time affects both the numerator and the denominator of a household's ratio of resources or consumption to needs.

Nonmarket time may also represent an important component, in and of itself, of a household's standard of living. Just as individuals require a certain minimum level of food, they require a minimum level of sleep, personal care, and leisure time.[52] And just as children have special needs for consumption of purchased child care and education, they also have special needs for the consumption of parental or family time.

Attention to these issues has been discouraged by lack of empirical data on time use. Today, however, many countries collect time-use diaries from representative samples of their populations. The statistical agencies of Canada, Australia, and the United Kingdom, among others, have published detailed summaries of the ways in which their citizens use their time outside paid employment.[53] Some time-use surveys have been conducted in the United States by independent research groups, and in 2003 the United States completed the first round of a regular American Time Use Survey (ATUS), which is appended to the annual Current Population Survey. Systematic analysis of these data could potentially improve measures of living standards.

Women and Nonmarket Work

Consideration of the value of nonmarket work is especially important because it has changed considerably over time, remains quantitatively significant, and varies considerably across households. Both women and men engage in nonmarket work, but women tend to devote a larger percentage of their time to this activity. In 2003 women ages fifteen and over averaged about thirty-three hours per week, and men about twenty hours per week. Their total hours of work (market plus nonmarket) were about the same at fifty-two hours per week.[54]

Many early censuses and labor-force surveys enumerated the number of women (and men) engaged in the occupation of housewife. In the not-so-distant past, a large proportion of adult women in the United States described their main activity as caring for family members, and many continue to do so today. Between 1972 and 1993 the Current Population Survey asked household members if they were "working," "looking for work," "going to school," "unable to work," "retired," or "keeping house."[55] The percentage of adult women between the ages of twenty-five and fifty-four who responded that they were keeping house declined from about 53 percent in 1972–73 to about 26 percent in 1992–93. In 2000, about 30 percent of all women over age 16 were engaged in "homemaking."[56] Nonmarket work remains the primary occupation of more than one quarter of all working-age women.[57]

Most empirical studies of the value of nonmarket work focus on national income accounts, noting that it represents between 40 and 60 percent of gross domestic product.[58] Less attention has been devoted to household level estimates, but one early study estimated that the value of home production among affluent white households amounted to 70 percent of their money income after taxes.[59] Estimates that take the value of household production into account lead to a picture of patterns and trends in standards of living in the United States that is very different from the one drawn by measures that rely entirely on market income. Imputing a value to women's nonmarket work reduces measures of inequality in "extended income" but does not counter the trend toward increased inequality over time.[60]

Although some households clearly enjoy more household production and consumption than others, their needs for nonmarket work also vary. On the one hand, failure to impute a value to nonmarket work understates the overall standard of living of households in which housewives and mothers (and sometimes others) specialize in the provision of nonmarket services. On the other hand, it also overstates the standard of living of adults who devote substantial time to the care of children or other family members and would, if they withdrew that time, be forced to purchase market substitutes for it. In other words, imputation of the value of time has implications for the distribution of well-being within households (between parents and children), as well as among households.

Nonmarket work, like work for pay, reduces the leisure time available to those who perform it and also generates a flow of services that increases the potential consumption of the household as a whole. If adult expenditures of cash on children are treated as a cost that reduces adult standards of living, adult expenditures of time should be treated in a parallel way. In 2003, according to the American Time Use Survey, women living in households with children under eighteen spent 12.6 hours and men 6 hours per week in direct care of household members.[61] The presence of children was also associated with extra hours of housework, especially for women.

Nonmarket Work and Expenditures on Children

Habits of thought tend to obscure the connection between nonmarket work and expenditures on children. Parental time is often taken for granted. Survey researchers have tried to devise subjective equivalence scales by asking questions such as: "Mr. and Mrs. Smith have three children and are generally considered prosperous. What is the lowest income they could have and still be considered prosperous?" Variations in the number of children referred to in this question can reveal a mental map of their perceived costs. Statistical analysis of answers to questions like this in the 1970s and 1980s suggested that the cost of a child was relatively low compared to that of an adult.[62] But asking the question in these terms, avoiding mention of whether Mrs. Smith is working outside the home, invites the respondent to assume that the mother of the house would be at home whether children were present or not.

When Mrs. Smith works for pay, as she is increasingly likely to do, she must shell out money for child care and other work-related expenses. Empirical studies of household spending show that increased hours of market work among women lead to significant increases in spending on food and clothing.[63] Households that devote more time to paid employment outsource more of the services that they once provided themselves by eating more meals out, paying for laundry and housecleaning services, and relying on even more upscale assistance such as therapists and personal trainers. Such expenditures have increased over time, canceling out some of the effects of increased household income.[64]

Few women reduce their hours of household work proportionately as they increase hours of market work, which complicates empirical analysis of the relationship between hours of employment and household outsourcing.[65] A significant part of the reduction in their standard of living comes from the reduction in their leisure time. Causality can also run the other way. Families who benefit from contributions of nonmarket work, such as a grandmother willing to provide child care at no cost, are likely to supply more hours to paid employment. Such hidden contributions from outside the household weaken the empirical correlation between hours of market work and purchases of substitutes.[66]

Toward New Equivalence Scales

How does the standard of living of households with children compare to that of other households in the United States today? It is hard to imagine a question more relevant to debates over family policy. Yet conventional answers are inadequate. Neoclassical models of happiness maximization not only make implausible assumptions; they assume that preferences for parenting are fixed. Most parents get great pleasure from parenting, but most wage earners also report getting great pleasure from paid work.[67] We do not conclude, as a result, that they should not get paid.

The costs of children should be defined in terms relevant to material standards of living. But standards of living must be broadly defined. Simple models of the ratio of household resources or consumption to needs understate the needs that children impose. Most emphasize necessary goods such as food, clothing, and shelter but neglect necessary services such as child care, education, and health care. More profoundly, conventional approaches ignore nonmarket work in the home, which both contributes to household standards of living and imposes costs on those who perform it on behalf of children and other dependents. There is no magic solution to the difficulty of specifying accurate equivalence scales. But greater awareness of existing problems should inform efforts to estimate the overall magnitude of resources devoted to children.

Appendix: Nonmarket Work and Living Standards

To illustrate the effect of nonmarket work on household consumption and needs, consider the stylized comparison of four two-person households with and without children and with varying levels of specialization in market and nonmarket work presented in Table 3.1. For the purpose of simplicity, assume that all households can earn a dollar for every hour of market work, that the value of nonmarket work is also one dollar per hour, and that all income and household production is devoted to consumption. Total consumption is defined as the sum of market income and the value of nonmarket work.

Household A has two adults, both breadwinners who work for pay 40 hours per week. Its market income and total consumption amount to $80 per week. Household B has two adults, a breadwinner who works for pay 40 hours a week and a homemaker who performs nonmarket work of 40 hours per week. Its market income amounts to only $40 per week, but the value of its nonmarket work also amounts to $40, allowing total consumption of $80 per week. Household C has one adult breadwinner who works for pay 40 hours per week and one child under the age of five. Its market income amounts to $40 per week and it devotes 20 hours per week to nonmarket work, allowing total consumption of $60 per week. Household D has one adult homemaker who does

Table 3.1 Stylized comparisons of the standard of living of four families

	Family A	Family B	Family C	Family D
Number of adults	2	2	1	1
Number of children	0	0	1	1
Total hours of market work	80	40	40	0
Total hours of nonmarket work	0	40	20	60
Market income	$80	$40	$40	0
Nonmarket income	0	$40	$20	$60
Total consumption	$80	$80	$60	$60
Market costs of child care	0	0	$20	0
Nonmarket costs of child care	0	0	$10	$30
Total consumption net of both market and nonmarket child care costs	$80	$80	$30	$30

Note: Assume that all families have the same number of members and earn $1 per hour for both market and nonmarket work.

not work for pay, devotes 60 hours per week to nonmarket work, and has one child under the age of five. Its market income is 0, but its nonmarket work and total consumption amount to $60.

Standard-equivalence scales divide household income by the number of adults and children without any consideration of the value of nonmarket work. Family A would be ranked twice as high as Family B in terms of its ratio of income to needs, because its market income is twice as high. This is misleading, because Family B is receiving the additional but uncounted benefit of 40 hours of nonmarket work provided by a homemaker. Its consumption is exactly the same. For instance, rather than spending money on restaurant meals, a housekeeper, and a gardener, Family B provides these services for itself. We do not know how consumption is distributed between the adults in either Family A or Family B, but it is possible that both adults receive equal shares.

The contrast is similar, but slightly different, for the single parents with children, Families C and D. Both single parents in these families work 60 hours per week, rather than 40. Although the single parent in Family C puts in 40 hours of paid employment, she also spends 20 hours a week in nonmarket work after she gets home from the office. Of this nonmarket work, one-half, or 10 hours, is devoted to meeting her child's needs. She must also pay someone to care for her child while she is engaged in paid employment, which costs her $20. Her market income net of working expenses is therefore only $20. Her family consumes goods and services equivalent to $60. But the adult in this household is unlikely to consume one-half of this amount because household income net of paid and unpaid child care is only $30. This remaining sum must pay for the housing, food, and clothing expenses of both adult and child.

The single parent in family D has no market income, but the value of her nonmarket work is $60. Half of the time she devotes to nonmarket work is child care. By conventional measures, Family C is better off, but Family D's total consumption is the same as that of Family C. For similar reasons—the demands of child care—her share of total family consumption is almost certainly less than half.

The comparison between Family B and C is even more striking. Both have the same market income and the same per capita market income. Using an equivalence scale that weights children less than adults would make Family C appear to have a higher standard of living than Family B. But because it enjoys the services of a full-time homemaker, Family B enjoys higher total consumption than Family C, even though the single parent in Family C works many more hours total per week. Also, Family B has no explicit child-care costs, whereas Family C has a market income of only $20 after child-care costs are paid.

These comparisons are obviously overly simple. In the real world, there is less-than-perfect substitutability between market and nonmarket work. Families cannot meet their needs with zero time devoted to either one, and they must combine the two. Furthermore, these comparisons omit any consideration of the value of leisure—they focus entirely on differences in the value of goods and services consumed. Nonetheless, they illustrate just how misleading measures of standards of living putatively based on the ratio between consumption and needs can be, especially for families with young children.

CHAPTER FOUR

Children and Family Budgets

Children are an expensive crop. The U.S. Department of Agriculture (USDA) estimates parental expenditures on children from birth through age seventeen in much the same way as amounts spent raising apple trees or cattle to maturity. By their calculation, a middle-income, husband-wife family with two children in 2000 could expect to spend about $165,630 per child over eighteen years.[1] This estimate omits consideration of the value of time and energy devoted to child rearing, as well as the costs of a college education. Even so, it represents a hefty sum. If these hypothetical parents chose not to raise those two children and reallocated those funds to investments enjoying an average 5 percent annual rate of return, eighteen years later they would have a sum of $545,284.[2] If they left that nest egg untouched until they retired, say twenty years later, they would have accumulated close to $1.5 million.

The costs of parental commitments deserve careful consideration. Neoclassical economic theory deflects attention from them, assuming that parents know exactly how much they will spend and will allocate their spending in such a way that no one can be made any better off without making someone else worse off. Whether or not parents succeed at this task, it is important to ask how much they spend. This question is difficult to answer with precision because the data sources at hand are limited and also because shared consumption is intrinsically difficult to measure. But even an approximate picture of expenditures on children helps explain why parents feel economic stress.

This chapter develops an institutional approach to family budgets and summarizes the strengths and weaknesses of methods used by the USDA to analyze consumer expenditure data. A descriptive picture of spending on young children sets the stage for an analysis of the average value of parental time in Chapter 6.

Allocation within the Household

If parents love their children, the money they spend on them is, in a sense, money they spend on themselves. But it differs from expenditures on bathrobes or beer because a child—another person—benefits. Family members may try to take one another's happiness into account, but both their willingness and their ability to do so is limited. Whatever their motivation, parents typically allocate money to their children that they could have spent on other things, with significant consequences not just for children but also for society as a whole.

Partly because altruism alone is unreliable, virtually all modern societies enforce basic parental obligations to children and mandate some basic level of school attendance. Many cultural norms reflect expectations about sharing that are likely to affect family behavior, especially regarding expenditures on shelter, food, and clothing for children. These norms narrow the range within which individuals make choices. Normative expectations regarding educational spending are probably affected by education itself, and its potential costs and benefits are hard to quantify. These institutional and behavioral complexities make it difficult for families to make efficient decisions.

Efficient Allocation?
Economists conventionally assume that families allocate resources among their members so efficiently that it would be impossible to make one family member better off without making another worse off (achieving what economists term Pareto optimality). If individual family members disagree, they are presumed to resolve their differences in efficient ways. For instance, an altruistic head of household can use his control over resources to elicit good behavior from a "rotten kid" who might otherwise reduce the welfare of other family members.[3]

Neoclassical theory does concede an important source of inefficiency: parents may not have sufficient income to pay for efficient levels of investment in their children's education. A traditional focus on the cost of higher education has been extended to consideration of early-childhood education.[4] Few low-income parents can pay for early-childhood education and college on their own—the costs represent an unrealistic proportion of their budget. Income constraints go well beyond lack of ability to purchase these specific services. Many low-income families cannot afford to buy or rent homes in good school districts, much less pay for private schools. Demanding work schedules that fall outside the standard 8:00 AM to 5:00 PM time slot, as well as constraints imposed by limited public transportation, make it difficult for them to exercise much choice over which schools their children will attend.

Family income can have more subtle effects. Parents try to shape children's preferences, encouraging them to care about other family members, including themselves.[5] Some parents are likely to be more successful at socialization than others. Relatively well-to-do parents can use their resources to exercise leverage over their children, as in "If you don't do your homework, I'm not buying you a video game." Low-income parents have a smaller repertoire of positive rewards to bargain with. Some express concern about their ability to compete with the expensive clothes and gadgets lavished on young boys who join a gang that engages in illegal activity.[6] Though negative sanctions such as physical punishment come cheap, they can have adverse effects on children.

Since highly trained economists constantly debate the cost-effectiveness of different educational arrangements, it is hardly surprising that most parents are uncertain about how best to spend their money. The effects of imperfect information are compounded by variation in cultural norms. Decisions to send children to preschool are strongly influenced by parents' own level of education. Highly educated individuals place great intrinsic value on schooling, and they are often confident that their own cultural values will pervade the classroom. Less well educated parents, though equally concerned about their children's future, may consider schooling less intrinsically desirable. Those who are members of racial or ethnic minorities or other culturally disempowered groups may fear that education will dampen their own influence or shortchange their children in other ways. They may prefer informal or kin-based care for toddlers even when these are less likely than center-based care to improve children's readiness for school.

How do parents determine what their children want? Like other well-meaning altruists, parents face the conundrum that it is impossible to compare the happiness of two individuals accurately.[7] Infants can only sleep or smile or scream. Some things that make toddlers happy in the short run make them unhappy in the long run. Teens have been known to change their minds about what they want on an hourly basis. Family members cannot read one another's feelings off a calibrated gauge that enables them to compare relative well-being.

Parents try to make good decisions. But this does not imply that they always make efficient ones. And because parents face formidable information and coordination problems, we should not be surprised if they rely heavily on moral prescriptions of what families should do and on social perceptions of what other families are doing.

Social Norms and Sharing Rules

Family law provides only basic guidelines for the support of children within families that live together. Parents are responsible for the basic health and well-being of their children, and spouses must help maintain one another.[8] But no legal rules stipulate how income should be shared unless a parent no longer coresides with a child under eighteen. (The child-support responsibilities of non-custodial parents are discussed in chapter 5).[9]

Parental neglect is a more widespread problem than child abuse, particularly among families that have a hard time making ends meet. Legal guidelines are not based on physical health alone. In the words of the Arizona Supreme Court, for instance, child neglect includes conditions in which a caretaker fails to provide "one or more of the ingredients generally deemed essential for developing a person's physical, intellectual, and emotional capacities."[10] The overall rate of official child maltreatment in the United States, based on registered complaints and actions by state child protective services, was about 12.3 children per 1,000 in 2002.[11] Over the eighteen years of childhood, such risks accumulate.[12] Poor monitoring and inadequate public assistance probably result in higher levels of maltreatment than those actually registered.[13]

If we could always rely on parents to make efficient decisions regarding their children's education, mandatory public education (as well as child labor laws) would be unnecessary. The widespread adoption of such rules makes it virtually impossible to determine what would have happened in their absence. Enforcement of school attendance has remained largely unchanged since the 1960s, even though average participation in both preschool and postsecondary training has significantly increased. In many European countries, on the other hand, official standards (if not actual requirements) have ratcheted upward. In France, for instance, the participation of children ages three to five in publicly financed early-education programs approached 100 percent in the mid-1990s, compared to 54 percent in the United States.[14]

Social norms define parental obligations. Most children live in the same house as a parent, share at least some meals with that parent, and dress in ways comparable to the way a parent dresses. If a family's standard of living falls below a certain threshold, however, we generally expect parents to sacrifice on their children's behalf, even if this lowers their own standard of living. Most parents feel responsibility to meet their children's basic needs for housing, food, and shelter before indulging their own desires for luxuries.

Normative sharing rules do not negate the role of individual decisions. Within a certain range, parents balance their own consumption against that of their children. But there may be a certain threshold of spending on children below which they will not go, not only because of their own preferences, but also because of cultural norms that vary according to community standards. Mothers and fathers may have different priorities, and education may affect what parents want for their children, as well as what they are able to provide.

Norms of fairness are likely to come into play in families, as well as in society as a whole, because they help solve coordination problems. Imagine a parent who has just bought ice cream cones for two twin children, a boy and a girl. The little boy stamps his feet, demanding a share of his sister's ice cream cone on the grounds that he likes ice cream more than she does. The little girl protests that is not true. Most parents would simply say, "You each have a cone, that's fair." Fairness trumps subjective claims partly because interpersonal comparisons of happiness are contentious.

Social Norms and Family Budgets
This normative approach to family decision making has implications for the conceptualization of family budgets. If parents rely on a normative standard of sharing, the percentage of total spending devoted to children is likely to be higher for low-income families who give their children's needs priority when facing tight income constraints. If such buffering takes place, children in low-income families are better off than the equal-sharing rule built into most stylized equivalence scales assumes, but their parents are worse off. Overall patterns of spending are likely to be affected by child-care costs, which in turn are related both to patterns of parental labor force participation and the availability of family and friends providing unpaid child care.

A norm-based approach also implies that gender, cultural background, and education affect parental priorities as well as income. As emphasized in Chapter 3, it is difficult to ascertain what share of housing and food expenditures is consumed by children. Analysis of data from Consumer Expenditure Surveys can approximate parental spending, however, and the USDA estimates referred to above provide a good starting point.

USDA Estimates of Parental Spending

For about forty years, the USDA has been publishing estimates of expenditures on children that are often headlined in the popular press and cited as a basis for public policies that set levels of payment for foster care and child support.[15] These estimates rely on simple assumptions regarding the allocation of household spending.

Consumer Expenditure Surveys

The U.S. Bureau of Labor Statistics (BLS) began administering consumer spending surveys around 1900, partly in response to trade union efforts to define a "living wage."[16] The growth of the life insurance industry also directed attention to the costs and contributions of individual family members. In their classic *The Money Value of a Man,* published in 1946, Louis Dublin and Alfred Lotka used the Federal Study of Consumer Purchases to develop one of the first estimates of family spending on an average child up to age eighteen.[17] The USDA has used the BLS Survey of Consumer Expenditures (CE) to provide regular estimates of expenditures on children since 1966.[18]

The current annual CE Survey interviews about five thousand consumer units representative of the total civilian noninstitutionalized population, asking detailed questions regarding their income and expenditures.[19] Among other uses, this survey provides the basis for updating the Consumer Price Index, which is used to adjust incomes for the effect of inflation. The CE survey was not explicitly designed to capture expenditures on children, and, like most household surveys, it suffers from many limitations.[20] Nonetheless, it provides an indispensable source of information on how people spend their money.

Allocating Spending on Household Public Goods

Most households with children pool most of their income and spend it largely on items that they consume jointly, such as housing. Only a few specific items, such as children's clothing, toys, child care, and education can be distinguished from adult consumption. Children don't take up as much space as adults, and they often have smaller bedrooms. On the other hand, two adults are more likely to share a bedroom than an adult and a child, and many parents opt for more expensive neighborhoods in order to gain access to better schools for their children. Many adults need cars to get to work; on the other hand, many children also need adults with cars to take them to school, not to mention baseball and soccer. Groceries and many restaurant meals are purchased for collective consumption.

The USDA method assumes that families allocate spending according to an equal sharing rule slightly modified by differences in needs. Food expenses of children and adults are allocated according to age-based guidelines for caloric requirements. Medical expenditures are allocated on the basis of costs revealed in more detailed surveys, which depart only slightly from per capita shares. Estimates of work-related transportation costs are subtracted to arrive at a measure of household-related transportation costs, which are then allocated on a per capita basis. Spending on housing and other goods and services that cannot be attributed to parents and children are allocated per capita, dividing expenses equally among household members. (For a more detailed discussion of allocation rules, see Appendix A to this chapter.)

Because the USDA method departs from a per capita rule in allocation of food, medical expenditures, and transportation costs, the amount of consumption attributed to children is slightly less than the 50 percent that a straightforward per capita allocation would yield for a two-parent, two-child family, about 42 percent The allocation rule determines how the addition of more children to the household affects the estimated share devoted to children. To illustrate, assume that children and adults each receive a per capita share of family consumption. In a two-parent, three-child family, each member receives 20 percent of the total, so children account for 60 percent of the total. In a two-parent, four-child family, each member receives about 17 percent of the total, so children receive about 68 percent of the total, and so on.

The allocation rule takes into account the additional expenditures associated with additional children, but allocates these equally across all household members. This is sometimes called an "average cost" approach, as distinct from a "marginal cost" approach, which assumes that an additional child only consumes only an amount equal to the additional expenditures. The limitation of this average cost approach is that it assumes equal sharing. But the limitation of the marginal cost approach is that it assumes no sharing at all. The marginal cost of a third child is much lower than the cost of the first or second child. But that does not imply that the third child actually consumes less; rather, the third child reduces the consumption of other family members, including the first two children. The average cost approach is more consistent with normative standards in our society, which hold that children are entitled to the same treatment whether they arrived first, second, or third.

Following similar reasoning, a per capita allocation can be interpreted as a simple rule for sharing the benefits of joint consumption or economies of scale. An example that does not include children helps clarify the rule. Consider a single adult contemplating a decision to share an apartment with another person. The marginal expenditure (for example, the cost of renting a two-bedroom apartment rather than a single-bedroom apartment) is probably less than the average expenditure the two roommates would make (the cost of a two-bedroom apartment divided by two). But unless there are big differences in the size or number of the rooms they will lay claim to, most adults would agree to split the rent and utilities on a per capita basis. This decision rule allows them to divide the gains evenly.

Special circumstances might lead to departures from such a sharing rule. For instance, if one person had a long-term lease on an apartment with a below-market rent, he or she could probably find a potential roommate willing to pay more than half the total rent, because this would probably cost less than other available options. In some households children may be confined to small rooms and not allowed in adult rooms, in which case their consumption of housing services would be smaller than a per capita allocation suggests (although teenagers, in particular, tend to make large claims on shared space). Children may also affect one another's consumption more than that of adults. For instance, when a second child is added to the household with two adults, the first child may be required to share a bedroom or a playroom, which would leave adult use of space largely unaffected.

Still, an average cost allocation for jointly consumed goods seems more realistic than a marginal cost allocation. The more complex budget-share methods based on Engel or Rothbarth equivalence scales discussed in Chapter 3 are sometimes referred to as marginal cost estimates. Though it is true that they represent efforts to estimate the effect of an additional child, they differ more fundamentally from the USDA approach in their use of budget shares for a particular item such as food or clothing as a proxy for household happiness or satisfaction of basic needs. The USDA approach avoids assumptions regarding subjective welfare or basic needs, relying instead on empirical evidence of actual expenditures. Given this profound methodological difference, it is interesting that USDA-style estimates of spending on children often fall in between those generated using Engel and Rothbarth scales.[21]

Estimates of Per-Child Expenditures

The USDA offers a straightforward estimate of spending on children in 2000, focusing on families with two children under the age of eighteen in three income groups, and on single-parent families in two income groups (since relatively few of these families reach the top income category).[22] As Table 4.1 shows, in the middle-income, married-couple families, expenditures per child came to about $9,202 per year. Expenditures in the top income category were considerably higher, at $13,432 per year, about twice the expenditures per child in the bottom income category. Expenditures for single parents in the bottom income category were slightly lower than for married couple families in the same category. Expenditures in the middle income category are not comparable because of differences in category definitions.

Overall expenditures per child tend to increase with the age of the child but to decline with the number of children in the family (Table 4.2). In two-parent families expenditures on a single child were about 1.24 times higher than expenditures per child in a two-child family, and expenditures per in a three-child family were only .77 times as much as in a two-child family. (Corresponding factors for single parent families

Table 4.1 USDA estimate of average annual money expenditures per child in two-child families by income category and family type, 2000

	Two-parent families	Single-parent families
Low-income families (income less than $38,000)	$ 6,735	$ 6,397
Middle-income families (income $38,001–$64,000 for two-parent families or greater than $38,000 for single-parent families)	9,202	13,495
High-income families (income more than $64,000 for two-parent families)	13,432	

Source: Lino, *"Expenditures on Children by Families, 2000,"* tables 1 and 7.
Note: Figures are based on 1990–1993 data converted to 2000 dollars, income before taxes; groups exclude households with adult nonparents.

Table 4.2 USDA estimates of variations in annual expenditure per child by age and number of children in married-couple, middle-income families, 2000.

	One-child family	Family with two children	Family with three or more children
Age of child			
0–2	$ 10,838	$ 8,740	$ 6,730
3–5	11,135	8,980	6,915
6–8	11,148	8,990	6,922
9–11	11,098	8,950	6,892
12–14	12,016	9,690	7,461
15–17	12,226	9,860	7,592
Total, ages 0–17	205,383	165,630	127,536
Average per year	11,410	9,202	7,085

Source: Calculations are based on Lino, "Expenditures on Children by Families," 7.

were 1.35 and .72.)[23] Families raising more than one child probably enjoy some economies of scale. But the entire reduction in spending per capita cannot be interpreted as the effect of increased efficiency because it may also reflect belt-tightening—everyone in the family making do with less space and less privacy.

These estimates of spending on children under the age of eighteen represent a lower bound, for several reasons. Many low-income families have access to in-kind benefits such as subsidized child care, food stamps and Medicaid, whereas many middle- and high-income families have access to employer-provided health benefits. (See the discussion in Chapter 8.) In-kind benefits reduce their out-of-pocket expenditures. These estimates also omit child-related savings and investments, such as money set aside for college even before children reach college age. They also omit consideration of the physical demands of pregnancy and childbirth, which are substantial. One indicator of these is the market price of surrogate motherhood services in 2000, about $15,000.[24]

Spending on Child Care

Most child-specific items, such as toys and children's clothing, represent a small percentage of overall expenditures and are also discretionary, varying considerably according to personal tastes and also region of the country. The most important—and most variable—category of child-specific spending is paid child care.

Mothers are likely to take the price of child care into account when considering how many hours they will work outside the home.[25] Causality clearly works the other way as well. The number of hours that mothers devote to paid employment affects the amount of money a household devotes to purchased child care. But the relationship between these two factors is weak, because parents can often rely on relatives or reschedule their own time using shift work in order to provide care.[26] All else being equal, mothers able to take advantage of free or low-cost assistance are more likely to seek paid employment than those who must pay for care. Child-care spending is also affected by who earns income: such expenditures tend to be mentally—perhaps even literally—subtracted from a mother's earnings, because she is the person who would likely care for the child if she were not working for pay.[27]

For families who must pay, the costs vary enormously by institutional setting and region of the country. In 2002 estimates for approximately full-time care (corresponding to a forty-hour workweek for a parent) ran from a low end of $3,600–$7,800 for a family child-care home, to $6,000–$9,000 for a child-care center to $18,000–$30,000 for a live-in nanny.[28] In recent years costs have risen considerably faster than the rate of inflation.[29]

Most studies of child-care expenses focus on "working families," roughly defined as those in which all parents present in the home are working for pay. A recent study based on the 1997 National Survey of America's Families (NSAF) found that 48 percent of working families with children under age thirteen had child-care expenses. Of those families who paid for care, the average monthly expense was $286 per month, or an average of 9 percent of earnings.[30] Among low-income families (defined as those with earnings no more than 200 percent of the poverty threshold), the percentage of earnings consumed was about 16 percent. Most of these families are purchasing far less than forty hours per week of child care.

Low-income working families are less likely to purchase child care than other families for several reasons. They may qualify for free or subsidized child-care assistance. Many simply cannot afford to pay for care out of pocket, so they are less likely to seek employment unless they have a partner, relative, or friend who can help them out. Finally, middle- and high-income families are more likely to send their children to child-care centers because they consider it advantageous for their children. This is especially true for children ages three to five, for whom child care is being redefined as early-childhood education.

Our analysis of the CE survey, considering all households with children under six in 1998–2000, provides some insights into these patterns. About 54 percent reported spending no money at all on child care during the year. About 20 percent of all households surveyed devoted less than 5 percent of their total spending to it, and about 25 percent of all these households devoted more than 5 percent.

Restricting our analysis to households with at least $1,000 in total spending who reported expenditures on child care, we examined the effect of total household spending, household composition, education of household reference person, maternal hours of employment, and total household spending on expenditures on child care (See Appendix B to this chapter.) We found that, controlling for other factors, spending increased only slightly with mothers' hours of market work.

Single parents tend to spend substantially more on child care than married parents. Household composition has somewhat contradictory effects—households with two children spend more on child care than those with only one, but households with three or more spend less, perhaps because older children can help babysit. The presence of another adult in the household does not have a significant effect on child-care spending. Many relatives who help families with child care, such as grandparents, are likely to live in separate households. Even controlling for many demographic and economic characteristics, education exerts the most powerful effect. Households with a reference person holding a college degree spent almost $600 more per year on child care than others with less education.

Other studies show that variations in household structure affect spending patterns. Cohabiting partners do not devote as many resources to children as married parents.[31] Mothers tend to devote more resources to children than fathers, and slight differences in spending on boys and girls are apparent.[32]

Where the Money Goes

Studies of household budgets, once prominent in economics, have been largely displaced by more abstract theoretical models of utility maximization that assume efficient decision making. This chapter challenges the usefulness of these abstract models and emphasizes the insights of an alternative approach. Annual data from the CE survey provide a rich source of information on patterns of household spending. The USDA has helped parents and potential parents understand the magnitude of cash expenditures on children.

Updates and improvements of the USDA approach could help show how spending on children varies with household characteristics and overall spending. Our analysis suggests that expenditures on child care should not be treated merely as a work-related expense. Growing participation in prekindergarten programs is changing expectations of performance for all children once they enter public schools. High-quality early-childhood education has an important influence on children's future capabilities. (See the discussion in Chapter 10.) Most important, household spending on children under eighteen represents only a portion of parental economic commitments to the next generation.

Appendix A: Allocation Rules

Spending on children as a percentage of total spending can be modeled in much the same way as total spending as a percentage of total income:[33]

Let C = spending on children

T = total spending

(1) C = a + b(T)

The intercept of this equation, a, can be interpreted as the component of spending on children that is independent of income, and b as the marginal propensity to devote consumption dollars to children. Under this simple assumption, spending on children as a share of total spending is represented by:

(2) [a + b(T)] / T

Some studies of consumer spending report that families with similar demographic structure (such as two married parents) devote about the same percentage of their total spending to children.[34] This implies that a, the component of spending independent of income, is close to zero, and that b, the marginal propensity to spend on children, is constant. This hypothesis is difficult to test using data from the CE survey because so much household spending is devoted to shared goods such as housing.

Any approach that relies heavily on a per capita allocation rule (like the USDA approach applied here) eliminates much of the possible variation in the marginal propensity to spend. Only large changes in the composition of spending (such as a reduction in the share of housing as a percentage of total spending, or an increase in the share of spending on child-specific goods) can lead to variation in marginal spending or average share.

Appendix B: Determinants of Parental Spending on Child Care

We restrict our analysis to households with at least one child under the age of six and at least $1,000 in total spending who reported positive spending on child care, and we estimate the following equation using ordinary least squares regression.

$$K = a + b_1 T + b_2 S + b_3 K_1 + b_4 K_2 + b_5 K_3 + b_6 A_{1+} b_7 E + b_8 G + b_9 M$$

Where:

K = household spending on child care
T = total household spending
S = dummy variable for single-parent household
K_i = dummy variables for number of children
A_1 = dummy variable for presence of a child ages three to five in the household
E = dummy variable for household reference person with college degree
G = dummy variable for presence of an another adult (other than a parent) in the household
M = mother's hours of market work

Table 4.3 Regression estimate of determinants of spending on child care (all households with total spending > $1000, at least one child under 6, and positive expenditures on child care), 1998–2000, in $2000 dollars)

Variable	Coefficient	Standard error
Intercept	−284.24	177.05
Total spending	.04*	.00
Single parent	328.90**	164.09
Two-child family	504.14*	127.06
Three-child family	−141.46	167.37
Four-or-more-child family	−85.50	250.14
Child ages 3–5 in household	−504.23*	110.47
Household reference person with college degree	599.66*	121.57
Presence of a nonparent adult in household	−184.10	283.26
Mother's weekly hours of market work	1.06*	.06
Reference person nonwhite	−185.25	134.61
F	102.34*	
R^2	.21	

*Significant at .001 level; **Significant at .05 level.
Source: Author's estimates based on the Consumer Expenditure survey

Children outside the Household

Children often enjoy substantial transfers of money and time from parents and other family members outside their own households. Most significant for young children are contributions from noncustodial parents, typically fathers. High school graduates generally hope for family assistance paying for college. Adult children from affluent backgrounds often receive gifts from their parents for special purposes such as a buying a home. Many inherit substantial assets when their parents die. The overall size of these transfers is large in relation to what families devote to coresident children under the age of eighteen. The pattern they take suggests that families tend to rely on sharing rules rather than trying to maximize collective happiness.

Economists have long debated whether individuals save money to provide for themselves in old age (life-cycle saving) or to bequeath money to their children (intergenerational transfers).[1] The first motive seems more self-interested, the second more altruistic. But these two motives are not mutually exclusive, and they may vary among individuals and over time. Both the fragility of altruistic preferences and the difficulty of acting on them in efficient ways help explain the importance of social norms, legal rules, and public safety nets.

This chapter applies an institutional perspective to analysis of child support, educational spending, and other transfers and bequests to adult children in the United States, summarizing existing research and exploring the implications for public policy. The conclusion calls attention to the ways public policies replicate social inequality.

Institutional Failures

In the United States today, a large percentage of children live apart from their fathers and receive relatively little money or attention from them. Economists offer useful explanations of child support enforcement problems that focus on information and coordination problems. They seem reluctant, however, to face up to the possibility that the altruistic preferences that we often take for granted can dissipate, which can lead to "family failure."

Other forms of institutional failure are widely acknowledged. Most introductory microeconomics textbooks devote considerable attention to the "market failure" that arises when consumers have inadequate information or make decisions that spill over on others. Most texts also emphasize that public intervention to compensate for market failures can lead to authoritarian control or bureaucratic inefficiency, a parallel case of "state failure."[2] Conservatives often invoke the latter category in their efforts to explain the problems that beleaguer families today, arguing that they result primarily from the intrusion of state policies such as social insurance and welfare.

But families are distinct from both markets and states, so we should not be surprised if they are vulnerable to a distinctive form of failure. Not everyone successfully develops the cognitive and emotional capabilities required to sustain caring relationships. Altruistic preferences may grow out of biological propensities, but they are influenced by many aspects of the social and cultural environment. Individuals may fear the loss of control that affection for others can bring, and they may choose to alter their relationships in ways that reduce their emotional vulnerability.

Social norms help individuals respond to these problems, providing prescriptive guidelines for appropriate behavior toward family members. Norms for sharing resources considered necessary to meet basic needs are stronger than those concerning luxuries. Most children under the age of eighteen enjoy the commitment of at least one parent. Family responsibilities to children over that age are less clearly defined. This variability adds a distinctive twist to analysis of institutional problems. Family failure, market failure, and state failure can intertwine in a complex causality that is difficult to untangle.

Altruistic Dilemmas

Hearts are muscles that can be wounded but also strengthened by disappointment. Adults, like children, engage in wishful thinking. Most women and men who become parents express the hope that they will form an enduring relationship with their offspring. Yet these hopes are often disappointed. If we believe that families always succeed in making their members as happy as possible, we should conclude that family dissolution is neither good nor bad: adults simply reveal their preference to exit the relationship. Such neutrality ignores the possibility that children will be adversely affected.

Families try to nurture and strengthen altruistic commitments. Some efforts are more successful than others, whether as a result of individual capabilities or through sheer luck. Many aspects of the economic and social environment also have a discernible influence. Shared moral norms probably reinforce altruistic preferences. If you believe you should love someone, you may be more likely to love that person (although such prescriptions can also backfire). Reciprocity probably helps reinforce altruistic preferences. If you behave in a loving way toward someone and he or she reciprocates, your feelings may grow stronger (although of course some love persists unrequited).

Reciprocity is affected by economic circumstances, including the potential cost of breaking promises. Mutual dependence reinforces reciprocity, whereas attractive alternatives may weaken it. Personal contact often increases trust and affection. Many studies show how these factors may alter the outcomes of stylized experiments and games that test how willing individuals are to contribute to public goods or share windfall gains.[3] Though most experiments are designed to explore the behavior of individuals who are strangers, some findings are relevant to family interactions.[4]

Most individuals derive intrinsic satisfaction from close personal relationships, but they are also wary of the risks involved. Falling in love with someone who does not reciprocate is a painful experience. Love for children creates vulnerability. The parent most willing to sacrifice for a child often becomes the one who makes those sacrifices. The metaphorical "weights" that family members place on one another's happiness may vary, and they may also change over time. If one parent or family member increases support for a child, another parent may withdraw it, in a private version of "crowding out."

Institutional rules such as marriage help reduce such risks and uncertainties. But such rules can also create problems of their own. Spouses who know that divorce is impossible may be more likely to abuse one another or to become depressed or demoralized. Recent historical evidence suggests that married women living in states that made divorce more difficult were significantly more likely to commit suicide than women in other states.[5] The specifics of divorce rules also matter. Parents may disagree over child custody as well as child support. The parent who most wants custody may be willing to bargain away his or her right to child support in return.[6]

Other incentive problems result from what critics of the welfare state refer to as the "Samaritan's dilemma." Altruists who take too much responsibility for others can undermine the incentives individuals have to take care of themselves.[7] This is exactly the dilemma that parents face as they try to help children make a transition to adulthood. Should they pay for a child's education, or expect that child to take out loans? Should they help out a son or daughter who seems especially needy, or would this penalize their other children who have worked hard to achieve more self-sufficiency?

Families and State Policies

Since both families and public welfare programs take responsibility for the care of dependents, it is not surprising that they suffer from similar incentive problems. The idealized family of neoclassical economic theory always succeeds in maximizing its happiness. As a result, it achieves an efficient equilibrium that is inevitably disrupted by transfers from outside. Theoretically, public provision of free school lunches for their children should lead parents to compensate by reducing their own expenditures on children's breakfasts. Theoretically, public transfers cannot improve children's happiness unless they are larger than the amount that parents can withdraw in response.

In practice, it seems unlikely, if not impossible, that parents either aspire to or achieve such "efficiency." Many are unable (or unwilling) to provide the level of support that children would prefer. Of course, public assistance may be partially neutralized by reduction in family transfers. A noncustodial parent may contribute less as a result of a social safety net. Parents may put less into their college fund because state universities are relatively cheap. Adult children may be less likely to take responsibility for aged parents if Social Security and Medicare provide adequate assistance.

On the other hand, private transfers can also create perverse incentives. A father may be more likely to abandon a child if he knows a mother will care for it. A parent may hold back support for college in the hope that a grandparent will help pay the bill. Large gifts and bequests to children may weaken the link between individual effort and economic success. As Andrew Carnegie famously put it, "Great sums bequeathed often work more for the injury than the good of the recipients."[8] Individuals who enjoy substantial transfers or bequests have less incentive to develop their own capabilities, and the free ride they enjoy may also discourage others who might otherwise seek to compete with them—hence the case for levying taxes on large gifts and bequests.

Both parents and the state must try to balance the benefits of transfers to children against the possible costs. Too small a transfer may leave children's needs unmet or their capabilities underdeveloped. Too large a transfer may undermine children's incentive to take responsibility for themselves, itself an important capability. Because children's needs and capabilities are difficult to assess, the "optimal" transfer is difficult to specify.

The difficulty is compounded by uncertainty about transfers from other sources. A noncustodial parent may worry about the effect of his contributions to children on those made by a custodial parent. Parents considering college costs are often unsure of what the state will provide—and the state is often unsure of what parents are willing to pay. Rapid economic change compounds such uncertainties. Child-support enforcement is a relatively new policy priority. A college education, once considered a luxury, is rapidly becoming a virtual necessity. Many public policies delivering to children, such as college financial aid, are difficult to understand, much less predict.

Child Support

Parents who do not live with their children contribute less money (and time) to their support than those who do. The economic effects are substantial. In 2001 about 28 percent of all children under twenty-one lived in families with a parent outside the home. Four of five of these lived with a mother but not a father. Only about half of custodial parents had child-support agreements (63 percent of custodial mothers and 39 percent of custodial fathers). Only half of those received the payments they were due. The average annual amount paid was about $5,800, often for the support of two or more children.[9]

The survey on which these estimates are based is far from perfect. It relies on the reports of custodial parents, and it probably understates the value of in-kind transfers. Almost a third of custodial parents claim they do not feel a need to make formal agreements, which suggests that they consider informal transfers a better arrangement.[10] Still, custodial parents almost always shoulder a heavier economic burden than noncustodial parents. Whether custodial parents are happier as a result is a separate question.

Parental Default

Not all children are conceived by a male and a female making an explicit commitment to raise a child together. The weakening of traditional social norms regarding sexual intercourse outside marriage has altered the decision-making environment, placing more responsibility for fertility decision-making on mothers, who become first movers in a strategic game. Once a child is born, fathers can withdraw support, enjoying some benefits of parenthood without paying any costs. Under these circumstances, failure to pay child support can be conceptualized as a form of default, like failure to make a payment on a loan.

It is easy to see why noncustodial parents might feel reluctant to provide financial support. When parents live together, they can monitor and influence the ways money is spent. When they do not live together, the noncustodial parent loses the ability to monitor or control family expenditures.[11] When dad sends a check, he may imagine mom buying racy new lingerie for herself instead of clothes for the children. Even in-kind transfers, such as bringing diapers and milk, or paying for after-school activities, can have the effect of crowding out expenditures by the custodial parent, leaving the child no better off. This aspect of family failure provides yet another example of the information and monitoring problems that make social norms and rules so important.

But child support breaks down for more profound reasons, reasons that are related to emotional and personal interactions that parents often cannot anticipate. Changes in the way that family members feel about each other are tantamount to what neoclassical economists would describe as changes in preferences. In 2001, for instance, 17 percent of custodial parents with no legal support agreement reported that they did not want to have contact with the other parent, and 17 percent could not locate the other parent.[12]

Child support flows most generously when noncustodial parents have developed and sustained strong emotional connections with their children. High paternal involvement before divorce is associated with a higher likelihood of later making child support payments, and divorced fathers who do not want contact with their children tend to be those who were less involved within marriage.[13]

Among couples negotiating child support, emotional dynamics greatly complicate financial bargaining. Mothers who fear for the quality of their children's relationship with their father may be reluctant to push enforcement issues. Mothers who succumb to anger and disappointment may use support enforcement (and child custody) as a way to retaliate against fathers. Under these circumstances, the assumption that parents are rational altruists who know exactly what they want seems particularly lame. Institutional rules for child support emerge precisely because it is so difficult for individuals to negotiate efficient solutions.

The stipulation and enforcement of institutional rules have a more important influence on the level of child support than any other discernible factor. Although the overall percentage of awards made and paid has changed little over the last twenty years in this country, this apparent stability conceals two countervailing trends. Significant improvement in support paid by unmarried fathers has been accompanied by an increase in the percentage of custodial parents who have never married, among whom support obligations are more difficult to establish. Even in the latter instance, however, public policies, such as increased efforts to register paternity, are having a marked effect.[14]

Whether custodial parents will receive support from noncustodial parents is largely determined by which state they live in. The percentage receiving the full amount they are due ranges from 14 percent and 15 percent in California and New York to 29 percent and 30 percent in Minnesota and Wisconsin.[15] Success is clearly related to the level of institutional effort. As one policy analyst puts it, in child support, "you get what you pay for."[16] In this case, it is important to note, the "you" is not a happiness-seeking parent but a political coalition seeking to modify state policy.

Income-Sharing Rules

Judicial discretion once played a large part in determination of levels of child support. Huge variation and conspicuous inconsistencies prompted passage of a federal law in 1984 requiring states to develop guidelines. These guidelines were strongly influenced by early empirical estimates of parental expenditures on children, which informed specification of explicit sharing rules.

Most states set levels of child support by reference to an income-sharing formula that allocates responsibility based on the relative contribution each parent makes to total family income, with extra consideration for child care and unusual medical expenses.[17] This approach relies on an estimate of the percentage of income that parents devote to children in intact families (an estimate based largely on research from the 1970s) that varies along with family income, ranging from 21.5 percent of gross income for one-child families in the lowest income category to 11.8 percent for those in the highest income category. (For two-child families, the percentage ranges from 24.2 to 18.3 percent.) The basic amount of money due the child is then prorated between both parents on the basis of their proportionate shares of income (taking into account the need for a "self-support reserve" for low-income, non-custodial parents.[18] This formula discourages custodial parents from increasing their income, because this lowers the contribution required by the noncustodial parent.

Other states use a fixed-percentage rule that requires a noncustodial parent to pay a fixed percentage of his income, no matter what the level. The state of Wisconsin is often cited as a model: noncustodial parents are required to pay 17 percent of their gross income for one child, 25 percent for two children, 29 percent for three, 31 percent for four.[19] This rule conforms to the principle that family members should share income, regardless of the level they enjoy. It has the advantage of simplicity, which makes implementation and updating easier. Yet the stipulated share is considerably lower than that typical of either two-parent or one-parent households with children.[20] Of course, when a parent lives with a child, he or she can share the benefits of spending on items such as housing. On the other hand, custodial parents devote far more time to children than noncustodial parents, and that time is worth a considerable amount of money (as the following chapters will show). Further, many states have proved reluctant to update their child-support guidelines despite evidence of increases in the costs of rearing children.[21]

Public and Private Incentives

State policies toward child support are difficult to change in part because they provoke distributional conflict. Custodial and noncustodial parents have different economic interests; each would like the other group to pay a larger share. But efforts to improve policy are also weakened by the problems highlighted in earlier chapters: poor understanding of family decision making and lack of adequate information on actual expenditures on children.

Many public policies create perverse incentives. Among families receiving Temporary Assistance to Needy Families, for instance, the child support payments that noncustodial parents make often go to defray state expenses, rather than benefiting children. Many states demand "payback" from the noncustodial parent for public assistance provided to the custodial parent. Under these circumstances, neither custodial nor noncustodial parents gain much from conformity to child support rules. States have a greater incentive to prosecute poor noncustodial parents than rich ones, in order to reap the bounty they are awarded. Some enforcement policies create more problems than they solve, such as those that that lead to incarceration of fathers who are then genuinely unable to pay accumulated child-support arrears.

Most discussions of child-support enforcement focus entirely on money expenditures, treating the issues of custody and visitation as separate. This focus should be broadened. Custody and visitation can strengthen the emotional ties that sustain altruistic commitments.[22] Yet both the income-support rules discussed above ignore the in-kind contributions made when a noncustodial parent spends more time caring for children, unless this accounts for more than 30 percent of all custody time.[23]

Most nonmarried or divorced parents bargain "in the shadow of the law." A prescribed formula for setting levels of child support represents a fallback imposed on those couples who fail to negotiate an agreement successfully. Greater emphasis on counseling and arbitration, rather than on adversarial proceedings in family court, could help many families. Making it easier to update and revise support agreements in tandem with visitation and custody agreements would also improve bargaining outcomes.

Higher Education

Parents sometimes begin saving to pay the future costs of college even before their children are born. Their expenditures on college, like other expenditures on children, are tallied in our national income accounts as a form of consumption or a simple transfer of consumption expenditures from one generation to another. In other words, they fall into the same category as spending on clothes and restaurant meals. Yet these expenditures represent investments in children's human capital that offer diffuse but important benefits to society as a whole.

Students invest in their own education with time and effort as well as money. This investment is not a simple decision based on anticipated rates of return to a college degree in the labor market. It requires complex strategic interactions with parents, educational institutions, and the state. Parents are not required to help pay for college, but the assumption that they will do so is built into the institutional structure of both public and private financial aid. Differences in parental ability and willingness to pay have momentous consequences for children, affecting the probability that they will go to college and the types of institutions they will attend.

Bargaining over College

"Is it so wrong to expect your kids to pay for at least some of their own college education?" Thus begins a recent article in the *Wall Street Journal* pointing to the increased stresses and strains imposed on parents by the escalating cost of higher education.[24] The question illustrates the difficulties of defining appropriate levels of parental altruism in a shifting economic environment. Most parents want their children to get a college education. But it is not clear what they should be willing to sacrifice to help pay for one.

Many states require divorced parents to contribute to college costs, which has prompted lawsuits complaining that no such requirements are imposed on parents in intact families.[25] But federal student aid procedures require parents (including stepparents) to file financial need statements. Existing rules make it difficult for prospective students under the age of twenty-four to qualify as financially independent of their parents.[26] Private institutions also make it clear that financial aid is based on parents' "ability to pay," not their "willingness to pay." This institutional environment puts considerable pressure on parents to contribute.

Yet not all parents are willing to cooperate. One online guide to financial aid devotes an entire section to the question "What can you do if your parents refuse to help?"[27] It is not uncommon for parents and students to disagree on educational goals, and empirical research shows that parental income has an effect on behavior different from that exerted by income under a student's own control.[28] A history of family instability often reduces the probability of support. Children of divorced parents are less likely to receive assistance paying for college than those from intact families.[29]

Virtually all institutions of higher education apply either a federal formula or an institutional formula for calculating an "expected family contribution" that is based on parental income and assets. Though the two formulas differ in their treatment of assets, they stipulate a similar requirement: a share of parental income that increases as income increases. For instance, in 2004 a married couple with one college-age child and one fourteen-year-old, a pretax income of $30,000 per year and no assets was expected to contribute about 4 percent of their income. A similar family with an income of $60,000 was expected to contribute about 16 percent, and one with an income of $120,000, about 29 percent.[30]

In practice, therefore, parents who hope to obtain financial aid for college have little choice regarding their contribution. Other family members, however, are not constrained. The income and assets of grandparents are not considered relevant to aid assessments. Financial advisers routinely suggest that grandparents avoid making transfers to a college savings account that would reduce aid eligibility. A direct gift, they point out, is much more cost-effective.[31] A recent survey of families saving for college revealed that about one-third expected financial assistance from grandparents and other relatives.[32]

It is easy to see the benefits of standardized sharing rules for financial aid. Without such rules, parents would be tempted to withhold support from their children in order to gain additional assistance. But the rules presume a specific level of familial altruism that may set the bar too high for some families and too low for others. Highly educated parents may be bound by a sense of intergenerational reciprocity, but parents who have not themselves received the benefit of a college education may feel less bound (as well as less financially able) to help their children out. Children with affluent grandparents can enjoy the best of both worlds, garnering both private and public assistance to pay for college.

Differences in the relative bargaining power of parents and children also deserve consideration. Parents with substantial wealth and income enjoy considerable leverage over their children. The threat of withholding support for college can be, and probably is, used to induce "rotten kids" to follow rules and perform well in school. Parents who cannot promise this assistance may have a harder time maintaining discipline, because their children have less to lose by defying their authority.

Who Pays for College?

The probability that a high school student will attend college has increased considerably over the last thirty years, as has the price tag for a college degree.[33] Parental contributions to higher education probably represent a growing share of the private costs of raising children. According to the Congressional Budget Office, parents paid about one-fourth of all college costs in 1999–2000 (including the value of room and board for children living at home). Students themselves paid another quarter, and public support or assistance covered the remaining one-half.[34]

In dollar terms, the average parental contribution for college students came to about $5,000 a year. For students who completed a degree in four years, the out-of-pocket expenses came to about $20,000 or about 12 percent of the estimate of total average expenditures on a child under age eighteen for a middle-income two-parent, two-child family presented in the previous chapter. The likelihood of receiving such assistance varies by family income, and also by number and age of parents.[35] During 1999–2000 parental contributions ranged from approximately 20 percent of costs for families with income less than $90,000 to 38 percent for those with higher income.[36] A majority of families with children with incomes over $50,000 report that they are saving for college. Below that level of income, however, a minority do so. The most common explanation offered is simply insufficient funds.[37]

Parental income has a strong effect on the probability that a child will attend college, which suggests that many families are constrained by lack of funds (and the difficulty of borrowing against future earnings). Differences in parental income at the time that students graduate from high school may be less important than earlier differences that reduce the quality of education that young children receive.[38] But enrollment of low-income students is very sensitive to increases in tuition.[39]

Assistance for middle-income families (such as the Hope Scholarships implemented under the Clinton administration) may do little to increase college attendance because the beneficiaries would have been willing and able to pay the costs themselves.[40] Similarly, public subsidies for state universities may simply reduce family contributions. On the other hand, there is no direct evidence that public spending on higher education crowds out private spending dollar for dollar. Families may reallocate their spending to help their children in other ways, such as helping to pay for graduate education or professional training.

Though parents of low-income students are expected to pay a smaller proportion of their income in order to garner financial aid, the actual amount of aid received tends to go up along with family income. Both federal and private financial aid subsidize the difference between expected family contribution and the price of tuition and fees, generating greater assistance for those who attend relatively high-priced private institutions. The share of low-income students attending private institutions has declined over time; most of these students attend relatively low-cost two-year community colleges and state universities.[41]

Children's financial contribution to their own education increasingly takes the form of loans that they will pay back after they have attained their degree. In 1999–2000, 64 percent of college students graduated with debt, on average about $17,000.[42] Students from low-income families shouldered the heaviest debt burden. Though such investments are likely to pay off for college graduates, survey data suggest that students both underestimate the effect of interest and overestimate the income they will earn upon graduation. College debt affects their family formation decisions and their ability to spend money on their own children.

Public Policies, Private Decisions

The economic benefits of higher education are easier to assess looking backward than forward. Though education increases potential productivity, its benefits within the labor market are partly positional. The payoff to one person's educational credentials depends on how many others with the same credentials are competing in the labor market. The increasing global supply of college-educated labor threatens to lower the relative benefits that U.S. graduates have enjoyed in the past. Though still quite high, the college premium has declined in recent years.[43]

Public subsidies of education reflect appreciation of its public benefits. But they also reflect distributional conflict among groups that benefit unevenly from current policies. Recent disputes over the appropriate definition and implementation of affirmative action represent the most visible example.[44] State university systems typically offer large overall subsidies to students from middle- and upper-income brackets. Affluent families have access to elite private colleges, which provide insulation from the budget pressures weakening many state university systems. Institutions that should be "engines of opportunity" look increasingly like "bastions of privilege."[45]

Transfers and Bequests

Although adult children are often a source of emotional support and physical assistance to their parents in old age, they do not come close to repaying the money parents spent on them. The flow of financial resources within families in the United States moves from the old to the young and transfers from parents to adult children are by far the largest component of financial transfers between households. Evidence from the National Survey of Families and Households indicates that among adults of all ages with at least one living parent, 17 percent received money from their parents, and only 4 percent gave money to their parents.[46] Even among adults aged fifty-five and over, only around 4 percent received financial assistance from their children and only around 20 percent received practical assistance.[47]

That practical assistance may have momentous consequences. For instance, elderly persons with no surviving children are significantly more likely than others to land in a nursing home financed through public assistance.[48] Women tend to provide more kin support than men. Daughters are more likely to help their parents, and elderly women are more likely to receive assistance.[49] Norms of reciprocity also come into play. Divorced parents who participate little in their children's upbringing are less likely to enjoy attention or assistance from them in old age.[50] Most parents hope for emotional rather than financial payback. Often their hopes are rewarded. But precisely because the fulfillment of their hopes is unpredictable, parents seem to reach for a balance between their own interests and those of their children that is calibrated by social norms.

Altruism, Exchange, or Norms?

If motives for transfers are altruistic, then parents should transfer more to children who are relatively needy. If motives are self-interested, then parents should transfer more to children from whom they hope to gain more in exchange (such as assistance in old age). If families behave as units that maximize their dynastic happiness, the consumption levels of different family members should be linked. For instance, if one family member's income goes down by $1,000, the consumption of all other family members should go down as they help buffer the loss. Because it is difficult to identify individual consumption within households (as emphasized in Chapter 4), this prediction is easier to test by looking at family members living in separate households.

A variety of empirical studies show that drops (or increases) in consumption across related households are not strongly related.[51] Nor do transfers from the government to one household seem to have much effect on family transfers to that household, as a model of "crowding out" would suggest.[52] If parents were altruistic, they would transfer more money to children with the least income, but transfers don't significantly reduce differences among siblings.[53] Adult children sometimes behave in ways that are consistent with self-interested motives, such as devoting more time and energy to parents who will potentially leave them bequests.[54] But parents don't seem to provide very large rewards—or incentives—for children to compete with one another to provide care and attention to them in old age. Most wills provide for equal division among surviving children.[55]

Parents may have paternalistic preferences, acting on what they believe is good for their children.[56] Parents may want to equalize their children's opportunities rather than their income.[57] Parents may not want to hurt their children's feelings by appearing to play favorites.[58] But reliance on specific assumptions regarding the nature of parental preferences raises the question of how these preferences are formed and reinforced. Directly asked, individuals concede that they often feel the pressure of moral obligations. Analysis of a special module of the 2000 Health and Retirement Study revealed that nearly a quarter of respondents did not disagree with the statement "My immediate family sometimes pressures me to do more than I want to do for them," and nearly a fifth did not disagree with the assertion "I sometimes have to ask over and over again to get my immediate family to help me."[59]

Magnitudes of Transfers and Bequests

Low-income households have more to gain than high-income households from the insurance that both altruism and reciprocity can provide. But because they lack the resources to provide financial transfers, they are more likely to provide informal types of assistance, such as child care.[60] Like spending on higher education, transfers and bequests to adult children tend to go up with family income.[61] One study found that parents in the top income quartile transfer about three times as much to children between the ages of eighteen and thirty-four as those in the bottom income quartile.[62] Gifts from parents are particularly important for home ownership. Among adults interviewed in the National Survey of Families and Households who had purchased a home since 1980, about 25 percent had received financial help mostly from parents, and the median amount was $5,000.[63]

The baby-boom generation stands to inherit a significant chunk of wealth from the generation born before 1945. But this wealth is highly concentrated. In 2001 about one-quarter of those born between 1946 and 1964 reported that they had received or expected to receive an inheritance. The median amount they had received was about $48,000 (in 2002 dollars). Of all those who had received an inheritance, only about 7 percent reported inheriting more than $100,000. Most large bequests were received by families that were already in the top 40 percent of the income distribution.[64] Black and Hispanic families are far less likely than white families to accumulate sufficient wealth to pass significant amounts on to the next generation.[65]

It is difficult to predict how much baby boomers will bequeath to their own children. The ongoing shift away from defined-benefit pensions (which offer no benefits to heirs) toward defined-contribution pensions (which create financial assets that can be inherited) may benefit the younger generation. Proposed changes in Social Security could have a similar effect. On the other hand, the pre–baby-boomer generation enjoyed particularly generous Social Security benefits relative to their contributions, which may have boosted their bequests. The health expenditures required to increase life expectancy in old age may continue to ratchet up, as they have in recent years.

The proportion of families receiving a bequest may well remain constant at about 25 percent. This is an important benchmark because it provides an indicator of the extent to which benefits currently enjoyed by the elderly will translate into improvements in the standard of living of the younger generation. Both transfers and bequests represent a form of intrafamily redistribution over the life cycle that implies that the younger generation will be better off than current cross-sectional differences in income distribution by age suggest. This redistribution also has macroeconomic implications: the younger generation as a whole inherits a liability to pay for public debt that currently helps finance the consumption of the older generation. Those who receive a private bequest enjoy a private asset that counterbalances this public liability.

Taxation of Transfers and Bequests

Political debate over the taxation of gifts and bequests in the United States has always reflected concern about incentive effects. If individuals could transfer unlimited amounts of money to others, including adult children, without incurring additional tax liability, they could use such transfers to avoid taxation. Largely for that reason, a ceiling has long been imposed on tax-free gifts to adult children and others, set at $10,000 per person in 2000 (and $12,000 in 2007). The rationale for taxing large bequests or estates rests on different arguments. Inheritance of large sums of money violates the principle that individuals should be rewarded primarily for their own efforts. Heirs enjoy windfalls. Personal fortunes of extremely high magnitude are not merely the results of individual effort; they reflect the implicit contributions of the social and economic infrastructure in which they were made, as well as good luck. By this reasoning, fellow citizens deserve a share.

The symbolic significance of the estate tax outweighs its economic implications. The estate tax in this country has typically been levied only on very large estates. In 2000 only about 2 percent of the estates of all those people who died were subject to it.[66] Further, most families that wanted to avoid paying this tax could do so by making large transfers before death, or by setting up trust funds. Nonetheless, political support for reduction of the tax has been quite strong. Now being phased out, it is currently scheduled for complete elimination in 2010 (although in the absence of new legislation it will be reinstated the following year).

Intergenerational Income Flows

Interhousehold income transfers represent an important dimension of the larger circular flow of resources to children within families. The failure of many noncustodial parents to provide adequate support for their children shifts the cost of raising the next generation toward custodial parents, primarily mothers. Among affluent families, expenditures on higher education represent a substantial sum, and the structure of financial aid for higher education encourages grandparents to contribute. In a highly competitive educational system in which success in high school is rewarded by financial aid for college, such family investments pay off. But they replicate preexisting inequalities, creating a kind of hereditary meritocracy.

The unequal distribution of both private wealth and bequests shows that cross-sectional comparisons understate the extent of lifetime income inequality among individuals currently under the age of eighteen. Though all these children will pay federal taxes to help support the elderly generation as a whole, only about 25 percent of them are likely to receive bequests from their elders. Intergenerational accounting should take such class differences into consideration.

CHAPTER SIX

Accounting for Family Time

Family time is harder to account for than family spending. Quantification is one way of making it visible. Time, like money, can be denominated in standardized units and tallied in spreadsheets. But an hour of time is not nearly as homogeneous as a unit of money, and many family activities are conceptually difficult to measure. Social scientists have less experience accounting for time than accounting for money. Measuring the amount of time devoted to housework is relatively straightforward. Measuring the amount of time devoted to the care of others is far more difficult, because care is an emotionally laden, complex interaction that is not always reported as a specific activity.[1]

Most empirical time-use surveys tally time that parents devote to activities with children under the age of eighteen. A glance at the numbers produced by these studies suggests that parenting is not very demanding. Mothers in the United States seem to devote, on average, less than two hours a day and fathers less than an hour a day to activities with children under the age of eighteen.[2] These studies understate the temporal demands that children impose. Ask the mother of a young son about her schedule and she may well say, "My time is his."[3] Even when parents are not engaging in activities with their children, their time is often constrained by them. Equating time spent in activities with children with child-care time is a bit like equating money spent on child-specific goods such as diapers and toys with expenditures on children. Just as children have a significant effect on the consumption of shared household goods such as rent, utilities, and transportation, they influence the larger allocation of family time.

Mothers are now far more likely to work for pay than in previous decades. But responsibility for children continues to reduce the amount of time women devote to paid employment. Studies of time use show that the trade-off between time devoted to paid employment and time given to child care is not as steep as many supposed. An additional hour of time devoted to paid employment reduces time spent in activities with children by far less than one hour. But mothers combine paid work and child care at considerable cost to their own leisure, sleep, and time spent with their spouses.

This chapter summarizes research on family time devoted to children in the United States, and it provides new estimates of parental time inputs to children from birth to age eleven that are based on time diaries administered by the Child Development Supplement of the Panel Survey of Income Dynamics (PSID-CDS), which complement the estimates of monetary spending on children described in the previous chapters. This sets the stage for consideration, in Chapter 7, of the monetary value of this time.

Family Work

The vocabulary of modern economics calls attention to the distinction between market and nonmarket work, making the market an arbiter of value. But most productive activities that take place outside the realm of market exchange today involve the provisioning and care of family members. Not all these activities have market substitutes, and many of them have distinctive characteristics. It seems more accurate and appropriate to refer to them as what they are, rather than what they are not, as "family work" rather than "nonmarket work."

Demand for the measurement of family work has a long history punctuated by protests from women's groups. In the nineteenth century Elizabeth Cady Stanton insisted that women's domestic work differed from men's wage work only because it was "unpaid, unsocialized, and unrelenting."[4] Elizabeth Blackwell challenged the notion that women who provided family care and domestic service were "supported" by their husbands, rather than bearing their fair share of joint burdens.[5] In 1878 the Association for the Advancement of Women, a group of highly educated feminists, sent a letter to Congress complaining of the Census Bureau's failure to acknowledge the productive value of the home and woman as home keeper. The letter failed to sway federal legislators, but it presented a point of view shared by the Massachusetts Bureau of Labor Statistics, which had begun collecting data in 1865 on the number of adults engaged primarily in housework. Some men placed themselves under this rubric, whereas the few married women (2 percent) who reported no paid or unpaid work were categorized as "wives, merely ornamental."[6]

In the early twentieth century the academic discipline known as home economics created a platform for bringing attention to family work. The first time-use surveys in the United States were administered to small samples of farm wives in the 1920s.[7] In their early tract on life insurance, *The Money Value of a Man*, Louis Dublin and Alfred Lotka lamented the lack of adequate data: "The mother, in the majority of cases, gives a full working day to home occupations of one kind or another. Had we a pecuniary measure of the value of these personal services, we should naturally add a pro-rata share of them in our estimate of the cost of raising a child. Unfortunately, such a measure is lacking."[8] In her classic *Economics of Household Production,* published in 1934, Margaret Reid emphasized the economic significance of child rearing and housework.[9]

On the other side of the globe, Soviet planners began administering time-use surveys as a tool for calculating the potential supply of labor.[10] In the early 1970s Alexander Szalai orchestrated a series of surveys in European countries.[11] In the United States, Thomas Juster and Frank Stafford at the University of Michigan took the lead in collecting and analyzing time-use data; they were followed by John Robinson and others at the University of Maryland.[12] Feminist activists all over the world began insisting on greater attention to women's invisible work in the home.[13] A large and growing literature examines the time spent in housework and the ways it is divided between men and women.[14]

Still, this research is in its infancy. Though at least twenty studies of parental time use have been conducted over the past twenty-five years, they often categorize child care in different ways and rely on small samples.[15] Most studies survey individual adults but fail to specify the number of children being cared for or their ages. Child-centered surveys, such as the PSID-CDS, provide a more accurate picture of the adult time children receive, but they focus entirely on children's activities, ignoring adults' supervisory and on-call responsibilities. In 2003 the U.S. Bureau of Labor Statistics (BLS) launched the first annual nationally representative time-use survey, the American Time Use Survey (ATUS), which offers a new window into the organization of family time. The availability of these data makes it all the more important to confront two important conceptual problems directly: how should family work and care be defined?

Defining Work

Time can be converted into money through the sale of labor services, and money can be used to buy time through the purchase of labor services. But it is difficult to distinguish between labor and leisure or between production and consumption. It is easier simply to assume that activities that are paid represent work, and those that are unpaid represent leisure (even if they sometimes feel like work). The easy assumption, in this case, is the most misleading one.

Labor versus Leisure?

Neoclassical economic theory defines work in terms of motivation. Work is a means to an end, an activity undertaken for the purpose of generating income. Leisure is an activity undertaken for intrinsic pleasure, an end in itself. These subjective definitions call attention to an individual agent's state of mind. Institutionalist approaches influenced by classical political economy, on the other hand, define work in terms of its results, rather than motives. Work is the creation of goods and services that meet human needs, for the benefit of oneself or others. Neither of these definitions is entirely satisfactory. Motivation is difficult to observe; human needs are difficult to define. Consideration of family care calls attention to this conceptual dilemma because it is more personal than most other forms of work yet more productive than most leisure activities.

Virtually all introductory microeconomics textbooks portray a graphical trade-off between labor and leisure that determines the supply of labor to paid employment, omitting even a mention of nonmarket work. This convenient simplification is inconsistent with modern neoclassical economics. As Gary Becker and others emphasize, individuals engage in many nonmarket activities in order to consume the resulting output. They face a three-way choice among market work, nonmarket work, and leisure.[16] Becker and other neoclassical economists treat family work exactly the same as market work (as though they were simply two different jobs), and they alter their interpretation of the labor-leisure trade-off accordingly. Individuals work as long as the happiness yielded by an additional unit of income or product exceeds the happiness they would receive from leisure.

This tidy resolution of the issue, however, is achieved by assuming that neither paid nor unpaid work yields intrinsic benefits, which is implausible. Most parents want to provide their children with the goods and services they need, but they also to want to experience the activity of parenting, whether because they enjoy it or because they believe it to be socially and morally worthwhile. Many people experience paid employment in similar terms, as a source of intrinsic satisfaction, self-expression, and meaning. They garner "process benefits" or "psychic income" as well as income from employment.[17] In one time-use survey in which individuals were asked to describe their feelings about their daily activities, work outside the home was rated about the same as the leisure activity of gardening, and slightly higher than other household work.[18] Even workers in low-wage occupations often take pleasure in their activities and pride in their efforts.[19] Parents sometimes describe the paid workplace as a less stressful and more personally rewarding environment than the home.[20]

Neoclassical labor economists acknowledge the intrinsic satisfaction paid work can yield when they explore the influence of individual preferences on occupational choice and relative pay. Some individuals may prefer low-risk jobs, accepting lower pay or a "compensating differential" in order to satisfy such preferences. Other compensating differentials may be related to the type of work performed. For instance, teachers and child-care workers may accept less pay than similar workers in other occupations partly because of the intrinsic satisfaction they derive from contact with children.[21] Paid work, like family work, reflects personal preferences and generates intrinsic benefits. Serious consideration of parenting challenges the assumption that work can be defined either as paid activity or as "that which we would really rather not do." How, then, should family work be defined?

The Third-Person Criterion

In her pioneering analysis of household production in the 1930s, Margaret Reid articulated what has come to be known as the "third-person" criterion.[22] Work can be defined as an activity that one could, in principle, pay a person outside the family (a third person) to perform. Leisure, unlike work, is an activity that that no one can perform on another's behalf. Using a slightly different nomenclature, the Australian economist Duncan Ironmonger defines work as an activity that creates a potentially transferable benefit. Outputs are objective and transferable; personal enjoyment is subjective and nontransferable.[23] Though these definitions draw upon the labor-leisure distinction described above (labor is outcome-oriented, and leisure is process-oriented), they differ from neoclassical definitions because they do not rest on assessments of individual motivation.

The third-person criterion classifies activities on the basis of their technical and social characteristics. Housework and child care are considered work because one could hypothetically hire someone else to perform them (or because they create a hypothetically transferable benefit). In practice, some parents might be willing to pay for child care as a substitute for their own time, and others might not. Furthermore, substitutability between money and time may be limited: mothers and fathers might consider purchased care a good substitute for their own time only up to a certain point. Individual preferences, however, do not affect the classification of child care as work.

The third-party criterion is not without inconsistencies. Some activities are not defined as work even though, in principle, a third party could be hired to perform them. Sexual services are commonly bought and sold. But consensual sex is usually undertaken with the presumption of mutual pleasure, and ideals of romantic love suggest that purchased sex is not a substitute.

Some activities fall into the category of things we would love to pay someone else to do for us but cannot. Studying is often subjectively experienced as work rather than leisure. Some of its benefits (such as a heightened appreciation of ideas) are nontransferable; others (such as resulting increases in skill and productivity) create transferable benefits. Time devoted to studying is often diverted from more immediately remunerative activities, so it clearly imposes an opportunity cost. The same is true of commuting time. These activities can reasonably be considered work even if they do not satisfy the third-person criterion.

Another classificatory dilemma is posed by sleep and personal care activities. Unlike leisure, sleep and personal care are necessary activities of personal maintenance. Most people who fail to sleep approximately eight hours of every twenty-four eventually suffer ill effects. Time diaries show some variation in the average amount of time that people sleep, which suggests that it lies within the realm of individual choice.[24] But, like time devoted to eating, bathing, and grooming, it represents an activity that probably contributes to the quality of both work and leisure but cannot be easily assigned to either category. As a result, time-use researchers often treat these activities separately.

Most contemporary studies of time use follow the precedents set by Alexander Szalai in time-diary surveys administered in the 1960s. Unpaid time devoted to activities of housework and care of family members is categorized as work. This categorization is only loosely justified by the third-person or transferable benefit criterion. Nonetheless, it represents an improvement over the traditional practice of treating all unpaid activities as leisure. As the women of the Association for the Advancement of Women insisted in 1878, parents perform especially important family work.

Defining Child Care

The flow of time can be measured objectively, but it is experienced subjectively. Furthermore, it is often remembered poorly. Asking a stylized question such as "How much time did you spend in child care last week?" often yields only a ballpark answer. The reports that family members give are not always consistent. For instance, husbands typically report doing more housework than their wives report them doing, and vice versa.[25] Survey responses are also subject to "social desirability" bias. Respondents eager to give a good impression are likely to exaggerate time spent in activities considered praiseworthy (such as child care) and to underreport time spent in activities considered unproductive (such as watching television).

No survey method can guarantee an accurate report, but the problems described above are minimized when respondents are asked to fill out a time diary describing activities during the previous day. Table 6.1 reproduces the survey administered to participants in the PSID-CDS, which was designed with special attention to activities that involved television, videos, and computer games. Some illustrative responses to the survey are shown in the table. Such responses are typically standardized when the survey is coded for analysis. For instance, activities such as "eating sandwich" or "drinking juice" would both be coded as "eating." Some national surveys include only a few categories of child-care activities; others go into considerable detail, distinguishing among developmental activities (such as reading aloud to a child), high-contact activities (such as feeding or bathing), and low-contact activities (such as monitoring children or making arrangements on their behalf).[26]

Table 6.1 Survey form, PSID-CDS, with sample responses

Time	What did your child do?	Time began	Time end	If watching TV, was that a videotape or TV program?	If TV, video, computer games, what was the name of the (program/video/game) child was (watching/playing)?	Where was child?	Who was doing the activity with the child?	Who (else) was there but not directly involved in the activity?	What else was child doing at the same time?
							Do not answer if sleeping or personal care		
1:00 PM	eating sandwich	1:00PM	1:20		.	kitchen	mother	sister	
	watching TV	1:20	2:30	video	101 Dalmations	living room		sister	playing with toys
	napping	2:30	3:45			bedroom			

Source: http://psidonline.isr.umich.edu/CDS/questionnaires/cds-i/english/Tdiary.pdf (accessed April 8, 2007).

Primary and Secondary Time

People tend to do more than one thing at a time, or to alternate between activities so rapidly that they seem to be doing many things at once. One can feed a baby a bottle while watching television, or talk to a toddler while cooking dinner. Some time diary surveys try to capture this complexity by distinguishing between a primary and a secondary activity. For instance, the PSID-CDS question "What did your child do?" yields a primary activity and "What else was child doing at the same time?" yields a secondary activity (Table 6.1).

Similar questions are often asked of adults in time-use surveys. But the distinction between primary and secondary activities varies considerably and is sensitive to the wording of survey questions. Parents almost always organize their time in response to their responsibilities for children. Child care, defined broadly, often takes place in the background. Data from Australia suggest that as much as three-quarters of all time spent in child care may be "secondary."[27] Canadian time-use data suggest something closer to two-thirds.[28] Most U.S. time-use surveys find that secondary time represents a much smaller percentage of the total, in part because questions are not as carefully designed to uncover it.[29]

Both primary and secondary activities are typically reported from the adult's point of view. But the total time that one adult spends in such activities may overlap to varying degrees with that of other adults. For instance, if both mother and father simply report spending ten hours in activities with children, this may represent ten hours of care time provided by two parents at the same time, or twenty hours of care time provided by each parent at different times. Time that a child spends with two parents may be of higher "quality" than time with one parent; it is certainly more costly.

A related issue concerns the number of children being cared for at one time. A parent who devotes ten hours to activities with children may be caring for one child or four. The ratio of adults to children, or density of care, has significant implications for its cost and quality. As more children are added to a household, the increment in adult care time associated with each child tends to go down.[30] But does an increase in the number of children per adult increase the efficiency of care or simply dilute its quality so that each child benefits less? The answer to this question almost certainly depends on the nature of the care activity.[31] Low care density matters less for supervisory or "on-call" care than for intensive activities such as reading to or talking with a child.

Supervision, Responsibility, and "On-Call" Time

As Margaret Reid pointed out long ago, time spent in *activities* with children represents a subset of all time that should be described as child care.[32] Leaving a child under the age of thirteen unsupervised for any significant length of time can be legally considered a form of child neglect. Even though legal standards vary, and many so-called latchkey children spend time at home alone, most parents devote considerable time and effort to meeting on-call as well as supervisory responsibilities.[33] Young children spend a large percentage of their time sleeping, often in a room separate from a parent. School-age children often spend time playing on their own, with siblings or with friends in a room separate from a parent. Under these circumstances, parents are unlikely to report that they are "engaged in an activity" with children.[34]

The diffuse character of parental responsibilities explains why stylized questions such as "How much time did you spend providing care for your children last week?" typically yield much larger estimates than time-diary questions about activities with children.[35] The 1997 Australian Time Use Survey seeks to capture supervisory time with a category called "Minding Children," defined as "caring for children without the active involvement shown in the codes above. Includes monitoring children playing outside or sleeping, preserving a safe environment, being an adult presence for children to turn to in need, supervising games or swimming activities including swimming lessons. Passive child care."[36]

After extensive field testing of various measures for the ATUS, the BLS decided to measure passive child care in the following way: after the respondent completes the twenty-four-hour time-diary activity report, the interviewer asks if, at any time during those activities, a child was "in your care." If a respondent is unclear about what "in your care" means, the interviewer specifies, "By 'in your care' I mean that you were generally aware of what your child was doing, and you were near enough that you could provide immediate assistance, if necessary."[37]

The ATUS approach represents an important supplement to activity-based measures, providing a clear picture of what might be termed passive care. It conceals, however, an important distinction between supervision and being on call and gives short shrift to the latter. For instance, the "in your care" measure excludes time that children are asleep during the evening or night, or time that parents are asleep. Yet babysitters are often hired to be on call for young children who are fast asleep in the evening. And parents are often economically constrained by the requirement that they sleep in proximity to their children. Most measures of passive care also ignore the additional burdens of housework that children impose.

Consider the analogies with a firefighter's job, which includes at least three different aspects. The *active* aspect is the actual fighting of fires. The *supervisory* aspect includes monitoring phones, radios, and other electronic apparatus and ensuring that equipment is maintained and ready. The *on-call* aspect requires being available to respond to an alarm during long periods that may include eating, playing cards, and napping. For both firefighters and parents, on-call time is less demanding than active or supervisory time, but it is nonetheless significant. Developmental psychologists testify to the importance of invisible forms of social support, the knowledge that a loved one is available nearby.[38]

In sum, studies that focus entirely on time parents and children spend engaging in primary activities together understate the demands of child rearing. Parental care falls into a number of different conceptual categories: participation with a child in primary activities, participation in secondary activities, supervisory responsibilities, being on call, and engaging in tasks that indirectly benefit the child (such as cooking, cleaning, washing clothes, or making appointments and arrangements for special activities).

Children's Effect on Parental Time

If time devoted to children is multifaceted, so too are the alternative activities from which that time is drawn. Paid employment is the most conspicuous; many women who become mothers modify their schedule of work outside the home. New parents tend to be most amazed (and befuddled) by their loss of sleep. With an infant in the house, parents find that some forms of housework (such as laundry) increase while others (such as cooking gourmet meals) decrease. Parents of young children seldom enjoy much leisure unaccompanied by care responsibilities. The temporal demands of child care deserve careful consideration.

Parental Employment

Children alter their mothers' schedules more visibly than fathers' schedules. Over the last forty years, the percentage of mothers working for pay outside the home has steadily increased. But perceptions of this trend are often exaggerated by reliance on the simple distinction of being part of the paid labor force or not. These in-or-out measures are better suited to traditional male forms of participation in employment than to female patterns, which have historically been far more diverse.[39] Unlike most fathers, who tend to have a job or not, many mothers vary their hours and weeks of employment, structuring paid employment around their family responsibilities.

A close look at labor-force measures reveals significant differences in the *extent* of married mothers' labor-force participation. In 1998, for instance, about 64 percent of mothers with children under six in the United States participated in paid employment, but only 35 percent worked full-time, year-round.[40] A study that tracked a representative sample of married-couple families between the late 1980s and early 1990s found that becoming a first-time mother decreases wives' employment by about eight hours per week, and having two or more within a four- to seven-year time span leads to a further reduction of about twelve hours per week. Fathers' hours of employment are unaffected by the first child, but increase by about three hours per week with additional children.[41]

International comparisons show that the effect of children on their mothers' participation in paid employment differs substantially across countries. In countries like Finland and France that provide high-quality universal child care, mothers of children under the age of six are more likely to work full-time in paid employment than in countries such as the United States and Great Britain.[42] On the other hand, many countries that provide universal child care also provide paid family leaves from work for both mothers and fathers for a significant period after birth. As a result, parents tend to spend more time with infants.[43]

Since there are only twenty-four hours in a day, any time that parents devote to paid employment reduces the time available for their children. But time commitments can often be rearranged in ways that protect the most important kinds of parental interaction. Employed mothers tend to draw first from the fund of time devoted to leisure, housework, and sleep.[44] Several different surveys of U.S. families confirm that increases in mothers' employment leads to relatively small reductions in the time they spend engaged in activities with their children.[45]

Parents make important choices about how to allocate their time. But their choices are significantly constrained by the institutional environment. About one-third of parents employed full-time in the United States report that they feel that they do not have enough time for their families because of their jobs.[46] Though increases in mothers' employment do not have much effect on the average time that fathers spend in activities with children, many dual-earning parents spread their time thinner, working in staggered shifts that reduce their opportunities to spend time with one another. Parents arrange paid employment around care responsibilities. Among dual-earner couples with a child under five in 1996, over one-third included a spouse who worked nonstandard hours (fewer than half of their hours worked in the week before the Current Population Survey fell between 8:00 AM and 4:00 PM).[47] The pattern was even more extreme among low-income, dual-earner couples. Increased time pressure exacts a psychological toll. Interviews with children of working parents show that they are less concerned about the hours their parents work than how tired and stressed out they are when they come home.[48]

Even parents who maintain a relatively high average activity time with children may lack access to paid or unpaid family leave to deal with unexpected problems such as illness. Low-income families are particularly likely to lack such flexibility. Few of the jobs they can obtain are family-friendly.[49] Single mothers are particularly constrained. For instance, evidence suggests that the paid work requirements imposed on recipients of Temporary Assistance to Needy Families significantly reduced breast-feeding, with negative consequences for infant health.[50]

Mothers and fathers at the high end of the earnings spectrum often have access to better family benefits. On the other hand, many professional career trajectories require a time commitment far exceeding forty hours per week. From an employer's point of view, an ideal worker is never absent from work, willing to travel on short notice, and always available to provide extra effort on nights and weekends. Obviously, such an ideal worker cannot raise children unless he or she has a partner willing to be an ideal parent, an extreme division of labor that puts the caregiver at a disadvantage.[51] Even when employers try to encourage work-family balance, competitive winner-takes-all dynamics penalize individuals who devote time to caring for dependents.[52] Women are more vulnerable to these pressures than men because professional demands are at their greatest during the period of their life cycle—their late twenties to mid-thirties—during which they are most likely to become mothers.

Housework and Leisure

In addition to direct care, children add to housework demands such as laundry and cleaning. Studies of their overall effect on hours of housework, however, reveal varying estimates, largely because of differences in survey design and definitions of housework. Data from the mid-1970s suggested a strong influence on mothers' housework time, but not on fathers'.[53] More attention has been focused on differences between husbands and wives than on the effect of children on housework, which may be mediated by a number of factors, including the extent to which families rely on purchased meals and other services.[54] The 2003 ATU Survey shows a difference of only about one hour per week in housework performed by women in a household without children and those that included a child under the age of six.[55]

The repercussions of children on housework are greater when comparisons are restricted to white, married women, or when they follow the same set of families over time. A study of families in the PSID from 1979 to 1987 shows that employed wives increased time devoted to housework by five hours per week when children were present.[56] A study based on the National Survey of Families and Households estimates that the transition to parenthood in married-couple families led to an increase in mothers' housework of about sixteen hours per week, whereas husbands' time devoted to housework remained unchanged.[57]

Changes in the absolute amount of time adults devote to housework may be less important than shifts in the composition of that work, away from activities designed to serve adults, such as cooking gourmet meals, and toward activities serving children, such as doing laundry. Few time-use surveys are designed to explore such shifts in the intrafamily distribution of services, because they seldom ask for whom household work is being performed. The presence of children clearly modifies the kinds of leisure activities that parents engage in, as well as the quantity and quality of the sleep they enjoy.[58] In general, parenting intensifies gender specialization in different tasks.[59] Not surprisingly, women who stay home often end up taking on more responsibility for work around the house. Though this may be an efficient decision from the point of view of the family as a whole, it increases mothers' economic dependency and vulnerability.[60]

Average Parental Care Time Per Child

The USDA has long used data from the CE Survey to estimate average parental spending on children up to age eighteen, as discussed in Chapter 4. Potential parents interpret these estimates as an indicator of the costs they will incur, and policy makers apply them to the design of rules for foster care, child-support enforcement, and social safety nets. Yet money expenditures omit consideration of the value of parental time. Reliance on them leads to inaccurate comparisons of economic well-being across households. It also distorts perceptions of the relative costs of children of different ages. Young children need less food and clothing than older children. But they need far more direct care.

The PSID-CDS makes it possible to construct parallel estimates of the average amount of parental time devoted to the care of children.[61] These estimates do not include indirect time demands such as housework. They do, however, include consideration of supervisory and on-call time, overlaps among care providers and recipients, and economies of scale within the household. They also take advantage of the child-centric structure of the data by offering estimates of time that noncustodial parents devote to activities with children.

The survey instrument asked parents, teachers, and children themselves (where appropriate) to designate the activity children were engaged in during two twenty-four-hour periods, one a weekday, the other on a weekend. For each activity, ten categories of people (such as mother, sibling, friend) could be listed as participating or engaged with the child in that activity ("Who was doing the activity with child?"), and one or more members of those categories could also be listed as available ("Who else was there but not directly involved in the activity?" (See the appendix to this chapter for details.)

Average Parental Care Time for Children from Birth to Eleven

To construct estimates that can be easily combined with the USDA's estimates of money expenditures, we first restrict our attention to children from birth to eleven in families with two children, distinguishing between two-parent and single-parent families. A general overview of children's time helps set the stage (Table 6.2). We categorize children's time in activities with parents and nonparents, in school, in child care, and with babysitters as "active care" and designate the time left over as "supervisory care"—time requiring adult supervision or on-call responsibilities.

On average, a child aged eleven or younger living with two parents in a family with another sibling engages in an activity with at least one parent 31.9 hours per week. Time with an adult relative accounts for another 3.4 hours per week, and time with an adult nonrelative other than a paid babysitter another 3.7 hours per week. Time in institutional care (school or child care) or with a babysitter amounts to 22.3 hours per week. Children are awake, but not engaged in an activity with an adult, for 27 hours a week on average. They spend about 79.7 hours per week sleeping or engaged in personal care.

In proportional terms, children living with both parents spend only about 19 percent of their total time engaged in activities with a parent. Institutional care such as child care and school accounts for the next largest component of their time, about 13 percent. Activities with adult relatives and nonrelatives each account for 2 percent of their time. Children spend 16 percent of their time awake but not engaged in an activity with adults. Overall, about half their time, 48 percent, is spent sleeping or in personal care (Figure 6.1).

Not surprisingly, children living in single-parent families spend less time in activities with a parent, about 9.7 hours fewer per week than those in two-parent families. They spend more time in institutional care or with other adults (Table 6.2). The younger the child, the greater the differences between those living in two-parent and one-parent households. Children living in single-parent households spend a significant amount of time with fathers, but about half as much, on average, as children in two-parent households spend with their fathers without a mother being present(Figure 6.2).[62]

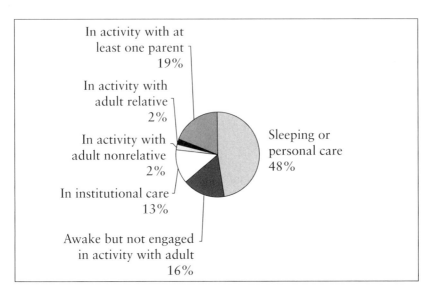

Figure 6.1 How children in two-parent, two-child families spend their time

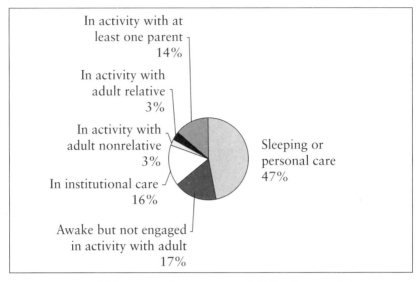

In activity with at least one parent 14%

In activity with adult relative 3%

In activity with adult nonrelative 3%

In institutional care 16%

Awake but not engaged in activity with adult 17%

Sleeping or personal care 47%

Figure 6.2 How children in single-parent, two-child families spend their time

Children of different ages receive different types of care (Table 6.2). Time engaged in an activity with at least one parent declines gradually as children grow older. Infants under the age of three are most likely to be engaged with parents, but they also sleep longer hours. Hours of institutional care increase somewhat for children between three and five and more sharply when children reach the age of six (at which most enter the first grade of elementary school). As children in two-parent households age, they spend less time engaged in an activity with a father when the mother is not present. The opposite holds for children in single-parent households. Older children are more likely than younger ones to spend time in activities with fathers, who are predominantly nonresident parents.

To develop an accounting framework that translates this descriptive information into an estimate of the average amount of parental-care work time per child, we make use of information regarding overlaps. More than one parent and more than one child can participate in an activity. In two-child households, about 35 percent of the total time children spend in an activity with a parent includes participation by another adult.[63] This implies that for every 100 hours in which a child is receiving active care from at least one parent, about 135 hours of adult active care are being supplied. Furthermore, in two-parent, two-child families,

Table 6.2 Care time devoted to children ages 0–11 in two-child families in 1997 (average hours per week per child)

	All	0–2	3–5	6–8	9–11
Children in two-parent households					
N	834	203	228	198	205
Passive care					
Sleeping or engaged in personal care	79.7	82.5	82.0	78.0	76.0
Awake but not engaged in activity with an adult	27.0	24.2	25.7	27.0	31.0
Active nonparental care					
In institutional or paid care (school, childcare, or babysitter)	22.3	15.1	19.4	25.8	29.2
Engaged in activity with adult nonrelative (unpaid)	3.7	3.5	3.0	3.8	4.4
Engaged in activity with adult relative (e.g., grandmother)	3.4	4.4	2.8	3.6	3.0
Active parental care					
Engaged in activity with at least one parent	31.9	38.3	35.1	29.8	24.4
Engaged in activity with father but not mother	6.2	7.9	6.9	5.7	4.3
Engaged in activity with mother but not father	16.4	19.5	19.0	15.5	11.4
Engaged in activity with both parents	9.3	10.9	9.2	8.6	8.7
Children in single-parent households					
N	237	49	59	58	71
Passive care					
Sleeping or engaged in personal care	77.9	83.0	81.4	77.3	71.9
Awake but not engaged in activity with an adult	29.8	22.5	28.2	32.1	34.4
Active nonparental care					
In institutional care (school, child care, or babysitter)	27.4	30.1	19.2	25.8	33.7
Engaged in activity with adult nonrelative (unpaid)	4.4	2.1	5.7	4.5	4.8
Engaged in activity with adult relative (e.g., grandmother)	5.2	5.4	7.3	5.5	3.2
Active parental care					
Engaged in activity with at least one parent	23.2	24.9	26.1	22.8	20.0
Engaged in activity with father but not mother	3.3	.2	2.7	3.1	6.1
Engaged in activity with mother but not father	19.0	23.2	22.5	19.1	13.1
Engaged in activity with both parents	.9	1.5	1.0	.6	.8

Source: Authors' Calculations.

a sibling is present about 26 percent of the time that a child is participating in activity with a parent, whereas in single-parent, two-child families, a sibling is present about 43 percent of time.[64]

The implications of these overlaps for the quality of care that children receive or the effort that parents offer are unclear. When many adults are present, responsibilities for children are diffused, and not everyone is working equally hard. To provide a lower-bound estimate of the average amount of active parental care work time per child, we assume that there is no value added from the participation of a second parent; even if both are engaged, the total active parental-care performed per child is no greater than what one parent alone could provide. We subtract half of the overlapping activity time with a sibling for each child. In considering passive care responsibilities, we assume that only one parent need be present, and we divide this time by half to arrive at average passive care time per child in a two-child family. We also exclude time children spend sleeping, on the assumption that parents are less constrained during these hours.[65]

This accounting yields lower-bound estimates of the average amount of active and passive parental-care time per child in a two-child family, expressed in both absolute and percentage terms by age in Table 6.3. Money expenditures on children in two-child families are also included in this table to illustrate the different patterns evident in these two types of expenditure as children age. In two-parent families, children two and under cost less than any other group in terms of money expenditures. They receive more hours of active parental care than any other age group, however. The pattern of passive care runs the other direction: very young children require less, and older children more. The average amount of parental-care hours per child from birth to eleven is about 41.3 hours per week.

Children living with a single parent receive about a third less active parental care time than those living with two parents.[66] Children from three to five seem to receive slightly more active care than children two and under, but otherwise the pattern is similar: young children require significantly more active and older children more passive care. Money expenditures are far lower for the youngest age than for other age categories. Measured in terms of money, infants and toddlers are cheap compared to teens; measured in terms of time, they are considerably more costly.

The USDA estimates of money spending on children include a consideration of economies of scale: differences in spending per child among

Table 6.3 Parental money expenditures and care work time per child, children ages 0–11 in the United States in 2000 (children in two-child families)

	Annual money expenditures	Age-specific money expenditures relative to children ages 0–2 (%)	Weekly average active parental care time per child (hours)	Weekly average active parental care time per child relative to children ages 0–2 (%)	Weekly average passive parental care time per child (hours)	Weekly average passive parental care time per child relative to children ages 0–2 (%)	Weekly average parental care hours per child (not including sleep)
Living in two-parent households							
All ages	$8,915	102	27.8	83	13.5	112	41.3
0–2	8,740	100	33.3	100	12.1	100	45.4
3–5	8,980	103	30.5	92	12.8	106	43.3
6–8	8,990	103	25.9	78	13.5	112	39.4
9–11	8,950	102	21.2	64	15.5	128	36.7
Living in one-parent households							
All ages	$6,048	115	18.4	94	14.8	131	33.2
0–2	5,270	100	19.6	100	11.3	100	30.9
3–5	5,950	113	20.4	104	14.1	125	34.5
6–8	6,710	127	17.9	91	16.0	142	33.9
9–11	6,260	119	15.7	80	17.2	152	32.9

Source: Figures for money expenditures from Lino, "Expenditures on Children by Families"; figures on time expenditures are authors' calculations.
Note: Figures for children living in two-parent households are for middle-income families with before-tax income between $38,000 and $64,000.
Figures for children living in single-parent households are for low-income families with before-tax income below $38,000.

Table 6.4 Variations in average active parental care time per child under twelve by number of children per family (expressed relative to children in a two-child family with same number of parents)

	One child (%)	Two children (%)	Three or more children (%)
Two-parent families	150	100	85
One-parent families	159	100	85

one-child, two-child, and three-child families. We construct a parallel approximation of the economies of scale in parental-care work time by examining families of different composition (Table 6.4). The typical only child under twelve enjoys far more time in activities with parents than the typical child in a two-child family. Children in two-parent, single-child families receive about 50 percent more active care time from at least one parent than those in two-child families; in single-parent families the differential is about 59 percent. Children in families of three or more children, however, receive only slightly less than those in two-child families: 15 percent less in both two-parent families, and single-parent families. This probably reflects the greater age difference among children with more than one sibling, which makes overlaps less likely.

Differences in Family-Care Time

Average parental-care time estimates can be misleading, because they conceal important differences in the time that mothers and fathers provide and obscure the different roles that family members play in providing care. The relative share of passive care time that mothers and fathers provide cannot be ascertained from the PSID-CDS. Relative shares of time devoted to *activities* with children can be estimated, however. Table 6.2 indicates that children in two-parent two-child families engage in activities with their mothers for 16.4 hours per week, with both parents about 9.3 hours per week, and with fathers about 6.2 hours per week. As is true of calculations of average time inputs, overlaps complicate the picture. How do we credit fathers for the time they spend together with mothers and children? Ethnographic and qualitative studies show that in most families, mothers take primary responsibility for activities with children, even when fathers are engaged.[67]

Since it is difficult to ascertain what this means in quantitative terms, we give fathers the benefit of the doubt, assume that they perform half the work when both parents are present, and credit them with one-half the hours that both parents provide together.[68] By this assumption, fathers in two-parent families provide, on average, 10.8 hours a week, or about one-third of the time that children in two-child families spend in activities with at least one parent. Using the same assumptions, we find that fathers in single-parent families (some of which are headed by a father) provide, on average, about 15 percent of total time. Taking these averages, adding those for children in one-child and three-or-more child families, and weighting all these by their proportions in the PSID-CDS yields the result that, overall, fathers provide about 28 percent of all the active-care time that children receive.

Since most studies of time devoted to children are based on parents' time diaries, they do not reveal the important role that other individuals play. As Table 6.2 indicates, children in two-parent, two-child families participate in activities with nonparental relatives for an average of 3.4 hours a week, and with adult nonrelatives about 3.7 hours a week (in both cases, with no parent present), for a total of 7.1 hours a week—more than the time that fathers spend with children without a mother present. Nonparents play an even more important role in the lives of children living in single parent-households, engaging in activities with them for 9.6 hours a week.

Racial and ethnic differences in the amount of time children spend with parents and nonparents are evident, but it is difficult to assess these in a relatively small sample. Other studies based on the PSID-CDS show that significant racial and ethnic differences in father involvement in two-parent families largely reflect differences in family composition and employment patterns.[69]

The Quantity of Parental-Care Time

Parents do more than merely devote time to their children. They work at the task of providing both active and passive care. Both types of care work can be quantified, and analysis of data from the PSID-CDS offers lower-bound estimates of the amount of parental-care work devoted to children of different ages in different types of households. In general, active parental care accounts for only about 20 percent of the time devoted to children under the age of twelve, and passive care responsibilities are substantial. Young children receive more active care than older children; they are the most expensive timewise, even though they are the least expensive in terms of cash expenditures. Children living in single-parent households receive considerably less parental-care time than those living in two-parent households, and that time overlaps more often with time their siblings receive. Only children enjoy significantly more time in activities with parents than those with one sibling, and children with two or more siblings enjoy slightly less. Mothers provide more than two-thirds of all the active parental care that children under the age of twelve receive.

Accounting for Parental Care

Parents should get credit for the work they do. Child care is often an obligation to be met, not just a pleasure to be fulfilled. It meets the third-person criterion, since someone else can be—and often is—paid to provide it. Child care also provides transferable benefits, not only to the most direct beneficiary, the child, but also to those who will benefit from that child's capabilities in the future.

Most parents work for pay and many find it difficult to balance paid work with family work. Institutional arrangements in the United States are poorly adapted to their needs. Mothers bear the brunt of this problem. Although fathers in two-parent households provide significant amounts of assistance, they are less likely to reduce their hours of market work in ways that reduce their future earnings. Fathers generally enjoy more uninterrupted leisure time than mothers do.

The time that parents devote to active care represents only a small portion of their commitments. The PSID-CDS, recording time allocation from children's point of view, reveals the quantitative dimensions of both supervisory care and time spent on call. The magnitude of these temporal demands suggests that the value of parental time represents a significant percentage of overall parental spending on children under the age of twelve. The next chapter offers a lower-bound estimate of the monetary value of this time.

Appendix: The Child Development Supplement of the Panel Income of Survey Dynamics (PSID-CDS)

Respondents to the Child Development Supplement have already been included in at least one PSID interview. The majority of respondents come from longtime PSID respondent families. Eligibility for the Child Development Supplement is based on the ages of the PSID family's children. (Details are available at the PSID-CDS website at www.isr.umich.edu.)

Time-Diary Data

The time-diary data have a unique case ID and multiple observations per child, each referring to activities over a twenty-four-hour period. Almost every child has two twenty-four-hour time diaries, one kept during a weekday and one during a weekend. Weekly averages are constructed by multiplying the weekday data by five and the weekend data by two.

Each activity associated with a child lists an activity code, duration for an activity, who is participating in the activity, and who else is available. Our examination of the data revealed that participating and available categories are not always mutually exclusive. There are 104 segments of child time in which a mother or father is coded as "participating" but also coded as "available but not participating." We believe this represents a coding error, and we recoded these activities as time "participating."

In most cases, missing values are coded as zeros so as not to reject child-level observations that lack only a small amount of information about specific activities. We found, however, sixteen cases in which no activity is listed for a child (code 481) for an entire day (over a span of twenty-four hours). In those cases, time that anyone spent participating in any activity with a child totaled zero for an entire day. We excluded these day-length records from consideration. Two children have both sample days excluded and were therefore removed from our data set.

The exclusion of activities of sleeping and personal care from consideration of participation or availability of other persons is apparent from the survey instrument itself, which explicitly states in the heading above the participation and availability columns in capital letters: DO NOT ANSWER IF SLEEPING OR PERSONAL CARE. These activities comprised seven specific activity codes.

Family and Household Structure

Ten categories of individuals could be coded as "participating" or "available": mother, father, sibling, stepmother, stepfather, stepsibling, child's friend, grandparent, other relative, or other nonrelative. Of these ten, only four (mother, father, stepmother and stepfather) refer to unique individuals. The other six categories could potentially include more than one person. We include stepmothers in the mother category, stepfathers in the father category, and stepsiblings in the sibling category.

In the PSID, each family unit has one and only one current head. The head must be at least sixteen years old and the person with the most financial responsibility for the family unit. If this person is female and she has a husband in the family unit, then he is typically designated as head. If she has a boyfriend with whom she has been living for at least one year, then he is typically head. If the husband or boyfriend is incapacitated and unable to fulfill the functions of head, however, then the family unit will have a female head.

The "other nonrelative" category may include a cohabiting partner such as a live-in boyfriend. An adult cohabiter is labeled a boyfriend or girlfriend (code 88) the first time he or she appears in the sample. But if the cohabiter remains in the family unit at the next interview, the label is switched to either "Wife" or "Head." Thus, cohabiters "disappear." Since the PSID-CDS is based on families who have already been interviewed at least once, it includes few cohabiters. (Only a cohabiter who joined a family unit since its last interview would show up as such.)

CHAPTER SEVEN

Valuing Family Work

Economists are sometimes described as individuals who know the price of everything and the value of nothing. Introductory textbooks invoke the diamond-water paradox: diamonds are virtually useless, yet expensive. Water is indispensable, yet often free. In a competitive marketplace, prices are set by the intersection of supply and demand. When goods and services are in generous supply, they come cheap. In our society, diamonds are marketed as a symbol of love. But love is much more like water: something that has been widely available but whose infinite supply is by no means naturally guaranteed.

When goods and services lack market prices, economists have methods of estimating or imputing them. The value that individuals place on a given activity can be imputed by asking what they gave up in order to engage in it, or the opportunity cost. But the value that individuals place on an activity is not necessarily the same as its value to society as a whole. This chapter provides estimates of the replacement cost of parental care time for children under twelve by asking the following question: "If parents were unwilling or unable to provide care to their children, what would society need to pay to provide substitute care of acceptable quality?"

This counterfactual question resembles those used in efforts to value environmental resources or services, such as "If we could no longer harvest timber from our National Forests, what would it cost us to purchase comparable quantities and qualities of timber on the market?" or "If we could no longer obtain clean water from our own aquifer, what would it cost us to purchase a comparable substitute?" It is meaningless to ask such questions about resources or services that are either infinite in supply or impossible to replace. Who could guess how much would it cost us to replace sunlight as a source of energy for life on earth? But as fertility decline and childlessness show, the services that parents provide are not in infinite supply. And though there is no perfect replacement for a parent, society can and does pay for substitutes when parents are not available.

We use a replacement cost approach to assign a value to the average estimates of unpaid time devoted to the care of children under twelve, combining these with estimates of money spending on children to provide a measure of the total value of parental expenditures on young children. However approximate the results, they offer a better guide to the economic realities of family life than measures based on money expenditures alone. They also reveal the shortcomings of conventional equivalence scales that assume that children require fewer resources than adults to achieve the same standard of living.

Imputing Value

Most empirical efforts to value parental time devoted to children have used opportunity cost: the market earnings that a parent forgoes. Yet broader imputations of the value of housework have focused on replacement cost, or what would be required to purchase a substitute for unpaid labor. Which is the more appropriate way of valuing parental labor time? The answer to this question depends on the purpose of the valuation. Precisely because child rearing is not a market transaction, there is no single price that can be assigned to it, and we cannot estimate the value of child rearing without specifying the value to whom. The value that parents place on their own time is likely to differ from its value to society as a whole.

The Value to Whom?

Neoclassical economists analyze household production as a metaphorical market. Children are the most direct recipients of care and, in this sense, represent the demand side of an imaginary market exchange. One can ask what a child would hypothetically pay a parent (perhaps via time travel) to do a good job raising her or him.[1] This question is obviously unanswerable. Parents who love their children try to internalize their children's welfare by asking what parental effort might be worth to children over their lifetime. Such altruistic considerations probably influence parental time allocation more profoundly than the more selfish pleasure of time with children. But as much as parents love children, they remain separate individuals. Therefore, it seems likely that the value to the parent of providing services differs from the value to the child receiving them (a point often obscured by the assumption that families act as if they are dynastic units).

Take Sue, a lawyer trying to decide whether to paint her own living room or hire someone to do it for her. Sue can ask herself what the opportunity cost of her time is. If, in lieu of painting, she would have put the extra hours in paid employment, her hourly earnings (after taxes) represent the hourly cost of her time. If Sue derives no intrinsic benefits from either activity, her calculation is a simple one. She compares her opportunity cost with what it would cost her to hire a painter to do the job. If the cost of hiring that painter is less than the opportunity cost of her own time, she should hire him to do the work.

Under these assumptions, if Sue chooses to do the painting herself, we can conclude that its value to her is at least equal to her opportunity cost. But the assumption that Sue derives no intrinsic benefits from the activity of painting seems implausible. Many people engage in nonmarket work activities for the same reason they engage in leisure—they derive intrinsic satisfaction from them. It is entirely possible that Sue likes painting so much (compared to her paid employment) that she does it even when it would cost her much less, in dollars, to purchase substitute labor. In this case the value to her is far greater than the value to others, who do not capture the intrinsic benefits. If Sue lives with roommates, for example, who are willing to give her something in return for her labor (such as a rent reduction), they are likely to place a value on her services approximately equal to the replacement cost, not her opportunity cost.

The reasoning above relies on the exchange metaphor. If Sue is both the supplier and the demander of her own labor, she is in a sense, making a deal with herself. Opportunity cost offers the best approximation of the value of her time. If Sue lives with roommates who are willing to give her something in exchange for the time she devotes to painting, she is making a deal with them. They probably don't care whether she derives intrinsic benefits, so replacement cost offers the best approximation of the value of her time to them.

Time devoted to the care of children offers a particularly striking example of the complexity of nonmarket transfers. Most parents enjoy the actual process of parenting, some more than others. When and if Sue makes a decision to reduce her hours of employment in order to mother a child, she almost certainly takes into account the intrinsic satisfaction she will enjoy. The opportunity cost to her in terms of earnings forgone may be significantly higher than the replacement cost of her time. But Sue is not simply making a deal with herself. She is also involved in an informal exchange with the child itself, another parent, other family members, and society in general. She may expect to get something in return from all these participants, whether in the form of financial assistance, social insurance, informal reciprocity, or personal appreciation. And all these participants may place a different value on her time.

A further complication is that one party's willingness to provide care may be affected by his or her perception of another party's willingness to provide it. Fathers would be less likely to abandon children if they believed that mothers would abandon them as well. Parents might be less likely to offer parental care at no cost if they perceived a social willingness to compensate them for their services. Such strategic considerations may explain why people often express discomfort at the thought of assigning a monetary value to parental time. On the other hand, neither parents nor society can make informed decisions about time and money to devote to children without a clear picture of the economic contingencies involved.

Valuing Labor Inputs at Opportunity Cost

Parental decisions to allocate time and money to children can be modeled in standard neoclassical economic terms as a form of happiness maximization.[2] This approach, however, relies heavily on the assumptions of perfect information and foresight criticized in Chapter 2. It offers few insights into the influence of children on the circular flow of resources through the economy or material standards of living.

Most studies of expenditures on children that take time into consideration rely on the value that mothers place on their own time, as revealed by their participation in paid employment. If a woman gives up an hour of paid employment to spend an hour with a child, she must value that hour at least as highly as her hourly wage after taxes. The total value of the time she devotes to children can be measured by her forgone earnings.[3] In their estimate of total expenditures on children, Robert Haveman and Barbara Wolfe assume that the total time that a mother spends in either child care or work is forty hours per week, and they estimate the reduction in paid employment hours due to children.

Fathers' child-care inputs, which are less likely to result in forgone earnings, are assumed equal to zero. On the basis of these assumptions, they estimate that the average value of parental time per child in 1992 was $1,693 (or, adjusted for inflation, about $2,078 in 2000).[4]

This measure of opportunity cost is incomplete because it fails to account for reduction in earnings over an entire lifetime. Even a brief period of time withdrawn from full-time paid employment has a significant negative effect on future earnings. Women who raise children tend to earn less than those who don't even when they don't significantly reduce their hours of paid employment.[5] Mothers may put less effort than other women into their paid jobs, or they may turn down promotions that they think could interfere with family responsibilities. They may also face some subtle forms of discrimination on the job. In any case, this reduction in earnings independent of hours worked contributes to what has been termed "family gap" and the "motherhood penalty." It adds up to a substantial sum of money above and beyond the costs incurred by simply going without a paycheck for a couple of years while taking care of an infant.

In the United States the relative importance of the motherhood penalty has been increasing over time, in part because other sources of difference in men's and women's earnings (such as overt discrimination) have declined. In 1991, by one estimate, motherhood accounted for more than 60 percent of the difference in men's and women's earnings.[6] The penalty is buffered to some extent by income pooling between married or cohabiting parents. Mothers tend to reduce their hours of market work, whereas fathers tend to increase theirs. If mothers and fathers share income, they also share the costs of forgone earnings.[7] But sharing may be influenced by relative bargaining power, and lower earnings leave mothers vulnerable to poverty when and if income pooling comes to an end. Divorce often has adverse consequences for women, not only because it increases reliance on their own earnings but also because it reduces their eligibility for benefits, such as pensions, that are based on their husband's earnings.

The size of the motherhood penalty varies with mothers' education. Higher-earning women pay a higher opportunity cost, and their career trajectories are often more adversely affected by taking time out. Public policies also have important ramifications. For instance, the motherhood penalty is larger in the United Kingdom, where part-time work is common, than in France.[8] In the United States the Family and Medical Leave Act has made it easier for mothers to resume paid employment with the same employer after twenty-four weeks, with positive effects on their earnings.[9]

Arriving at better estimates of the motherhood penalty—and devising ways to reduce it—is an important goal. But the value of time devoted to parenting cannot be reduced to estimates of forgone earnings. Caring for children also reduces the time available for productive household activities, leisure, and sleep. As was emphasized in Chapter 6, mothers' employment leads to relatively small reductions in the time they spend engaged with their children. Parents often face financial constraints that force them to spread their time thinner, which reduces their opportunities to spend time with one another. The value that Haveman and Wolfe set on the opportunity cost of parental time would have purchased only about 403 hours of replacement child-care time at the federal minimum wage in 2000, considerably less than one and one-half hours per day. As the time-diary results from Chapter 6 make clear, this estimate of the quantity of parental time is unrealistically low.

Valuing Labor Inputs at Replacement Cost

National income accounting relies on measures of market transactions rather than individual happiness. Similarly, most estimates of the total value of family work rely on measures of replacement cost rather than opportunity cost.[10] That is, they are based on the wage rate required to hire a replacement, rather than the actual or potential wage rate of the person doing the work. The replacement cost approach offers a better estimate of social value: as shown in the house painting example above, Sue's roommates are less interested in what Sue herself would be willing to give up in wages than in what it would cost them to hire someone else to do the job.

A replacement cost approach strips away the intrinsic value that the individual performing the work places on it, relying instead on an impersonal market substitute. It is consistent with the approach applied in wrongful death suits, which makes a distinction between lost services that would "have pecuniary value irrespective of the relationship between the deceased and survivors" and those that have value "only because of the love and affection that existed" between them.[11]

The relative size of estimates based on replacement and opportunity cost depends partly on the difference in wage rates between the person performing work and his or her potential replacement. Among highly educated and experienced wage earners, opportunity cost is likely to be higher for all but the most skilled forms of household work. On the other hand, opportunity cost is often applied only to time that is actually withdrawn from paid employment. For nonmarket activities such as parenting, this captures only a small portion of total time. Whether a replacement cost or opportunity cost is used, the wage rate is typically based on a female occupation and may reflect the effects of discrimination—and even, ironically, the motherhood penalty described above. Hence, it should always be construed as a lower-bound estimate.

The most accurate replacement wage for family work would be based on the costs of hiring a specialist for each separate activity performed. For instance, hours devoted to cooking would be multiplied by the wage of a cook of commensurate skill, and hours devoted to child care multiplied by the wage of a child-care professional of comparable education and experience. In practice, it is often difficult to determine the relevant levels of skill and experience and to match them with the appropriate wage rates.

Most estimates rely instead on an approximation, the wage rates of a generalist rather than a specialist. An early study by the National Bureau of Economic Research used the average wages of domestic servants to estimate that housewives' services amounted to 30.7 percent of market national income in 1909.[12] Robert Eisner used a similar approach in his estimates of the value of nonmarket work in the United States in the 1980s.[13] The national statistical agencies of Canada and Australia have constructed supplements to their national income accounts that impute a value to nonmarket work that is based on generalist wages.[14]

These estimates show that nonmarket activities valued solely on the basis of labor inputs account for a sizeable proportion—between 40 and 60 percent—of the total value of all market output.[15] The child-care component of these estimates, however, relies only on time devoted to active child care, which leaves passive care out of the picture. As a result, these estimates significantly undervalue family work.

Valuing Outputs at Replacement Cost

Both opportunity and replacement cost methods have typically been used only to impute the value of the labor devoted to family work and other nonmarket activities. They omit any consideration of the contribution of other inputs, such as capital and raw materials. An alternative approach, developed by the Australian economist Duncan Ironmonger and applied by the Office of National Statistics of the United Kingdom, asks what it would cost to purchase a replacement for the *output* of nonmarket work rather than the labor used to produce it. For instance, the value of a home-cooked meal can be equated with the cost of a similar restaurant-produced meal. Taking that value and subtracting the cost of the raw materials and capital used up provides an estimate of the value of the labor. The value of the child care provided at home can be equated with the cost of placing a child in a child-care center for an equivalent number of hours. This includes the value of passive care, which considerably boosts estimates of the total value of nonmarket work.[16]

This approach raises an interesting conceptual issue. The final "output" of child care is not merely a child-care service that could be purchased in the market, but the child itself, for which there is no market equivalent (unless one accepts the notion that a child can be assigned a value equal to its future lifetime earnings, as discussed in Chapter 2). Still, asking what it would cost to place a child in a child-care center for twenty-four hours a day provides an interesting measure of the replacement cost of care, which includes consideration of the value of capital and raw materials as well as the labor involved. This approach, however, cannot easily be combined with the USDA's traditional estimates of parental expenditures. As a result, this chapter focuses more narrowly on an estimate of the replacement cost of parental time.

The Replacement Cost of Parental Time

Different measures of the value of parental time are appropriate for different purposes. Replacement cost is an appropriate measure of cost to society as a whole. If parents were unwilling or unable to provide care to their children, what would it cost to provide substitute care of acceptable quality? The answer to this question hinges on how acceptable quality is defined. In most cases, there is no perfect substitute for parental care. A secure, long-term relationship with a caregiver is crucial to a child's emotional well-being and capacity for cognitive development.[17]

One could argue that foster care represents the basic replacement cost of a parent, since many children are placed in that arrangement when family care is not available. Most states provide very low stipends for foster care, which are based on estimates of cash expenditures that omit consideration of the value of care time. Though annual maintenance rates for children in foster care vary considerably across states, they averaged $4,644 for two-year-olds and $4,848 for nine-year-olds in 2000.[18] These amounts are well below the level of money expenditure per child characteristic of low-income single parents reported in Chapter 6. One result of these low stipends is that many foster parents must take in a large number of children to make ends meet. The quality of care is uneven, turnover rates are high, and outcomes for children are deplorable.[19]

A more reasonable minimal replacement standard is provision of an equivalent number of hours of active care by a person earning a wage equal to that of an average child care worker, and an equivalent number of hours of passive care (not including sleep) by a person earning at least the federal minimum wage of $5.15 and supervising two children at once. The wages of child care workers in 2000 were quite low: $7.43 per hour, compared to a median hourly wage for all workers of $13.74.

These low wages reflect the fact that the occupation is dominated by women who have traditionally been discouraged from entering more highly paid jobs. But they also reflect the large supply of unpaid family labor. If all parents suddenly withdrew their parenting services, the demand for child care would go up, which would increase the demand for child-care workers, which would increase their wages. This is another reason why the hypothetical valuation presented here represents a lower bound.

Components of Replacement Time

Using the estimates of time use described in Chapter 6, we include only time that a child is awake and not engaged in an activity with a nonparent adult or in institutional care. Sleep time is excluded on the grounds that it largely coincides with parental sleep time. In our valuation of active care, we include only time in which at least one parent is participating in an activity with a child, ignoring the additional value a second participating parent might offer. Our analysis of overlaps shows that of all the time children in a two-child, two-parent family spend with at least one parent, another child is present 26 percent of the time. We assign half of this overlap to each child. Thus, the total time that one child engages in an activity with a parent, minus 13 percent, represents the parental activity time input per child. Of all the time children in a two-child, single-parent family spend with a parent, another child is present 43 percent of the time. We subtract 21.5 percent from the time a child in a one-parent family spends with at least one parent. We multiply these hours by the average hourly wage for child-care workers in 2000, or $7.43 per hour. Again, this average hourly wage represents a lower-bound estimate.

We assume that more than one child can be supervised at once, and that replacement supervision would be paid for at the minimum wage in 2000 of $5.15 per hour. In a two-child family, one hour of supervision for one child is valued at one-half the minimum wage, or $2.58 per hour.

Most estimates of the value of family time devoted to children focus exclusively on parents. To take advantage of the information regarding participation of other family members in unpaid care activities, which are particularly relevant to single-parent households, we include a measure of this time, valuing it (like parental time) at the average child-care worker's wage. (We assume that this time is not remunerated by cash or in-kind transfers from parents.) The total value of family-care time represents the sum of time children spend participating in activities with parents, time children spend in activities with adult relatives, and passive care.

Valuation of Replacement Time

The average value of parental time per child under the age of twelve for children living in two-parent, two-child families, calculated in this fashion, amounted to about $276 per week (Table 7.1). The comparable number for children in single-parent, two-child families was lower, about $212 per week. Since relatives help single parents more, differences in the value of total family-time inputs for children in two-parent and single-parent families are slightly smaller, about $301 per week compared to $251. Converted to annual amounts, these estimates suggest a lower bound for the replacement cost of parental services per child in a two-parent, two-child family of about $13,352, and in a one-parent family, $11,024.

How different would these estimates be if different assumptions regarding the value of parental time were used? We offer a "high variant" of the value of parental services, counting all parental time rather than all non-overlapping parental time and applying a higher wage rate.[20] We do not term this an upper bound because it does not include any consideration of child-specific skills, the emotional benefits of long-term relationships, or any valuation of passive care time while children are asleep. Both parental time and time of adult relatives are valued at the median wage in 2000 of $13.74, rather than a child-care worker's wage of $7.43. These steps are presented separately in Table 7.2, in terms comparable to those in Table 7.1. The high-variant imputation of the replacement cost of parental services per child in a two-parent, two-child family comes to an average of over $23,000 per year.

Table 7.1 Lower-bound imputation of the value of four categories of family time per child aged 0–11 in two-child families (per week, in 2000 dollars)

	All	0–2	3–5	6–8	9–11
Children in two-parent households					
N	834	203	228	198	205
Passive care hours: child awake but not engaged in activity with an adult, divided by 2 (assuming 2 children supervised at once) valued at minimum wage of $5.15 per hour	$ 70	$ 62	$ 66	$ 70	$ 80
Parental-care activities: hours of time with at least one parent, minus 13% to account for overlaps with sibling, valued at the average child-care worker's wage of $7.43 per hour	206	248	227	193	158
Nonparental relative care activities: hours child engaged in activity with a nonparental relative, valued as above.	25	33	21	27	22
Total imputed value of family care: sum of categories above	301	343	314	289	260
Imputed value of parental care: passive care plus parental-care activities	276	310	293	262	238
Children in single-parent households					
N	237	49	59	58	71
Passive care hours: child awake but not engaged in activity with an adult, divided by 2 (assuming 2 children supervised at once), valued at minimum wage of $5.15 per hour	$ 77	$ 58	$ 73	$ 83	$ 89
Parental-care activities: hours of time with at least one parent, minus 21.5% to account for overlaps with sibling, valued at the average child-care worker's wage of $7.43 per hour	135	145	152	133	117
Nonparental relative care activities: hours child engaged in activity with a nonparental relative, valued as above	39	40	54	41	24
Total imputed value of family care: sum of categories above	251	243	279	257	229
Imputed value of parental care: passive care plus parental-care activities	212	203	225	216	205

Source: Author's calculations.

Table 7.2 High-variant imputation of the value of four categories of family time per child aged 0–11 in two-child families (per week, in 2000 dollars)

	All	0–2	3–5	6–8	9–11
Children in two-parent households					
N	834	203	228	198	205
Passive care hours: child awake but not engaged in activity with an adult, divided by 2 (assuming 2 children supervised at once), valued at minimum wage of $5.15 per hour	$ 70	$ 62	$ 66	$ 70	$ 80
Parental-care activities: hours of time with at least one parent, minus 13% to account for overlaps with sibling, valued at the median wage of $13.74 per hour	381	458	420	356	292
Nonparental relative care activities: hours child engaged in activity with a nonparental relative, valued as above	47	60	38	49	41
Total imputed value of family care: sum of categories above	498	581	524	475	413
Total imputed value of parental care: passive care plus parental-care activities	451	520	486	426	371
Children in single-parent households					
N	237	49	59	58	71
Passive care hours: child awake but not engaged in activity with an adult, divided by 2 (assuming 2 children supervised at once) valued at minimum wage of $5.15 per hour	$ 77	$ 58	$ 73	$ 83	$ 89
Parental care activities: total hours of time with either mother or father, minus 21.5% to account for overlap with sibling, valued at the median wage of $13.74 per hour	250	269	282	246	216
Nonparental relative care activities: hours child engaged in activity with a nonparental relative, valued as above	71	74	100	76	44
Total imputed value of family care: sum of categories above	398	401	454	404	348
Total imputed value of parental care: passive care plus parental care activities	327	327	354	329	304

Source: Author's calculations.

Costs of Parental Time Compared to Money Expenditures

Even the lower-bound estimate of the average replacement cost of parental time is large in relation to average money expenditures. This can be added to estimates of money expenditures provided in Chapter 6 to estimate average total family spending of money and time per child under 12 in 2000 (Table 7.3). This total comes to approximately $23,253 per year per child in two-parent, two-child families, and about $17,125 per year in single-parent, two-child families.[21] Overall, the time costs, measured in this fashion, represent about 62 percent of total expenditures (money plus time) on children in two-parent families, and about 65 percent in single-parent families. In both kinds of family, the percentage share of time costs declines as children grow older, but it remains well over 55 percent even for children aged nine through eleven.

As emphasized earlier, much depends on how replacement cost is defined. Nonetheless, it is difficult to imagine a more cautious lower-bound estimate than the one presented here. This estimate nonetheless

Table 7.3 Lower-bound imputation of the annual value of parental time compared with annual cash expenditures on children aged 0–11 in 2000

	Cash expenditures	Imputed value of parental time	Total expenditures	Time costs as percentage of total
Children living in two-parent households				
Average	$8,915	$14,338	$23,253	61.7%
0–2	8,740	16,101	24,841	64.8
3–5	8,980	15,226	24,206	62.9
6–8	8,990	13,632	22,622	60.3
9–11	8,950	12,353	21,303	58.0
Children living in one-parent households				
Average	$6,048	$11,077	$17,125	64.7%
0–2	5,270	10,595	15,865	66.8
3–5	5,950	11,648	17,598	66.2
6–8	6,710	11,200	17,910	62.5
9–11	6,260	10,672	16,932	63.0

Note: Imputed value of parental time based on annualization of figures in Table 7.1. Figures for children living in two-parent households are for middle-income families with before-tax income between $38,000 and $64,000. Figures for children living in single-parent households are for low-income families with before-tax income below $38,000, as in Table 6.3.

more than doubles the estimated cost of children. If parents withdrew their services, the total cost of replacing their contributions would be more than twice as high as widely used estimates of money expenditures on children under twelve.

The Aggregate Value of Parental Resources Devoted to Children

Placing a monetary value on parental time does not imply that we should pay all parents a wage. It does imply that conventional measures of living standards—which ignore the time costs of children—overstate parental standards of living and understate the extent of their contribution to the economy as a whole.

Parents devote more resources to children than have previously been acknowledged. Using only women's current forgone earnings as a measure of opportunity cost, Calhoun and Espenshade estimated the value of parental time at between 7 and 27 percent of total parental spending, Haveman and Wolfe at 22 percent.[22] These estimates imply that measures of cash spending alone should be multiplied by about 1.25 to arrive at an estimate of total parental spending. The lower-bound estimates of the value of parental time provided here, representing slightly over 60 percent of total parental spending, imply that cash expenditures of middle-income families should be multiplied by a factor of about 2.5 to arrive at a measure of parental contributions. Since the amount and value of time devoted to children varies less than the amount of money devoted to them, this factor should probably be larger for poor parents and smaller for affluent ones.

The value of time devoted to child care should be included in estimates of the relative standard of living of households with children. Specific revision of the equivalence scales criticized in Chapter 5, however, will require further research on how households use time and money. Estimates of money expenditures on children can be subtracted from total expenditures to arrive at a measure of adult consumption. But the value of time devoted to children represents an answer to a counterfactual question, and it cannot be meaningfully subtracted from parental income. It should be assessed in relation to the value of a household's "full income"—the value of its money income plus the value of the times its members devote to the production of household goods and services. Such assessments will require concerted efforts to measure and value all household activities.

Perhaps the estimates presented here can help motivate further efforts in this direction. From the point of view of the economy as a whole, expenditures of money and time on children represent investment in the future. The portion of this investment measured by Haveman and Wolfe represents a sum of money equivalent to about 15 percent of the GDP. The broader assessment presented here suggest that it represents a sum of money equivalent to more than 30 percent of the GDP—even ignoring the costs of college and other transfers to children over eighteen. The willingness of adults to undertake child-rearing commitments—and the efficacy with which they do so—has obvious implications for our collective standard of living.

The Many Values of Parental Time

No single dollar amount can represent the value of the time parents devote to rearing the next generation. From the point of view of individual children, such value is probably infinite. Likewise, many parents feel that the opportunity to spend time caring for their own children is priceless. But even crude approximations of the social value of family work, used judiciously, can help call attention to its contributions.

Market prices are an indication of individual willingness to pay for goods and services. Some people are always willing to pay more than others, for reasons related to their resources, their preferences, and their perception of what others are likely to pay. The same is true of time devoted to children. Parents are usually more willing to give up their time to take care of their children than anyone else. Mothers and grandmothers are usually willing to give up more than fathers or grandfathers. High-wage individuals give up more than others in forgone earnings when they reallocate time from paid work to family work.

Estimates of the opportunity cost of time devoted to child care are important and interesting, especially when they include time withdrawn from activities other than paid employment and consider indirect and long-term effects. But estimates of the replacement cost of parental-care services are better suited to valuation of the activities of the "household sector" in terms consistent with national income accounts. Considerable future research will be required to develop more precise estimates of the relative standards of living of parents and nonparents. Still, the numbers provided here provide a valuable reference point for consideration of the repercussions of public policies.

PART THREE

Public Spending on Children in the United States

CHAPTER EIGHT

Subsidizing Parents

In recognition of the important work that parents do, the United Nations Convention on the Rights of the Child, ratified by all nations except Somalia and the United States, stipulates that "the nation shall provide appropriate assistance to parents in child-raising." What exactly is appropriate assistance? Most northwestern European countries offer family allowances and paid parental leaves from work as well as publicly supported child care and education.[1] Even these benefits, the most generous in the world, cover only a small percentage of parental expenditures. As a result, they lower the overall cost of children only slightly. Yet policy makers often express surprise that they do little to boost overall fertility rates.[2]

Subsidies to parents have emerged from a hodgepodge of concerns about children's well-being, marriage rates, and birthrates, rather than explicit consideration of the appropriate level of support for parenting. International comparisons are often misleading, focusing on cash benefits and ignoring tax benefits that have the same effect of increasing disposable income. (See the appendix to this chapter). Parental-support programs everywhere suffer from a bewildering variety of provisions, but the United States stands out in its level of programmatic complexity and inconsistency. The distributional effects are perverse: many affluent families receive benefits that are surprisingly similar, in absolute terms, to those that poor families receive. Middle-income families typically receive less.

This chapter describes subsidies to parents that directly affect the disposable income of families with children in the United States. It provides a broad historical overview, situating the most important programs within an international context. It compares the tax benefits, public assistance, and social insurance available to families at different income levels in 2000 and examines public benefits and transfers related to parental leave, child care, and college financial aid.

Public Subsidies

Current forms of support for child rearing in affluent countries such as the United States cannot be explained simply as compensation for market failures. Although standard microeconomics texts seldom include children on a list of goods with spillover effects for society as whole, public policies themselves reflect commitments to children as public goods. Substantial cash subsidies (distinct from the in-kind programs that are the topic of Chapter 9) fall into three categories: direct subsidies through taxes or transfers, social insurance for retirement, death, and disability, and means-tested benefits targeted at low-income families.

Tax Benefits and Family Allowances

Anxiety concerning the effect of wage employment on the family has long etched public policy. In the early twentieth century, debates over family benefits were shaped by attitudes toward the value of paid and unpaid work, as well as the relative power of trade unions and women's groups.[3] Both minimum wages and family allowances were widely adopted by countries in the forefront of industrial development, partly out of fear that growing reliance on individual wages rather than household-based production would put parents at a disadvantage.

Most European countries, as well as Canada and Australia, began providing a fixed payment per child in the 1930s and increased these payments considerably in the aftermath of World War II. Levels were low; the total allowance for two children seldom amounted to more than about 10 percent of average annual manufacturing wages.[4] The level of European family allowances relative to average wages has changed surprisingly little over the last fifty years, although eligibility has expanded and is now less conditional on employment status.[5] In eighteen member countries of the Organization for Economic Cooperation and Development (including the United States) the average benefit increased from about 8 percent to about 12 percent of an average production worker's earnings between 1950 and 1990.[6]

In the United States the prominent senator and economist Paul Douglas (best known for his formulation of the Cobb-Douglas production function) made a case for family allowances in 1925.[7] Though his specific policy recommendations were never implemented, family benefits were carved into the U.S. income tax system through standard and personal deductions that allow families to deduct significant amounts from their taxable income depending on their size and structure.

The value of deductions depends on the marginal tax rate, which, with a progressive-rate structure, increases along with income. The combined value of standard and personal deductions was initially high enough to shield most families with children from income taxes, but was steadily reduced by inflation, which led to bracket creep. As nominal incomes rose, so did susceptibility to higher marginal tax rates. The real value of the standard and personal deductions declined substantially between 1960 and 1986, the year that they were indexed to inflation.[8]

The personal deduction applies not only to children, but also to spouses, including those who earn no market income themselves. Historically, most spouses not engaged in paid employment took direct responsibility for dependents; the tax subsidies for them indirectly subsidized family care. Yet the spousal benefit was not typically tied to the presence of children or other dependent family members. In a low-fertility society with a high level of nonmarital births, the personal deduction for a nonemployed spouse subsidizes marriage, not child rearing. Partly for this reason, many European countries have reduced marriage subsidies relative to child benefits.[9]

The U.S. federal income tax structure creates a marriage bonus when one spouse does not work for pay and a penalty when both spouses work for pay. (The penalty was attenuated but not eliminated by changes in the tax code adopted in 2004.) In 2000, more families enjoyed a bonus than a penalty, a bonus particularly large and accessible for affluent couples. Low-income couples seldom enjoy the option of allowing one person to specialize in nonmarket work; those receiving government assistance are particularly vulnerable to the marriage penalty because higher earnings reduce their eligibility for benefits, effectively increasing their marginal tax rate.[10] Both the bonus and the penalty affect wives (who are more likely to be second earners) more than husbands, which discourages women's paid employment, reduces their lifetime earnings, and increases economic vulnerability in the event of divorce.[11]

Recent changes in the tax code have significantly increased subsidies for child rearing. The Earned Income Tax Credit, a benefit for poor families discussed later in more detail, has effectively become an income-tested and employment-tested family allowance. In 1998 Congress enacted the Child Credit, which allowed most families to subtract $500 per child from taxes owed. In 2001 the Child Credit was increased to $600 per child, and in 2003 to $1,000 (but with a sunset clause that threatens to reduce it in future years).

Recent changes also make a portion of the credit potentially refundable to low-income families who would not otherwise benefit because they do not owe federal taxes.[12] If the United States moved toward complete refundability, a Child Credit of $1,000 per child (not counting the value of other tax benefits) would offer support greater than family allowances provided in most European countries. In 2002, for instance, the per child Swedish allowance amounted to about $950 per child, and the French allowance to less than $600.[13]

Family Leaves from Employment

The paid parental leaves from employment that evolved alongside family allowances in much of northwestern Europe have different implications from those of annual transfers. They are generally awarded only once per child, rather than being distributed over eighteen years, although some Nordic countries allow parental leave to be drawn down until a child has reached a certain age (in the case of Sweden, when a child has reached the age of eight). Paid family leave essentially defrays opportunity costs. Most parental leaves are reimbursed at a percentage of workers' wages, ranging from about 50 percent to 100 percent. Although this replacement rate sometimes varies along with wage level and is subject to caps, higher wage earners generally receive a higher benefit.[14]

If parental leaves are extended over a long period, as they are in the Nordic countries (often more than a year for maternal and paternal leave combined), payments can add up to a large amount of money. In the Swedish case, for instance, the benefit ranges from a floor of $10,342 to a ceiling of $35,204.[15] At a minimum, in other words, its value is ten times greater than that of the family allowance of $950 in one year (and at a maximum, thirty-seven times greater!). Even though it is paid only once, whereas the family allowance is paid annually, it represents, for most Swedish families, a greater source of support, especially when future family allowance payments are discounted to reflect their present value. Similarly, Canada offers 55 percent of earnings for up to fifty weeks in combined maternal and paternal leave benefits, up to a maximum of U.S. $17,500, which is substantially more than the discounted value of the maximum Canadian Child Credit over eighteen years. Most countries offer shorter leaves and lower replacement rates.[16]

Unlike family allowances, parental leaves from work have direct and significant effects on the supply of labor to paid employment. Women in these countries have a powerful incentive to wait until they have a job to bear a child, a factor that may help explain low teen pregnancy rates in countries like Sweden. On the other hand, the potential for long paid maternity leaves discourages private employers from hiring women and reduces women's job experience and lifetime earnings.[17] In many countries, only mothers are offered paid leave; even when fathers are offered paid leave, they are often less likely to use it.

The United States is the only major industrialized country that does not offer paid parental leaves from work. Federal legislation provides only twelve weeks of unpaid leave, and that only for employees of firms with more than fifty employees, about 60 percent of private sector workers. Five individual states offer some wage replacement for maternity benefits through Temporary Disability Insurance programs. Many private firms offer paid leave or additional unpaid leave, but highly educated women are far more likely than others to enjoy such benefits.

Many parents patch together benefits such as sick leave or paid vacation time to meet their needs. In the mid-1990s, only about 43 percent of women employed during their pregnancies received paid leave of any type during the first twelve weeks after childbirth.[18] Single mothers and low-income families are most likely to feel the economic bite of childcare responsibilities. Middle-income families may suffer a higher percentage loss because they typically enjoy higher earnings and are less eligible for forms of public assistance such as food stamps or Medicaid.

Social Insurance
Many of the social insurance programs implemented by the modern welfare state were a response to forms of market failure such as unemployment. A number of specific policies, however, such as transfers to protect mothers from the economic risks of widowhood, divorce, or abandonment, can be interpreted as a response to family failure. Most northwestern European countries, as well as Canada and Australia, gradually adopted such policies along with unemployment and disabil-

ity insurance. Social insurance buffers children from financial losses from the death of a wage earner, and it also offers pension benefits that reward nonmarket work. In some countries, but notably *not* in the United States, social insurance protects parents and children who fail to receive adequate financial support from a noncustodial parent.

Social insurance has been strongly influenced by the male family wage model; it offers so-called breadwinners extra benefits if they are supporting dependents. Though such patterns remain evident in northwestern Europe, most countries there offer at least some universal benefits that are not linked to labor-force history or marital status. In the United States, by contrast, many families rely on employer-provided pensions and health insurance that benefit adults who are not working for pay only if they are married to a wage earner.[19]

Emphasis on marriage as a criterion for social insurance was embedded in the Mothers' Pensions and Old Age Pensions adopted by many states between 1910 and 1920 as a precursor to federal policies put in place with the Social Security Act of 1935. That act established a safety net for widows and orphans distinct from that provided for children born out of wedlock; it also established an old-age pension system that, although linked to wages, provided greater benefits for married than for unmarried workers. Both Survivor's Insurance and Old Age Security were established as entitlements that initially covered only a small set of wage earners but were expanded during the postwar period to include virtually the entire labor force.

Survivor's benefits are provided only to married spouses and their children, at levels determined by the earnings of the covered worker. The level of support varies, but it has always been and remains much higher than the level of support provided by means-tested cash assistance to single mothers. Furthermore, few requirements, restrictions, or time limits are imposed on receipt of this form of assistance. Although the number of families with children receiving Survivor's Insurance per year is far lower than the number receiving Temporary Assistance to Needy Families, the higher levels of support make Survivor's Insurance a bigger component of the federal budget.

Social Security retirement benefits for spouses specializing in nonmarket work have always been substantial. From the outset, a married man and his never-employed wife were given retirement benefits 50 percent greater than those of a single man with exactly the same earnings and contribution history. Married women's rapid entrance into wage employment during the postwar period injected new funds into the system, as wives began paying Social Security taxes that partially offset their spousal benefits. As coverage expanded, the provisions of Social Security were made gender-neutral (providing spousal benefits to husbands based on wives' earnings as well as vice versa). Individuals were allowed to choose between a benefit based on their own earnings and one based on those of their spouse. Because most married women took time out of the labor force to raise children and earned lower wages than men, most could look forward to greater benefits based on their spouse's earnings than their own. The taxes these women paid into Social Security effectively subsidized the benefits enjoyed by housewives and lowered their own net earnings.

Social Security deploys a regressive tax and a progressive benefit structure whose effects largely countervail one another for individual wage earners. Life expectancy is an important determinant of net benefits. But when family benefits, rather than merely individual benefits, are taken into account, the picture changes. Since spouses can receive benefits that are based on their partner's contributions rather than their own, spouses of high-wage earners receive a particularly large direct transfer from the government. Social Security provides a higher rate of return on contributions for a one-earner family receiving the top benefit than it does for two-earner families in which both workers have low wages.[20] No spousal benefits are provided for those married less than ten years, although a majority of divorces take place within this period. Poorly educated single mothers with irregular histories of paid employment are unlikely to be eligible for benefits high enough to protect them from poverty in old age.[21]

Most other countries with social insurance systems provide some pension compensation for people who leave the labor force temporarily to care for young children.[22] The United States does not. Likewise, most European countries provide insurance against parental default or failure to pay child support in the form of special assistance for single parents. In a world in which most married women stayed home to raise children and few mothers were unmarried, Social Security helped underwrite a significant portion of the costs of raising children. Today the family wage embodied in our social insurance system provides more benefits to the affluent than to the poor, leaving many children in single-parent families living in poverty.

Public Assistance

Public assistance that takes the form of transfers to individuals with family income below a certain level is described as *means-tested*. Its success can be measured by the difference between pretransfer and post-transfer poverty. Most European countries, as well as Australia and Canada, provide transfers that significantly reduce poverty among families with children, especially those with single parents. The United States does not.[23] Much of the explanation for this lies in the evolution of the social insurance policies described above.

The Social Security Act provided an entitlement for widows and orphans (regardless of income), but it offered only means-tested assistance for mothers who were unmarried or who had been deserted by their husbands, through the welfare program that came to be known as Aid to Families with Dependent Children (AFDC). Cash benefits available to single parents with children were never high compared to other forms of assistance such as unemployment insurance.[24] After the mid-1970s, their real value was heavily eroded by inflation. These declines were only partially countervailed by the growth of a form of near-cash assistance, the food stamp program, which subsidizes food purchases.

In 1996 the AFDC program was converted to Temporary Assistance for Needy Families (TANF). Strict time limits and rules requiring recipients to work for pay contributed to dramatic reductions in welfare rolls.[25] These rules vary across states, but they mandate work (as defined by states) after a maximum of two years of benefits. The lifetime limit on federally funded aid (as of 2005) was five years, though up to 20 percent of the caseload is eligible for exemption because of hardship. TANF, like AFDC, has been supplemented by food stamps, as well as some in-kind benefits such as health care and child care (discussed in Chapter 9).

The biggest increase in means-tested assistance in the 1990s came through the expansion of the Earned Income Tax Credit (EITC), a program that now commands a larger share of the federal budget than TANF. The EITC benefit formula was designed, in principle, to encourage low-income parents to work, offering a subsidy theoretically sufficient to allow one full-time minimum-wage worker to support three dependents at an income above the poverty line. Benefits are closely tied to earnings, and they phase out steeply after family income reaches that line; a penalty is often imposed on recipients who marry someone working full-time.

The EITC is sometimes described as a wage subsidy program because a family must *earn* income to receive it. It more closely resembles a family allowance with a family cap, however, because benefits for families without children are extremely low, whereas those for families with one or two children are substantial. No extra benefits accrue for additional children. The EITC provides a substitute for earlier spending on TANF, encouraging paid employment and discouraging mothers from rearing more than two children. Yet its benefit structure penalizes married couples when both partners work for pay.

Another family insurance system, which provides a fallback for children whose families are either unable or unwilling to care for them adequately, is provided by public foster care and child protection programs. Such assistance is highly decentralized, and regulations and payments vary considerably among the fifty states. Eligibility is largely limited to the poor, and African American children are heavily overrepresented in foster care; more than three times as many children participate as would be predicted from their share in the population alone.[26] Children who spend significant amounts of time in either foster or institutional care are often developmentally disadvantaged. They are more likely than other children to drop out of high school and to experience incarceration.[27]

The structure of federal reimbursement encourages states to spend more on foster care than on assistance to children living with parents experiencing economic stress.[28] Family members who are not parents are often eligible for greater support through the foster care system than parents could receive through TANF. Since 1996 an increasing percentage of foster children has been placed with kin, such as grandparents.[29] Many kin foster families are also recipients of TANF grants made for children alone, an increasing share of all TANF grants.

Child Care and Education

Most advanced industrial countries provide for the care and education of children from a very young age through postsecondary education, at little cost to parents. In the United States, by contrast, parents typically pay high out-of-pocket costs for both preschool and college. Federal tax benefits help defray these costs. The Dependent Care Credit, which allows parents to deduct a percentage of child-care costs from their taxes, is limited to a small percentage (no more than 30 percent) of an amount capped at a low level relative to what many parents spend.[30] A less well-known but more generous subsidy takes the form of dependent care pretax accounts, which allow working parents with child-care expenses to set aside up to $5,000 per year in an employer-sponsored account that is exempt from both income and payroll taxes.

Though considered a laggard in the international child-care arena, the United States has a strong state university system and relatively high rates of college enrollment. Federal subsidies have played a historically important role. Like the Social Security system put in place in 1935, the GI Bill (officially known as the Servicemen's Readjustment Act of 1944) provided a virtually universal entitlement. Its most celebrated provision was a federal commitment to subsidize tuition, fees, books, and educational materials—as well as to provide a stipend for living expenses—for veterans at the educational institution of their choice. The bill contributed to burgeoning college enrollments in the 1940s and 1950s, and it continues to provide substantial assistance to veterans today.

In 1965 Congress passed the Higher Education Act, whose Title IV provisions made an explicit commitment to "need-based" assistance, corresponding to what is termed "means-tested" assistance in the world of social insurance. This spawned a variety of programs, including Pell Grants for low-income students and subsidized and unsubsidized loans for both parents and students. It also authorized programs funded by the federal government but administered by schools, or campus-based aid.

The Pell Grant remains the hallmark and bellwether of trends in need-based federal assistance.[31] The values of both the maximum and the average benefit have declined only slightly in real terms since the mid-1970s. The average cost of attending an institution of higher education, however, has increased significantly.[32] As a result, Pell Grants offer less assistance paying college bills than they have in the past. In 1980 the maximum grant covered about 70 percent of the average price of tuition, fees, and on-campus room and board at a public four-year institution; by 2000 it covered less than half.[33]

Students remain highly dependent on Title IV assistance. In 1999–2000 almost 25 percent of all undergraduates received either a federal Pell Grant or federally funded campus-based aid.[34] Increased financial aid from states and private institutions has lessened the ramifications of escalating tuition and fees. The net price of attending college (taking average financial aid into account) is far lower than the sticker price. A declining proportion of all federal, state, and institutional aid is based on financial need, however.[35]

The biggest boost to families paying for college in recent years has come from tax credits and deductions designed to benefit those in middle-income brackets. Like tax credits for children, these new benefits represent a shift away from means-tested assistance. Under the Clinton administration, the U.S. Congress passed two federal income tax credits in 1997 designed to help middle-class families pay for college. The

Hope Scholarship tax credit allowed families to subtract up to $1,500 in expenses for students in their first two years of college from their taxes, and the Lifetime Learning Tax Credit allowed credits of up to $1,000 for students in later years.[36] About 46 percent of undergraduates took advantage of one of these credits in the 1999–2000 year.[37]

These credits have since been supplemented by 2001 legislation providing new tax incentives for college saving as well as a federal income tax deduction of up to $3,000 for tuition and fees for those who do not claim one of the credits described above. These new benefits also favor families with higher incomes.[38] Overall, about 70 percent of undergraduate students and families in the United States receive federal assistance in paying for postsecondary education.[39] Though the complexity of these benefits makes it difficult to determine their distributional effect precisely, children from low-income families benefit least for the simple reason that they are least likely to attend college.

Tax Benefits, Transfers, and Social Insurance

How can federal subsidies for child rearing in 2000 be summarized in dollar terms? Since most families pay taxes as well as receive benefits, the best measure of subsidy would be the difference between taxes paid and benefits received over the life of a child. In the absence of data that allow such an estimate, a telling picture emerges from comparisons of the important benefits available to those at different income levels in 2000. Whether they have the word child in their name, all the programs described above provide benefits that are based on the presence and number of children. Their dollar value varies considerably depending on marital status, participation in paid employment, and family income.

Tax Exemptions and Credits versus the Earned Income Tax Credit
Child-related benefits are strongly affected by family income. Compare benefits available to married couples filing a joint tax return in 2000 at three different income levels: (1) paying no income taxes but eligible for the maximum EITC; (2) in the lowest bracket (with an income well above the poverty line but less than about $44,000); and (3) in the highest bracket in which exemptions and credits did not phase out (with an income between about $106,000 and $110,000 and facing a marginal tax rate of 31 percent).

A family with one child receiving the EITC in 2000 could have received a maximum net benefit of $2,000 (Table 8.1), although relatively

Table 8.1 Maximum child tax exemptions and credits for married couples filing jointly and raising one or more children in 2000

	Total	Percentage of midpoint of income bracket	Amount per child
Earned income tax credit (maximum child-related credit available to families with incomes between $9,720 and $12,690; smaller amounts available to families up to $30,000)[a]			
one child	$2,000	17.8%	$2,000
two children	3,535	31.5	1,768
three children	3,535	31.5	1,178
Personal exemptions for children plus child credits, 15% tax bracket (taxable incomes up to $43,850)			
one child	920	3.3	920
two children	1,840	6.5	920
three children	2,760	9.8	920
Personal exemptions for children plus child credits, lower portion of 31% tax bracket, (taxable incomes between $105,950 and $110,000)[b]			
one child	1,368	1.3	1,368
two children	2,736	2.5	1,368
three children	4,104	3.8	1,368
Personal exemptions for children and spouse plus child credits, lower portion of 31% tax bracket (taxable incomes between $105,950 and $110,000)			
one child	2,236	2.1	2,236
two children	3,604	3.3	1,802
three children	4,972	4.6	1,657

a. The maximum amount of the EITC for families without any children, $353, was subtracted from the total maximums for families with children.
b. The lower portion of the 31 percent tax bracket is chosen because this is the range in which the value of the dependent exemptions and child-care credits is at a maximum.

few families received the maximum. The personal exemption, set at $2,800 in 2000, had a value equal to the taxes that would have been paid if that sum had not been exempt from taxation. Each child under the age of eighteen could be claimed as an exemption, and each child under the age of seventeen qualified the family for a child tax credit of $500. Neither the exemption nor the credit was of any value to families who did not owe taxes. A family in the 15 percent tax bracket could have claimed an exemption worth $420 per child and a credit worth $500 per child, for a total of $920 per child. A family in the lower end of the 31 percent tax bracket could have claimed an exemption of $868 and a credit of $500 for a total of $1,368 per child.

In other words, families paying taxes in the 15 percent tax bracket received less assistance than poor families who could take advantage of the EITC or rich families whose exemptions were worth more. Figure 8.1 illustrates the resulting U-shaped pattern for married couples filing jointly, which has been described as a "middle class parent penalty."[40] The differences in level of support were even greater for families with three or more children. Since EITC benefits did not rise for additional children, benefits per child in these families—but not in more affluent families—decline. Benefits for heads of household (mostly single parents), not explicitly discussed here, follow a similar pattern.

More than a third of all children in the country in 2000 lived in families with three or more children. Not surprisingly, these children were susceptible to significantly higher poverty rates. If a family in the top bracket included a spouse who did not work for pay because she or he was providing child care, the additional personal exemption it could claim further accentuated the differences in benefit levels across income categories. The size of the Child Credit, at $1,000 per child, is now high compared to the EITC benefit. Future debates over the universality, level, and refundability of this credit will have momentous consequences for low-income families.

A broader view of the inconsistencies in tax benefits is offered in Figure 8.2, which pictures the overall shape of changes in benefits along with increases in family income for a typical married-couple family. This figure also illustrates the effect of the EITC phaseout that penalizes marriage among low-income couples. The benefit was designed to reach a plateau close to the point where a single mother with two children working forty hours a week, fifty-two weeks per year at the federal minimum wage of $5.15 per hour could receive the maximum benefit. If she married and continued to work for pay, as she would be likely to do at

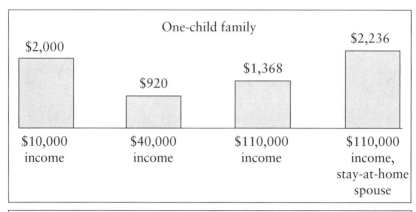

One-child family

$2,000 — $10,000 income
$920 — $40,000 income
$1,368 — $110,000 income
$2,236 — $110,000 income, stay-at-home spouse

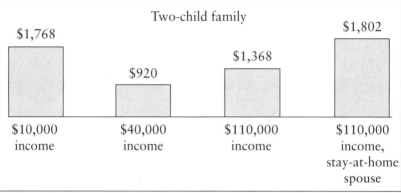

Two-child family

$1,768 — $10,000 income
$920 — $40,000 income
$1,368 — $110,000 income
$1,802 — $110,000 income, stay-at-home spouse

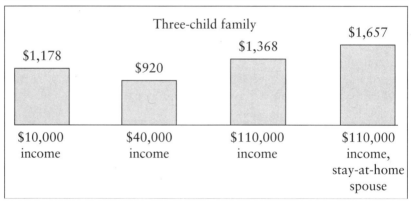

Three-child family

$1,178 — $10,000 income
$920 — $40,000 income
$1,368 — $110,000 income
$1,657 — $110,000 income, stay-at-home spouse

Figure 8.1 Tax benefits per child available to a married couple in 2000

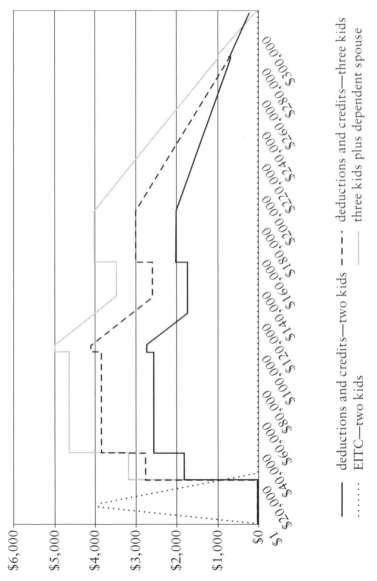

Figure 8.2 Child-related tax benefits and taxable income, married couples filing jointly in 2000

this income level, the additional income would almost certainly push her beyond this point. For instance, if she married a man working full-time at $7.00 an hour, her benefit would fall to $1,255, which is slightly less than a married couple with two children, filing jointly, with a combined income of $31,150 could receive through the combined benefit of dependent deductions and child credits.

Social Security versus TANF

Another telling illustration of the strange relationship between family income and public subsidy emerges from a comparison of the social safety net features of Social Security compared to TANF. Children are eligible for Social Security payments if a parent dies, becomes disabled, or reaches retirement age. About 7 percent of all children under eighteen received such assistance in 2000, more than the percentage receiving welfare through TANF.[41] At first glance, this seems surprising, since about ten times as many children live in households headed by an unmarried or divorced parent as in those headed by a widowed or disabled parent.[42]

But children in the larger category are subject to strict rules and time limits that reduce the period during which they receive assistance. Families of children covered by Social Security receive assistance for a much longer period of time, and they enjoy significantly higher levels of assistance. Survivor's benefits are paid as long as the surviving spouse is caring for a child under sixteen. Unmarried children receive benefits until they reach eighteen, or until age nineteen if they are in school.[43] Eligibility for survivor's benefits is virtually universal; under a special rule, benefits can be paid if the deceased worked for one and one-half years in the three years just before death. Benefits are set at 75 percent of the deceased's basic Social Security retirement benefit.

In contrast to TANF, neither surviving spouses nor disabled parents are required to work for pay in return for benefits. Indeed, their benefits are reduced if their earnings exceed certain limits or, in the case of surviving spouses, if they remarry. The combined face value (or potential payout) of insurance against disability and death for a young worker with average earnings, a young spouse, and two children in 2001 was more than $700,000.[44]

Children clearly have an important economic stake in the Social Security system. In 2000 the average benefit for a widowed mother or father plus two children was about $20,060 per year.[45] On a per capita basis, this amounts to about $6,687 per child. Average benefits for disabled and retired workers with a dependent spouse and children were slightly smaller. Since benefits are based on wages, they are considerably higher for survivors of high earners. Many families receiving these benefits had relatively low incomes, however, and children living in them were slightly more likely than all children to live in poverty.[46]

Comparisons of benefits available to children through Social Security and through TANF reveal striking disparities. Benefit levels for TANF, like those for its predecessor, AFDC, vary considerably by state.[47] The average benefit per family in 2000 was about $4,445 per year.[48] About 80 percent of TANF recipients also received food stamps, the value of which averaged about $2,736 per year.[49] Adding these two together, the average amount of means-tested cash assistance for single-parent families with two children was about $7,181. On a per capita basis, this amounts to about $2,394 per child. In other words, these families received assistance amounting to about a third of that provided by survivor's benefits—for a much shorter period. Families of color were, in general, far more dependent on lower and more restricted TANF than on survivor's benefits.[50]

In short, parents and children in this country enjoy much more generous insurance against demographic accident—death or disability—than against family failure, which is an equally serious problem. Discrepancies in benefit levels and rules intensify existing inequalities in income security among children.

Foster Care

Since foster care represents the fallback for children whose families are eligible for public assistance, the remuneration it provides also deserves close consideration. The low level of assistance provided by TANF constrains the level at which foster care can be reimbursed, since parents balance their desire to maintain custody against the possibility that their children might be economically better off in foster care. Newspapers report heartbreaking stories of parents who lack adequate resources or insurance to treat their children's mental health problems as a result of inadequate health insurance; some relinquish custody to ensure that their children will receive publicly subsidized treatment.[51]

Payments for in-home care by foster parents vary widely across states, but they are based on calculations of the cost of specific items such as room and board, supervision, and clothing. A lower-bound estimate of the national average for 2000 was about $5,000 per year.[52] This amount is significantly higher than the average per child support offered through TANF. As mentioned earlier, many states offer lower levels of foster care reimbursement for kin, but even these levels tend to be higher than family-based public assistance. For instance, in 1996 two children living in Maryland with relatives licensed by the foster care system would have received over $1,000 a month, compared to only $282 per month through that state's AFDC program.[53]

Many states use the USDA estimates of expenditures on children as a guideline for setting reimbursement, yet average foster care payments are considerably lower than the cash expenditures that low-income families make per child according to those estimates, not even including valuation of the care time that foster parents provide. Studies show that the number of children in foster care is rising much faster than the number of families willing to take them in, the result often being an increase in the number of children per foster family and a decline in the quality of care.[54]

Child Care and Higher Education Tax Credits

The decentralized, tax-based structure of public support for child care and higher education also results in uneven benefits. Employed parents who spend considerable money on child care derive important benefits. In 2000 the credit amounted to 20 to 30 percent of child-care expenses (depending on family income level), up to $2,400 for one child under thirteen, and up to $4,800 for two or more children if these expenses were incurred as a result of parental work for pay.[55] Thus, it offered as much as $720 per child, though the average amount paid was considerably lower, and most families were reimbursed at only 20 percent. But since this credit was not refundable, it offered no tax benefit for most families that had less than $15,000 in income.

Relatively few families take advantage of dependent care accounts, which allow working parents with child-care expenses to set aside up to $5,000 per year in an employer-sponsored account that is exempt from income and payroll taxes.[56] Here again, the value depends on a family's marginal tax rate: a family in the 31 percent federal income tax bracket in 2000 could claim a subsidy amounting to $1,550, not counting the benefit of exemption from Social Security as well as income taxes. In sum, the range of tax subsidies available for paid child care ranged from $480 a year (20 percent of $2,400) to a high of more than $1,500 (the benefit to a family in the highest tax bracket of a fully utilized dependent-care tax account). Affluent families were—and are— the clear winners.

The structure of the largest cash benefits available to college students resembles the social insurance benefits described above: Like TANF and the EITC, Pell Grants are based on assessment of family resources. All federal need-based college assistance relies on the same formula for determining eligibility; it is based on an expected family contribution that phases aid out as family income goes up. Both the Hope and Lifetime Learning Credit are based on the same principle as the Child Credit, although high-income families are more quickly cut off from receiving it.[57]

On average, the Hope Credit covered about 20 percent of the cost of tuition and fees for dependents who received it (and about 30 percent of those costs for independent young adults who received it).[58] Empirical studies confirm that students with family incomes between $40,000 and $80,000 were most likely to take advantage of these tax credits, and they also received the highest average benefits. Only about 14 percent of all students received both need-based aid and tax benefits, and generally in small amounts.[59]

Except for those few families who took advantage of dependent care pretax accounts, the potential tax benefits for college expenses exceeded those for child care, about $1,000 per child per year compared to $750. The full value of these benefits kicked in only at a fairly high level of family income, as did the opportunity to take advantage of them.

Who Benefits?

The United States provides more cash support for child rearing than is commonly recognized. A variety of tax deductions and credits, significantly boosted by changes since 2000, amount to a de facto family allowance similar in magnitude to that provided by many European countries. This cash subsidy ranged from about $920 to $2,200 a year per child in 2000, not counting the benefits of tax subsidies for a portion of child-care and college expenses, which could account for as much as $1,000 per child. But this benefit defrays only a small percentage of the costs of raising children even to age eighteen alone: between 10 percent and 25 percent of the average annual parental cash expenditures on a child under eighteen in a middle-income two-parent family (Table 7.3), and between 4 percent and 10 percent of average costs when the lower-bound replacement value of parental time for a child under the age of twelve is included.

The most significant difference between the United States and other industrialized countries lies in the absence of any federal provision for paid family leaves from work. Another important difference lies in the shape of public support for child rearing, as pictured in Figures 8.1 and 8.2. As a result of heavy reliance on tax deductions and credits, middle-income families are subject to a notch effect that lowers their potential benefits, whereas many high-income families reap significant gains. The structure of social insurance, as well as the increasingly rule-bound and limited nature of public assistance, reduces benefits available to low-income families, who have less access to marriage-based benefits and are also more vulnerable to an EITC-related marriage penalty.

The level of support for low-income families, whether provided through TANF and food stamps or through the EITC, is low in absolute terms, compared to other countries. The United Kingdom, Australia, and Canada, all with a political structure and culture similar to ours, have chosen to target low-income families with children, phasing benefits out steadily as income increases. By contrast, the United States provides greater benefits for higher-income families than for many in the middle of the income distribution.

Indeed, in 1999 the absolute level of benefits for families with income under $20,000 was lower in the United States than in these three countries, while the absolute level of benefits for families with income over $60,000 was higher.[60] Since that time, both the United Kingdom and Australia have initiated major policy changes aimed at further improving the position of low-income parents.[61] In the United States, by contrast, policy changes have not been aimed at reducing poverty.

Appendix: Cash and Tax Benefits for Families with Children

Both cash benefits for families, which take the form of direct transfers, and tax benefits, which represent indirect transfers, have the same effect: they increase disposable family income. Yet tax benefits receive far less attention both in international comparisons and in discussions of U.S. family policy. The result is often a distorted picture of relative levels of public support both among and within countries.

The two most widely cited data sources for international comparisons of support for child rearing focus entirely on cash benefits: Social Expenditure Database (SOCX), 1980–2001, of the Organization for Economic Cooperation and Development (OECD), and the U.S. Social Security Administration's series "Social Security Programs Throughout the World." A consideration of these makes Nordic countries such as

Sweden stand out from other countries such as the United States. But though Sweden offers generous family allowances, it offers virtually no tax breaks for child rearing. The United States, on the other hand, provides no family allowances, but it offers tax exemptions and credits of comparable value. In 2000 the potential value of tax benefits per child for many U.S. families was higher in dollar terms than the Swedish family allowance per child. The Swedish per child family allowance, according to laws implemented in 1999, came to 950 kronor per child per month. At the exchange rate of $1 = 7.31 kronor, this comes to $1,559.50 per year per child.[62] The Swedish family allowance is both universal and easy to understand. But its overall level is low.

Most discussions of the U.S. welfare state focus on means-tested benefits. But tax benefits and social insurance also reflect transfers between residents of the United States and their government. Like public expenditures on programs targeted to the poor, tax exemptions and credits cost taxpayers money and increase the disposable income of those who receive them. (Both expenditures and tax benefits have incentive effects that make it difficult to ascertain their exact incidence.) Poor families seldom pay very much in federal taxes, but state and local taxes take an especially large bite out of their income.[63] Though budget accounts for Social Security are kept separate from other government spending, they too are financed out of tax revenues.[64] More than two-thirds of U.S. households pay a higher percentage of their income in payroll (Social Security and Medicare) than in income taxes.[65] The complexity of the tax-benefit system makes it difficult to compare the total value of the social insurance families receive to the taxes they pay. But it also belies the notion that low-income families enjoy a free ride.

CHAPTER NINE

Public Spending on Children's Education and Health

Federal, state, and local governments in the United States spend a considerable amount of money on children beyond the specific benefits that parents receive through public transfers and tax breaks. Government spends even more on the elderly, in both absolute and per capita terms. The relative size of these age-targeted transfers has begun to receive considerable attention, eliciting warnings about the "graying of the budget" and a tug-of-war between the young and old. Though such a tug-of-war is taking place, the groups pulling on the rope cannot be characterized simply in terms of age.

The lack of public debate (much less consensus) on the extent to which support for dependents should be socialized has accentuated the influence of political power on policy outcomes. The elderly as a group have been better positioned than children to claim social insurance because they are relatively affluent, and, unlike children, have the right to vote. Transfers to the elderly have been framed as entitlements earned by years of paying taxes into Social Security and Medicare. Transfers to low-income parents, on the other hand, have been pictured as welfare rather than as compensation for producing the next generation of taxpayers.

This chapter examines the ways in which public spending redistributes money by age. It describes important differences in race, ethnicity, and political voice between the young and the old and summarizes what we can learn from analysis of government budgets. It also places U.S. spending on children and the elderly in an international context.

Age and Family Demographics

Age is an important determinant of political identity. As the demographer Samuel Preston pointed out long ago, "The elderly are a very peculiar kind of special interest group, quite unlike Teamsters or Southerners or the National Rifle Association. They are a group that almost all of us can confidently expect to belong to someday. Most programs for the elderly are to some extent perceived as a social contract whereby we transfer resources to ourselves over the life cycle."[1]

This social contract has been negotiated by groups with varying levels of political power; more attention has been paid to short-run benefits than to long-run sustainability. In the United States, age intersects with class, race, and ethnicity in ways that increase children's political vulnerability.

Who Raises Children?

In 2000 a large majority of all residents of the United States (about 62 percent) were of working age, between eighteen and sixty-four. The remainder of the population could be described, approximately, as dependents. Among these, children under the age of eighteen outnumbered the elderly about two to one, representing 26 percent of the population, compared to 12 percent for those sixty-five or over. The large size of the baby-boom generation, born after World War II, increased the relative share of today's working-age population. As this generation ages, the overall dependency ratio is likely to increase, along with the share of the elderly in the total population.

Most individuals—all but the homeless and those in military barracks, jails, or dormitories—lived in households. About 31 percent of these households did not include families (as formally defined)—they consisted of individuals living alone or with roommates or unmarried partners. About 36 percent of all households included children under the age of eighteen.[2] Among households with children, one- and two-child families were about equally common (41 percent and 38 percent, respectively). About 20 percent of all families with children lived with three or more of them.[3] The U.S. population can be divided into three groups of households of approximately equal numbers: those who do not live with family members, those who live with adult family members, and those who live with children. These three groups are affected in different ways by social and family policy.

African Americans and Hispanics are far more likely to live with children than non-Hispanic whites. Their average age is younger. (Immigration accentuates this effect among Hispanics.) They also tend to become parents at an earlier age and to have slightly higher fertility rates. At the same time, higher rates of mortality among African Americans and Hispanics lead to a lower life expectancy, which reduces their representation in older age groups. As a result, the white population is significantly older, on average, than the rest of the U.S. population. Whites represented about 70 percent of the total U.S. population in 2000, but they constituted 83 percent of the elderly and only 63 percent of all children. The proportion of whites who were over age 65 was almost twice the proportion of African Americans (15 percent compared to 8 percent) and three times greater than that of Hispanics (15 percent compared to 5 percent). The Asian population, which includes many immigrants, is also relatively young. One way to simplify racial and ethnic comparisons is to contrast white non-Hispanics with all others. In 2000 about 37 percent of all persons under eighteen were people of color, compared to only 17 percent of all persons sixty-five and older (Table 9.1).

Children's Political Voice

Children can't vote, and in the United States today a large percentage of their parents can't vote either. In 2000 about 33 percent of adult Hispanics and 36 percent of adult Asians were immigrants who had not yet attained citizenship and therefore lacked the right to vote.[4] Many other low-income parents lacked the right to vote because they were in jail and or had been convicted of a felony. Forty-seven states bar felons, and at least eleven bar ex-felons, from voting. Felony convictions have risen dramatically since 1972; as a result, over 4 million citizens, more than 2 percent of all voting-age adults, are currently barred from voting.[5]

Table 9.1 Distribution of persons by race and ethnicity within major age groups in the United States in 2000

	All ages (%)	<18 (%)	18–64 (%)	65+(%)
White	70.2	62.6	71.0	82.8
People of color	29.8	37.4	29.0	17.2
African American	12.6	15.4	12.2	8.3
Hispanic white	12.3	16.6	11.7	5.7
Other	4.9	5.4	5.1	3.2

Source: Author's analysis of 2001 Current Population Survey.

Taking both age and citizenship into account, persons in low-income groups are less likely be eligible to vote than those in high-income groups. They lack the financial resources to invest in electoral campaigns. With less voice, they are also less likely to participate. Education exercises significant influence: in 2000, 82 percent of those with advanced degrees voted; 38 percent of those with nine to twelve years schooling and only 53 percent of high school graduates voted.[6]

Differences in geographical distribution also affect political voice. African Americans, Hispanics, and Asians are concentrated in the South and West in densely populated states that are underrepresented by a political system that gives each state two senators regardless of population. Within many of these states, including California, Texas, and Alabama, adults of color represent large minorities whose numbers nonetheless fall short of majority status. About half of all children in the country live in the South and West, but about two-thirds of all low-income children and over 71 percent of children of color live in those regions.

Lack of voter support for public spending on children makes it difficult to improve the quantity and quality of public services, ranging from early-childhood education to local primary and secondary schools, to community colleges and state universities. Affluent parents respond by increasing their purchases of private services. They then have less to gain by supporting public services. As Eugene Steuerle puts it in his description of "the incredible shrinking budget" for working families and children on the federal level: "Programs for the politically disadvantaged wear stone slippers in the dance of legislation."[7]

Accounting for Age-targeted Spending

Governments generally tax the working-age population to help support both children and the elderly. Yet neither government budgets nor household surveys track public spending on individuals over their life cycles. Much of what appears to be government spending is simply a redistribution of one person's earnings over time. Susie Q. Citizen receives tax benefits as a child, grows up and pays taxes, raises children of her own, and then receives tax benefits when she retires. Many of the taxes she pays as an adult help finance the benefits she and her family received or will receive.

Because existing sources of data are limited, interpretations of them are often confusing and misleading. The amount government spends on programs targeted to children differs from the amount that families with children receive, after taxes, from the government, which differs from the amount that individual children actually receive. The amount spent on children and the elderly at any one time does not reflect what is spent on them over their lifetime. (See the appendix to this chapter.)

Public Spending

Analysis of government budgets provides useful insights into the forces shaping public policy. The federal government targets more spending to the elderly, whereas state and local governments target more spending to children, primarily through education. Most assistance to the elderly is provided through universal social insurance programs, such as Social Security and Medicare. Expenditures on children, on the other hand, tend to be either means-tested or significantly influenced—as in the case of public education—by the wealth of the community in which children reside.

Public provision for retirement has a long history in the United States. Veterans of the Union Army who fought during the Civil War received pensions that benefited a significant proportion of the elderly in the late nineteenth century. Many states began providing old-age assistance in the early twentieth century. Both these programs prefigured the Social Security Act of 1935, which provided pensions as well as survivor's benefits for employees that were based on the family wage model described in Chapter 8.

Like most public pension systems, Social Security was set up on a "pay as you go" basis, whereby contributions from all currently employed workers provide the funds to pay for the elderly. The Social Security Act proved politically popular, and both coverage and benefits increased substantially in the late twentieth century. Retirement benefits for federal employees, including the military, also grew during this period. Initially, the size of the cohort paying taxes was large compared to the size of the cohort receiving benefits. This has changed over time as a result both of fertility decline (which reduces the size of younger cohorts) and increases in life expectancy (which increases the size of older cohorts). These demographic changes, combined with the expansion of eligibility and benefits, have increased the fiscal demands of Social Security and generated concerns about its future.

In principle, Social Security is funded by contributions from both employers and employees of 6.2 percent of wages up to a ceiling ($76,200 in 2000; $97,500 in 2007). The incidence of the tax falls largely on workers, who are effectively paying 12.4 percent of their earnings into Social Security. In practice, Social Security taxes and implicit liabilities are simply part of a larger federal budget. Efforts to set aside a surplus by setting taxes higher than payouts in recent years have essentially been neutralized by the current deficit in federal spending as a whole.

Most working-age individuals in the United States have already planned for their retirement on the basis of assumptions about the Social Security they will receive, which has created resistance to any abrupt changes. As mandatory entitlements with a large political constituency, they are not likely to decrease in years to come. Even if Republican efforts to partially privatize Social Security were successful, they would do little to diminish the long-term implicit liabilities built into the system.

In 2000 an estimated $379 billion were spent by the federal government on individuals age sixty-five and over, not counting medical expenses. This spending amounted to about $10,900 per person in that age category, and it accounted for about 21 percent of the federal budget.[8] Federal direct spending on children takes a very different form, primarily means-tested assistance for children through Medicaid, TANF, the EITC, food stamps, Child-Care Assistance to States, and education. The Congressional Budget Office does not include the value of the dependent exemption and child credit in their tally of direct spending. But even adding that in yields a total of about $3,583 per child in 2000, less than one-third of per capita federal (non-health-related) spending on the elderly in that year.[9]

Higher levels of spending on the elderly have translated into improvements in their standards of living. Official poverty rates increased slightly for children after 1966 (the first year they were calculated), from about 18 percent to about 20 percent in 1999, and fell slightly by 2005 back to about 18 percent. Official poverty rates declined dramatically among the elderly over the same period, from about 29 percent to 10 percent in 2005.[10] Many elderly women living alone have incomes only barely above the poverty level. In general, however, federal policy provides better protection for the old than for the young.

Public Spending on Health

Modern health care delivers important benefits that are not captured by national income accounts. Most people would be willing to pay a large amount of money for an additional year of life, but significant increases in life expectancy over the twentieth century don't show up as an output of economic growth. Only the inputs, such as spending on new health technologies, are registered.[11] Increases in health insurance coverage since the 1960s have helped extend the benefits of medical innovation. Uneven coverage, however, remains a major source of public concern.

Although virtually all other affluent countries provide either universal health care or single-payer insurance, the United States continues to rely on a patchwork of public and private provision that imposes high administrative costs. Employers have long had an incentive to provide health insurance for their employees, which increases compensation without incurring either payroll or income taxes. Like employer-provided pensions, however, employer-provided health benefits were gradually retracted over the last decades of the twentieth century.[12] Those companies that still offer it typically require employees to pay a larger share of the cost than previously.

The three major programs directly financing health care for children and the elderly are Medicare, Medicaid, and the State Children's Health Insurance Program (SCHIP). As is true of programs providing direct cash benefits, the evolution of these programs reflects a complex interaction between age targeting and entitlement. President Johnson signed both Medicare and Medicaid into effect in 1965 as part of the Great Society. SCHIP was implemented during the Clinton administration, in 1997. Medicare represents an entitlement for virtually all U.S. residents over age sixty-five, financed partly through a payroll tax.

Though Medicaid is not a discretionary program that comes up for approval every year, it is a means-tested program dependent on budget allocations from the states as well as the federal government. It is designed to meet the needs of the poor, both young and old. The Congressional Budget Office estimated Medicaid spending on the elderly at $33 billion and on children at $23 billion in 2000.[13] On average the differences are even greater: about $950 per elderly person compared to $330 per child.

A large percentage of Medicaid expenditures on the elderly take the form of reimbursements for nursing home expenses. Many persons over the age of eighty—predominantly women who have outlived their husbands—require nursing home care for at least some period. They must pay for this care themselves until they have spent down their assets, including the value of their homes, to become eligible for assistance. Federal funding accounts for almost 40 percent of all spending on nursing homes, and reimbursement rates are set at low levels, which results in poor-quality services.[14] Low reimbursement levels for Medicaid services for parents and children also have adverse effects on care quality.

In the aftermath of a failed effort by the Clinton administration to implement a national health insurance system, Congress moved to remedy glaring disparities in coverage of children and the elderly in 1997 by extending public insurance to families with incomes 200 percent or less of the official poverty line. Like Medicaid, the SCHIP program offers the states matching funds for their own expenditures. This program suffers from a number of administrative problems, but it has significantly improved health insurance coverage for children.[15]

While most poor and near-poor children in the United States are covered by either Medicaid or SCHIP, most children in families with incomes above 200 percent of the poverty line are covered by private policies, paid for by parents or parents' employers. In 2002 only about 11 percent of children in this country lacked health insurance, a substantial decline from preceding years.[16] Still, this percentage does not compare favorably with the virtually universal coverage for the elderly provided through Medicare. It represents more than 8 million children who lack access to important health care services and are likely, as a result, to experience worse health outcomes.[17]

Health insurance coverage varies enormously by race, ethnicity, and citizenship, as well as by family income.[18] A period of no insurance coverage was reported for 23 percent of African American and almost 37 percent of Hispanic children in 2003. The especially poor coverage of Hispanic children likely reflects restrictions on the eligibility of immigrant children for public assistance.

The limited reach of the SCHIP program is also felt by working families with incomes close to but slightly above 200 percent of the poverty line. A few extra dollars of earned income can eliminate their eligibility. Like families in the 15 percent tax bracket in 2000, described in Chapter 8, they pay a middle-class penalty. Without access to public assistance, they are also less likely to enjoy a large tax-subsidized, employer-provided health care package. The health care premiums they are required to pay are likely to increase significantly over time.

In December 2003 Congress voted to add an expensive new entitlement to Medicare, guaranteeing coverage for most of the cost of prescribed medications for the elderly. Both Medicaid and SCHIP, by contrast, remain vulnerable to the ups and downs of state budgets, many of which have not yet recovered from the fiscal pinch of the 2001 recession. The asymmetry in spending has led many public health experts to express concern about generational equity in access to health care, emphasizing the particular vulnerability of children living in low-income families.[19]

The exact distributional effect of spending targeted to children and the elderly remains fuzzy, but the political trend is clear. Between 1960 and 1997 federal government spending targeted to children increased at about the same pace as economic growth, remaining at about 2 percent of the GDP. By contrast, spending targeted to the elderly through Medicaid, Medicare, and Social Security increased over the same period from about 2 percent to 8 percent of the GDP.[20]

Public Spending on Education

State and local governments spend more on children than the elderly, because they provide most of the dollars devoted to public education. In 2000 average expenditure in public elementary and secondary schools came to about $8,212 per pupil enrolled (slightly less than the estimated average value of parents' expenditures on children under twelve presented in Chapter 4). Educational expenditures raise the total amount of nonmedical government spending per child above the total non-medical government spending per elderly person.[21]

The largest component of educational spending is devoted to public primary and secondary schools, which accommodate over 85 percent of all students. Average total expenditures per student enrolled have increased steadily since 1950; between 1980 and 2000, for instance, the increase above and beyond the rate of inflation was 2.6 percent per year.[22] Over the same period, high school completion rates have improved markedly and college enrollments have increased.

The costs of education have risen substantially over time, for a variety of reasons. The increased opportunities available to educated women, who were once channeled almost exclusively into teaching and nursing, have diminished the occupational segregation that once kept teachers' wages artificially low. Students' needs have also intensified: Higher levels of immigration have brought more non-native speakers into school. Between 1979 and 1999 the proportion of children who speak a language other than English at home almost doubled, from about 9 to about 17 percent.[23] High levels of poverty, combined with both family and residential instability, make children more difficult to educate. Federal legislation requires schools to accommodate children with disabilities. Additional costs were imposed in 2003 by the testing mandates of the No Child Left Behind Act.

Significant inequalities in educational spending per student were institutionalized at an early date by reliance on local property taxes.[24] Affluent communities could spend generously on their schools, even with a relatively low tax rate, because of the high value of the property base to which that rate was applied. Good schools, in turn, increased the demand for housing in those communities, driving prices up. In recent years, highly educated, two-earner families have bid up the prices of homes in good school districts.[25] Low-income families can seldom afford to locate in them.

The heightened economic importance of education, along with the heavier tax burden of funding education, has intensified distributional struggle over spending. Progressive educational reform groups invoking ideals of equal opportunity have demanded redistribution of local property tax revenues to poor communities. Before 1980 legal decisions in both California and Texas led to major changes in the allocation of funds within those states, and by 2000 the disputes had widened to include Connecticut, New Jersey, and New York. Between 1989 and 2004, plaintiffs won twenty-four of the twenty-nine lawsuits filed against states for inadequate school funding.[26]

Equalization of spending per student is moving forward in many states, along with increased school choice that weakens the link between property values and educational quality. But the effects of school finance reform on student outcomes are complicated: equalization can backfire if it causes affluent families to defect from the public education system and support cutbacks in public spending.[27] Moreover, inequalities across states remain significant. In 2000 average spending per pupil in daily attendance ranged from $4,282 in Utah to $6,588 in Texas to $10,504 in New Jersey.[28]

The distribution of spending on pre-kindergarten, community colleges and universities is also hotly contested. As emphasized in earlier chapters, child care for toddlers is increasingly being defined as early-childhood education and children's attendance at organized center-based care and nursery school is no longer strongly related to maternal employment.[29] In 2000 about 64 percent of children in the U.S. between the ages of three and five were enrolled in kindergarten or nursery school. Most kindergarten was publicly funded, whereas funding for nursery schools—roughly equivalent to center-based day care—was evenly divided between public and private.[30]

Prekindergarten or nursery school attendance is strongly linked to family income. In 2003 only 41 percent of three- and four-year olds from families with income less than $20,000 attended, compared to 62 percent from families with incomes over $50,000. Children from low-income families were far more likely to rely on publicly funded facilities.[31] Inequality by income group was most pronounced for three-year-olds, and least pronounced for the five-year-olds, who are able to take advantage of publicly provided kindergarten in most states.[32]

Federal and state funding for child care in the United States is primarily funneled through the Child Care and Development Fund and TANF block grants, both created in the aftermath of 1996 reforms in public assistance. By increasing emphasis on maternal participation in paid employment as a requirement for public assistance, the Personal Responsibility and Work Opportunity Reconciliation Act highlighted the need for greater public provision of child care, and expenditures in this area increased dramatically after 1996. By 2000 the federal government was devoting $6.5 billion to child care, and states were spending an additional $2.5 billion, for a total of $9.0 billion.[33] Spending leveled out in 2001.[34] Most of this assistance was aimed at low-income families.

Yet eligibility for this means-tested assistance also grew over the period, and problems with both quality and service delivery meant that only a fraction of those eligible—between 12 and 18 percent—received assistance in 2000. A combination of waiting lists, low eligibility standards, high copayments, and sheer administrative hassle made it difficult for many poor parents to enter the system, problems that have persisted in subsequent years.[35] Like the federal Head Start program, which offers more-comprehensive services to low-income children, federally subsidized child care falls short of its own professed goals.

Uneven and unequal access also characterizes public higher education. The federal government provides student aid and tax breaks on terms described in Chapter 5; states provide highly subsidized services through public universities and community colleges. In 2000 college students received, on average, a public subsidy of about $10,000 a year while in school. Trends in total expenditures on higher education vary across states, but overall costs have increased at rates substantially greater than rates of inflation. At the same time, increasing pressure on state budgets (rising Medicaid expenditures in particular) have prompted many states to reduce their share of support for public institutions, which dropped from 63 percent of state university budgets in 1980–1981 to 51 percent in 2000–2001.[36]

One result of declining public support has been a rapid increase in the cost of tuition and fees at state universities, only partly counterbalanced by increases in financial aid. As a result, out-of-pocket expenditures by students and their parents have increased substantially in recent years and show every sign of continuing their climb.[37] Attainment of a college degree is now widely seen as the only ticket to middle-class income security. Yet relatively few students from low-income backgrounds are able to buy in. In 1999–2000 only 7 percent of youth from low-income families (those with incomes below $33,902) reaching age twenty-four had achieved a bachelor's degree, compared to 52 percent of those from high-income families (those with incomes higher than $86,223).[38]

International Comparisons

Income inequality is greater in the United States than in the United Kingdom, Canada, and Australia. The underlying cause—lack of policy effort—can also be described as an effect. Inequality makes it harder to build the kinds of political coalitions that can accomplish redistribution. A large share of public spending is devoted to life-cycle redistribution toward the elderly. The combination of means-testing for the poor and tax subsidies for the affluent leaves many middle-income parents in a difficult position, vulnerable to the threat of job transitions, unemployment, divorce, or major health problems.

Differences in the structure of spending on children have momentous consequences. Like most of the countries of northwestern Europe, the United Kingdom, Canada, and Australia all have either single-payer or national health insurance systems that represent a universal entitlement. Although their overall levels of educational expenditure per student are lower, there is less variation in amount spent per student.[39] Also like most of the countries of northwestern Europe, the United Kingdom and Canada provide more generous public subsidies for child care than the United States. In short, children in most other affluent countries enjoy more egalitarian patterns of public spending.

Poverty

Poverty rates among children are famously higher in the United States than in countries with more generous public assistance and social safety nets.[40] Because women are more likely than men to assume financial responsibility for children, poverty rates among women compared to men are also relatively high in the United States.[41] The United States is bigger than most other countries, and regional differences are greater. State-level variations in children's standards of living are conspicuous. In 2000, for instance, about 10 percent of children in New Hampshire lived in families with incomes below the official poverty line, compared to about 28 percent in New Mexico.[42] In the same year only about 6 percent of children in Vermont lacked health insurance, compared to 25 percent in Texas.[43] These state-level differences partly reflect differences in state policy packages, some of which are far more generous than others.[44]

Still, national averages are both relevant and telling. A recent UNICEF report notes the stark contrast between child poverty rates of less than 3 percent in Denmark and Sweden and those of more than 20 percent in the United States and Mexico. Comparisons reveal the tremendous influence of public policy. On average, public spending in countries that are members of the Organisation for Economic Co-operation and Development (OECD)reduces the rates of child poverty that would result from market forces alone by 40 percent. No country that devotes less than 5 percent of its GDP to social spending has a child poverty rate lower than 15 percent, whereas no country that devotes more than 10 percent has a child poverty rate greater than 10 percent.[45]

Inequality

Poverty is only one dimension of income inequality. Data from the Luxembourg Income Study, which harmonizes income data from a large number of countries in order to ensure their consistency show that in 2000 children were more likely to be found at the extremes of the income distribution in the United States than they were in relatively similar economies (Table 9.2). About 22 percent of all U.S. children lived in low-income households (those households with incomes below 50 percent of the median), compared to 17 percent in the United Kingdom, and fewer than 15 percent in Canada and Australia. A high percentage of children in the bottom category is associated with a high percentage in the top category as well, which indicates a greater inequality of income. The contrast with the Nordic countries such as Sweden is sharp. In none of these countries did more than 5 percent of children live in low-income households—most families live in households squarely in the middle of the income distribution. The countries of Continental Europe were only slightly more unequal than Nordic countries. Only in Mexico and Russia, relatively less prosperous countries, was the percentage of children living in low-income households greater than in the United States. In those countries, concentration at the top was even greater. Yet as the example of Taiwan shows, some less prosperous countries are as egalitarian as those of Continental Europe.

When estimates of the value of noncash expenditures on education and health are factored in, the picture changes. Since a larger percentage

Table 9.2 Distribution of children across household income groups: cross-national comparisons (disposable income)

	<50% median (%)	>150% (%)
Major English-speaking countries		
United States, 2000	21.9	16.5
United Kingdom, 1999	17.0	16.8
Australia, 2001	14.9	14.2
Canada, 2000	14.9	13.8
Nordic countries		
Sweden, 2000	4.2	10.6
Norway, 2000	3.4	8.9
Denmark, 2000	2.7	7.6
Finland, 2000	2.8	10.1
Continental Europe		
Germany, 2000	9.0	12.2
France, 2000	7.9	14.5
Austria, 2000	7.8	9.4
Belgium, 2000	6.7	14.6
Less prosperous countries		
Mexico, 2000	26.9	24.9
Russia, 2000	22.2	32.6
Taiwan, 2000	8.0	17.5

Source: Luxembourg Income Study (LIS) Key Figures, at www.lisproject.org/keyfigures.htm (accessed April 7, 2007)

of its public spending on children takes these forms, the United States looks better in comparative terms. Indeed, this country is so rich that its absolute levels of public spending per child (converted to purchasing power parity) were higher than those of any other country in the late 1990s. What stands out in the United States is inequality. The economic distance in household incomes between families in the top 10 percent and the bottom 10 percent after taxes and benefits are taken into account is greater than in the United Kingdom, Canada and Australia, as well as in Belgium, France, Germany, Netherlands, Finland, and Sweden.[46]

Health

Higher but more unequal spending also characterizes health care. The United States spends more money per capita on health care than any other country in the world, yet in 2000, at least twenty-four countries ranked better than the United States in child mortality. Similarly, because of the uneven coverage of children and their families, the United

States ranked lower than sixtieth internationally in immunizations against diphtheria, polio, and hepatitis.[47] Lack of paid parental leave for work discourages breast-feeding, particularly among low-income mothers, with adverse consequences for children.[48] Across developed countries, access to paid parental leaves from work is associated with significant improvements in child health.[49]

The causal relationship between income inequality and poor average health outcomes for children is a complicated one. That many low-income families are unable to pay for health insurance is one factor. Broader environmental factors such as educational attainment, parental stress, unsafe neighborhoods, poor air quality, and smoking and alcohol abuse are also relevant.[50] The U.S. Centers for Disease Control document a clear educational gradient in the probability of pregnant mothers receiving early prenatal care: 91 percent of mothers with some college education receive care during the first trimester, compared to 68 percent with less than a high school diploma.[51]

Reproducing Inequality

Generational conflict alone cannot explain patterns of public spending on children in the United States. Age-based interests play a role that is mediated by differences based on class, race, and ethnicity. Even the affluent elderly receive generous entitlements, whereas children in low-income families receive conditional, incomplete, and unreliable forms of assistance. Overall patterns of spending on children, like the patterns of public support for parents described in Chapter 8, do little to remedy existing inequalities.

Outdated and incorrect theories also create political drag. Mainstream economics reinforces the tendency to view child rearing as a private family responsibility, just another discretionary form of consumption. Conventional analyses of the welfare state lump all social spending in the category of unproductive spending. The sheer complexity of the programs described here and in Chapter 8 makes it difficult for voters to see who gets what.

Appendix: Defining Public Spending on Children

Even simple comparisons of direct spending on children at one time run into definitional problems. Some programs provide benefits that are explicitly linked to the number of children present, such as TANF, food stamps, or the survivor's benefits provided through Social Security. Other spending takes the form of tax benefits linked to number of children, benefits that do not always show up in comparisons of direct spending even though they have basically the same effect. As Chapter 8 emphasized, the greater significance of tax expenditures in the United States impinges on—and often vitiates—simple international comparisons.

In a classic article calling attention to generational conflict, Samuel Preston cited studies showing that public spending on the elderly in the 1960s and 1970s was about three times greater than spending on children, and he argued that the difference widened in the 1980s.[52] All these studies were based on spending explicitly targeted to children, and Preston's analysis focused on those components of public spending targeted at the poor—in particular, the composition of spending on Medicaid, the major means-tested program providing subsidies for health care.

Children in the United States are now much more vulnerable to poverty than the elderly. But simply looking at money targeted to the young and the old *once they are poor* is misleading. A large proportion of the most visible forms of public spending on children are means-tested programs, such as TANF and the EITC.[53] Yet the total value of tax expenditures that nonpoor families with children enjoy is also significant, as was shown in Chapter 8.

Some studies examine broader forms of direct and indirect spending targeted to families because of the presence of children regardless of their income.[54] Even this broader scope understates relative spending on children because it ignores the effect of intrahousehold transfers. Individuals under eighteen are more likely to live with working-age adults than are individuals over age sixty-two. To the extent that income sharing takes place within those households, children enjoy a share of public benefits whether they are provided *because* of their presence or not. High-income families with children derive important benefits not only from the dependent exemption and the child tax credit but also from tax subsidies for employer-provided health insurance and the mortgage interest tax deduction. The value of these tax expenditures is comparable to those enjoyed by families receiving Medicaid and public housing assistance.[55]

Both the tax exemption for a stay-at-home spouse and spousal benefits under Social Security were originally justified as part of a family wage system that would help support children (as emphasized in Chapter 8). Even though these benefits are increasingly unlinked from child rearing, they provide some indirect support for it. The amount of unpaid family care that the elderly receive from working-age adults is much smaller. Therefore, the exclusion of indirect subsidies for family work from the comparison makes spending on children seem smaller than spending on the elderly.

An example from the European context helps drive home the nomenclatural confusion. International comparisons conducted by UNICEF to analyze the effect of public policies on child poverty, like the U.S. studies above, define spending on children as that which is targeted to them. Expenditures on paid parental leaves from work are excluded on the grounds that they benefit parents rather than children.[56] Yet children are also the obvious beneficiaries. The best-known efforts to develop life-cycle comparisons under the rubric of intergenerational accounting simply compare the percentage of lifetime earnings that today's elderly paid in taxes to the percentage of earnings that today's working-age population will pay in taxes before they retire.[57] Such comparisons look at only half the picture, ignoring the distribution of benefits. A more satisfactory method would compare net benefits received by families with children with net benefits received by families with elderly persons. Unfortunately, such methods have not been widely applied, and they suffer from lack of accurate data.[58]

The Incidence of Net Benefits

A complete intergenerational accounting framework would also take intrafamily transfers into account. Just as a tax levied on a business may be passed on to a consumer in the form of higher prices, a benefit provided to a family may be passed on to individual family members. Once intrafamily distribution is considered, it is incorrect to conclude that "transfers away from the working-age population to the elderly are transfers away from children."[59] Affluent grandparents often help finance college for their grandchildren (as described in Chapter 5), and a small minority provide other substantial transfers and bequests. Even in a country as poor as South Africa, social pensions have a discernibly positive influence on the well-being of grandchildren.[60]

More important, the provision of both retirement security and survivor's benefits not only lessens the burden on working-age parents of supporting their elderly parents; it also lessens the need for them to save for their own retirement, which frees up resources for them to spend on their children. Working-age parents are probably more willing to spend money on their children's higher education when their security in old age is assured.

Neoclassical reasoning predicts that public transfers to children will be crowded out by a reduction in family spending on them, much as the public transfers to the elderly can be countervailed by reallocation to the younger generation.[61] But crowding out of public transfers may be mediated by social norms and competitive pressures. Though Social Security has probably reduced intrafamily cash transfers to the elderly, public support for higher education has probably led to increased parental spending.

Like the valuation of parental-care time, estimates of the effect of government transfers depend on a hypothetical counterfactual question. How much less would parents spend on their own children if they were required to help provide for their own parents as well as save for their own old age without the benefit of a generous social safety net? No one knows the answer to this question. Most measures of spending on children examine only current expenditures (see Chapter 4). More empirical research on the circular flow of resources within the household sector described in Chapter 1 is sorely needed.

CHAPTER TEN

Who Should Pay for the Kids?

Parents in general and mothers in particular pay most of the costs of raising the next generation. Employers and taxpayers—as well as children themselves—derive important benefits. Like the natural assets and ecological services provided by Mother Nature, parental services represent indispensable inputs into our market economy. The provision of these services is not motivated by market logic, but it is nonetheless affected by increases in the costs and risks of raising children. These costs and risks are strongly affected by institutional arrangements over which individual families have little control.

During the 1970s there was widespread concern that parents, heedless of the social costs of population growth, would raise too many children. Now that fertility rates have dropped below replacement levels in many areas of the world, demographic concerns have reversed. Concerns about the "baby bust" and "the empty cradle" have displaced fears about the "population bomb."[1] Some reduction in global population will offer long-run ecological benefits. But it will also diminish the supply of labor and reduce tax revenues from the working population even as the relative size and needs of the elderly grow. Immigration will probably not provide a sustainable solution to this problem.

Low birthrates are only the most dramatic manifestation of institutional changes in the relationship between the family and the economy that both create a need for public spending and fuel distributional conflict over it. The disjuncture between the private costs and public benefits of successful child rearing leads to outcomes that are both inefficient and unfair, and it requires creative thinking about institutional design. Who should pay for the kids?[2]

This chapter outlines three related but distinct reasons for public spending on children: social investment, intergenerational reciprocity, and moral obligation. Summarizing the findings of preceding chapters, it argues that better systems of social accounting could strengthen awareness of the benefits of intergenerational reciprocity. A review of policy strategies that have been put into effect in other countries or proposed for the United States points to the need to look beyond direct support for children to the larger structure of the welfare state.

Why Public Spending?

Economists have typically been reluctant to assign an economic value to children. Thomas Schelling summarizes the predominant view when he writes, "Though children are not pets in the United States, they are more like pets than like livestock, and it is doubtful whether the interests of any consumers are represented in a calculation that treats a child like an unfinished building or some expensive goods in process."[3] The words he chooses imply that ordinary people are simply consumers, rather than producers of the next generation. Treating children as livestock is not the only alternative to treating them as pets. Recognizing the social payoff to spending on children does not imply that children are merely another form of capital. Rather, it calls attention to the size and direction of intergenerational income flows that will strongly affect our future standards of living.

Social Investments

In a competitive market, the individual who invests money is normally the person who claims the return on it. Likewise, adults who invest in their own training and education expect to garner an individual return. But parents, communities, and taxpayers invest in children, and both the costs and the benefits of this investment spill over into the economic system as a whole. The empirical estimates of private and public spending on children developed in the preceding chapters demonstrate the magnitude of this hidden investment.

Economists often restrict the term "investment in human capital" to education. But if parents don't create and nurture children, schools can't educate them, employers can't hire them, and governments can't tax them. As a recent National Research Council report puts it, "It would be logical to treat the physical production of children—the 4 million infants who are born in the U.S. each year—as a component of the human capital produced in the home. If some are inclined to question whether these births represent real investment, they might consider the economic situation in year t + 20 in the event there were no births in year t."[4]

Estimates of the value of human capital that simply calculate the net present discounted value of future earnings are too narrow.[5] They exclude the value of the nonmarket work devoted to the production of children themselves, as well as the intrinsic value of human capabilities. Good parents don't necessarily earn higher salaries than bad ones. Indeed, they often earn lower salaries precisely because of the time and effort they devote to their children.

Some of the benefits of spending on children can be measured precisely in terms of improved educational outcomes, reduced social expenditures on drug use and crime, and enhanced productivity. But other benefits represent spillovers that escape a narrow market metric. Education may improve citizenship and parenting, as well as earnings. Payoffs to education may depend on economic context, particularly the opportunity to work with other highly educated workers.[6]

Payoffs may also depend on social context: individuals who believe they have a fair chance to succeed may work harder than those who perceive a tilted playing field. Furthermore, many individuals may choose not to maximize their earnings. Individuals who care for others not only volunteer time and money but often accept lower-paying jobs in order to perform work they consider intrinsically valuable.[7] As Jim Hightower, a former agriculture commissioner of the State of Texas, puts it, "It's easier to count the seeds in the apple than the apples in the seed."[8]

Still, specific studies of specific payoffs yield important results. An emerging consensus suggests that well-managed and well-funded early-childhood development programs provide benefits that far exceed their costs.[9] The benefits are often defined in social as well as individual terms. The oft-cited High/Scope study of the Perry Preschool in Ypsilanti, Michigan, tracked the performance of children from low-income black families against that of a control group, finding that participants were more likely to graduate from regular high school, more likely to earn $2,000 or more a month, and less likely to be arrested five or more times by age twenty-seven.[10] By one estimate, the real internal rate of return on investment for this program was 16 percent, higher than that typical of most local economic development initiatives.[11]

One of the most important benefits of early-childhood education is improved performance in later years of school. As a result, rates of return to all levels of education are closely linked. The effect of improved equality of opportunity at younger ages depends in large part on opportunities at older ages, as well as vice versa. Education develops capabilities that are more profound than the ability to find a higher-paying job, including the potential to help us solve the many unanticipated natural and social problems that are coming down the road.

Payoffs to investments in children's health also reach far beyond potential effects on lifetime earnings. Prenatal exposure to drugs, alcohol, and tobacco increases infant mortality. Childhood access to adequate nutrition and protection from infectious disease and environmental toxins heavily influence adult vulnerabilities. Eating and exercise habits formed in childhood have long-lasting effects.

The U.S. health care delivery system, oriented toward treatment rather than prevention of disease, discourages attention to children.[12] The health insurance system provides greater remuneration for treatment of complicated but rare diseases than for the chronic ailments that are most likely to affect low-income children. Child health problems with environmental causes are increasing in both absolute and relative importance. Asthma rates among children have risen from 3.7 percent in 1980 to 12.7 percent in 2000; obesity rates have risen from 5.7 percent in 1980 to 15.3 percent over the same period.[13] Unhealthy physical and social environments take a costly toll.

Child education and health are coproduced by families, communities, and public programs. Gains in one arena can be neutralized by lack of progress in others; increased public spending on education and health may have little effect unless accompanied by reductions in poverty and inequality.[14] Longitudinal studies tracking family members over a long period suggest that acute and prolonged poverty in early childhood has harmful effects.[15] The effect of family income is mediated by other factors, including parental efficacy.[16] On the other hand, many adult behavioral problems may be rooted in poorly understood effects of economic inequality and stress.

Randomized experiments provide a way for researchers to assess the effects of public policy packages on outcomes for children. For instance, the New Hope experiment conducted in Milwaukee, Wisconsin, between 1994 and 1998 provided a wage supplement, health insurance, and child care, as well as after-school programs for parents and other adults who worked full-time.[17] Children of families randomly selected to receive this economic treatment fared better over time in school than children in the families who were not. Boys, in particular, earned higher grades, were less likely to get in trouble, and developed higher aspirations for the future. In addition to measuring the quantitative dimensions of the gains that children enjoyed, New Hope researchers highlighted the gains that were more difficult to measure, including improvements in the quality of family life.

Intergenerational Reciprocity

The prospect of a high social rate of return does not guarantee a high level of social investment. Incentives to invest depend in part on who captures the benefits. Sociologists describe the ways in which economic development has reduced the relative importance of family life and altered the very meaning of marriage.[18] Economists describe the difficulties of negotiating efficient contracts: parents may be unwilling or unable to make optimal investments in children. Government can tax the entire working population to help finance those investments, offering taxpayers, in return, a future claim on earnings of more productive adult workers that will help support their retirement in old age.[19]

But though the modern welfare state represents an adaptive response to both market and family failure, its policies have emerged piecemeal, buffeted by the power of specific interest groups. The social contract that we rely on, combining market competition with a democratic state, leaves many aspects of family life out of the picture. Children are neither sovereign consumers nor voters, and parents produce an important good to which our economy assigns no market value. The political coalitions shaping our institutional environment have often lacked a clear understanding of the potential gains from collaboration. The terms of intergenerational transfers have never been explicitly discussed—much less publicly debated.

Federal and state governments provide more reliable income and health support for the old than for the young. Despite its many successes, the current structure of Social Security does not evenly share economic risks.[20] Commitments to children have become increasingly costly, yet the elderly population has little direct economic incentive to invest in the younger generation.[21] Today's adults have the power to incur both financial and ecological debts that children will be required to repay.[22]

Generational reciprocity can be defined in two different ways: paying back and paying forward. We could, as adults, repay the older generation (both parents and nonparents) for what it spent on us. Alternatively, we could repay the gifts made by the older generation, making equivalent gifts to the next generation.[23] Most of us already engage in both forms of transfer to some extent. But we do so unevenly, in an institutional structure that reproduces existing inequalities and rewards reproductive free riding.

Moral Obligation

Formally, children owe their parents and forebears nothing. They did not, after all, bargain to be born. But the lack of an explicit contract does not absolve us of implicit responsibility. Social systems require social commitments that reach beyond calculation of individual rates of return. An ethic of responsibility should inform the development of all our social institutions, including those that reward nonmarket work and affect intergenerational transfers.

Children are not merely commodities to be bought and sold or demographic outcomes to be subsidized or penalized. Parental efforts should be rewarded in ways that both honor and reinforce the profound moral commitments they represent. Family policies should reach for a balance between individual rights and social obligation that can strengthen trust and care.

We may never be able to guarantee children perfect equality of opportunity. Such an idealized goal is difficult to define, much less implement. But in the United States today, many forms of social investment in children intensify rather than mitigate preexisting inequalities, discouraging motivation to succeed. Children who are expected to compete in a modern economy deserve a fair start and a level playing field. Those who suffer from illness or disability deserve an opportunity to develop their talents and enjoy their lives fully. Our children's capabilities have intrinsic value.

Accounting for Children

A better understanding of current intergenerational transfers could help us design better ones. Placing expenditures on children within the larger circular flow of the economy outlined in Chapter 1—and assigning values to the flows of money and time that are devoted to them—requires a fundamental change in national income accounting and the structure of federal, state, and local budgets. Whether it moves through the family, the market, the community, or the state, spending on children should be treated as investment, not consumption. Both the cost of producing children and many different ways of valuing their future contributions should be integrated into macroeconomic theory. We need to develop better ways of monitoring both what we spend on and what we get from the next generation. We also need a better understanding of the relationship between economic and demographic change.

National Income Accounts

The estimates presented in Chapter 7 show that combined family spending on children under the age of eighteen, including the value of family time, averaged about $20,000 per child per year in 2000. Some of this family spending was subsidized by government transfers, and government spending on in-kind programs such as health and education represented additional investment. As Chapter 9 indicated, about $3,500 was spent per child on the federal level and about $8,200 on the state and local level for education: about $11,700 per child per year. A ballpark measure of average private and public spending per child (accounting for some overlap between the two) comes to about $30,000. In 2000 about 72.4 million individuals under eighteen lived in the United States.[24] This implies total spending on children (not counting college students and those 18 and over) of about $2.2 trillion dollars. In the same year, estimated gross investment in the U.S. economy came to about $1.7 trillion.[25]

Our current definition of gross investment in the United States is far too narrow. National income accountants have long noted that much government spending, including spending on education, is arbitrarily defined as consumption, even when it increases productive capacity. Many categories of household spending are devoted to capital used in nonmarket work, such as cars, computers, and household appliances.[26] If we take the metaphor of human capital seriously, we should characterize both public and family spending on children as a form of investment.

Taking human capital seriously would also change our international balance of payments. Adult immigrants bring human capabilities that were produced elsewhere—by families and schools in their countries of origin. As a result, they provide a literal transfer of capital that helps counterbalance our trade deficit.[27] Though the long-term effects of immigration on other groups within the U.S. labor force remain unclear, this transfer of human capabilities substantially boosts the overall output of the U.S. economy, often at substantial cost to the countries—and family members—that immigrants leave behind.[28]

A better accounting system would monitor all public and private expenditure on children through age seventeen, in addition to all spending on education and training past that age. The development of systematic human capital accounts would require careful consideration of how to treat both maintenance and depreciation of adults, defining investment in net terms. The advent of new forms of data collection such as the American Time Use Survey creates the potential to measure the amounts of time devoted to nonmarket work. But time-use surveys will not reach their full potential until they are combined with surveys that measure household expenditures and monitor outcomes for both adults and children.

Public Finance and Social Policy

Life-cycle record keeping could improve our systems of public finance. Current methods of accounting for social spending conceal the extent to which individuals and their families benefit from the family welfare state. Most individuals know what they earn and approximately how much they pay in taxes. But few if any have a clear picture of how much public money was devoted to them before they began paying taxes on their own, or how much they will benefit in retirement.

Most studies of intergenerational transfers understate the money and time that both families and government devote to children. The best-known intergenerational accounting models use stylized assumptions to compare the net taxes (taxes minus specific government benefits) paid by different cohorts. The resulting estimates suggest that adults today will fare much better than their counterparts in the future; we have saddled future generations with considerable public debt.[29] But these estimates ignore differences between parents and nonparents.[30] The net benefits of "borrowing from the future" are unevenly distributed.

Measures of poverty among dependents such as children and the elderly are a fundamental guide to social policies. Yet current measures of poverty rely on equivalence scales that assume that children require fewer resources than adults and treat households as units, ignoring possible differences in the standard of living of parents and children or men and women. These assumptions yield the misleading impression that households with children need fewer resources to achieve a given standard of living than adult-only households of the same size.

When family members allocate time to care for a child they often reduce the time they devote to other productive activities such as paid employment and housework. If they reduce time in paid employment, they incur an opportunity cost that is approximated by what they could have earned. If they reduce time in housework, they either purchase substitutes for the services they once provided or make do with fewer of these services. In either case, their material standard of living is reduced. Yet policy makers and researchers persist in using poverty lines for families with children that are the same regardless of parental hours spent in paid employment.

This reluctance to value nonmarket work depresses the level of assistance that public policies provide to families with children. Examples include reimbursement rates for foster care, child-support requirements for non-custodial parents, and levels of assistance provided through TANF. None of these policies provides adequate assistance for families with children.

Public support for child rearing in the United States takes an unnecessarily complex and inconsistent form. Even highly trained experts have a hard time deciphering who gets what. Most people probably cannot assess the extent to which government programs and tax benefits will subsidize their parental efforts. Nor can they easily discern the effect of the taxes they pay now on their future security in old age.

The legacy of a family wage system that rewards marriage rather than child rearing has perverse effects. In the United States today, unmarried parents who devote a substantial share of their money and time to child rearing are eligible for public assistance only if their income falls below a specific amount and they work for pay. The public benefits for which they are eligible in retirement are determined only by their individual earnings. By contrast, married persons can claim significant tax and social insurance benefits that are based on a spouse's earnings record, even if they devote no money or time to children.[31]

Despite much talk of marriage promotion, existing policies impose a proportionately greater marriage penalty on the poor than on the affluent. Most of the benefits for which low-income families are eligible, including the EITC, phase out steeply as their incomes increase. When two low earners marry, their pooled income is often sufficiently high to significantly reduce their eligibility for benefits. Yet few low-earning men earn enough on their own in the labor market to be able to support a spouse who is a full-time homemaker. As a result, they cannot take advantage of the tax exemption that higher-income families can claim. Low earners are also much less likely than high earners to have access to tax-free employer-provided health and pension benefits that provide coverage for spouses and children.

Economics and Demographics

Conservatives tend to blame government intervention and popular culture for declining commitments to families, but the process of economic development itself set these forces in motion. Corporate capitalism has largely displaced family business, and the demand for skilled labor has dramatically increased the importance of education. Women's entrance into paid work reflects the larger expansion of individual wage employment. Increased life expectancy itself, surely one of the most important benefits of economic growth, expands the demographic burden of the older generation.

Neoclassical economists have often argued that the traditional gender division of labor, in which females specialize in family work, emerged because it was efficient. Males have more physical strength, women have a comparative advantage in infant care, and specialization improves overall efficiency.[32] But specialization was never based on efficiency alone. Historically, it has been reinforced by patriarchal rules that restricted women's property rights, access to education, and opportunities for skilled employment, which have made it difficult for them to choose anything other than specialization in family care.[33]

Women now enjoy more economic freedom but less reliable support for the task of caring for dependents. Nonmarriage and divorce have increased the percentage of children being raised by mothers alone. Many highly educated women, finding it difficult to reconcile family responsibilities with career success, opt out of motherhood. Many less well educated women with poor economic opportunities choose motherhood despite the attendant risks of poverty for their children and themselves. A large percentage of men default on parental responsibilities, failing to provide adequate financial support or active care for their children. Current trends in family structure are exacerbating inequalities in child outcomes such as educational attainment.[34] These demographic changes threaten our economic future more profoundly than the prospect of rapid fertility decline.

Reframing Public Policies

Though many aspects of the social welfare state have come under attack in recent years, spending on families with children is on the increase. Most advocates of increased spending single out one of the rationales described above—investment, reciprocity, or moral obligation—and emphasize one policy instrument that fits that rationale. The limitations of such approaches are painfully apparent. Even those who endorse a broad set of policies tend to confine their attention to those that relate specifically to parents and children. Improvements in the interface between families and the market economy require bolder thinking about the structure of the welfare state.

Policy Strategies

Proponents of the investment model tend to worry most about the quantity and quality of human capital, often calling for investments in early-childhood education. The policy principle is straightforward. Public spending should be invested in ways that yield the highest social rate of return. Defined in these terms, investments in low-income families may be the most productive. But who defines the social rate of return, and what incentives do competing individuals and groups have to maximize it? This approach sidesteps issues of distributional conflict and political power.

Proponents of reciprocity highlight these distributional concerns, seeking to offer some principles for reconciling them. In the United States today, individuals with the same earnings history and marital status receive the same Social Security and Medicare benefits, even though some have devoted far more than others to the production of the generation that will finance those benefits. The disjuncture between the private costs and social benefits of child rearing could, theoretically be solved by privatizing the benefits rather than by further socializing the costs. Some argue, for instance, that parents should be offered a legal claim over their children's earnings to supplement or replace Social Security.[35] Others propose that adults who raise children could be relieved of a large portion of their responsibility for paying Social Security taxes.[36]

This approach evokes traditional neoclassical confidence in individual decision making, but it ignores many contractual and coordination problems described in earlier chapters. Both the costs and benefits of children are complex, diffuse, and difficult to pin down. Some families will be lucky; others will not. Privatization may offer higher benefits to some but impose higher risks on all. If parents capture the economic benefits of their children's future contributions, why should taxpayers without children help pay for education?

Other dimensions of social inequality can be interpreted as failures of reproductive reciprocity. Mothers tend to pay a higher price for parenthood than fathers. Immigrants tend to pay substantially more in taxes relative to lifetime benefits than native-born workers. The current generation of adults as a whole may fare better than future generations, who will have to pay for accumulating debt, environmental degradation, or both.

The sheer complexity of competing demands may help explain why many advocates make a case for greater public support for children as a moral obligation.[37] From this perspective, the precise allocation of resources is less important than basic principles such as child protection, equal opportunity, and public recognition of parental contributions. The potential benefits of social investment and intergenerational reciprocity suggest that respect for such moral obligations serves our long-run economic interests.

Family Policy Packages

The difficulty of framing specific solutions for interrelated problems explains the appeal of broad family policy packages. Simple cash incentives to child rearing seem to have little effect.[38] The countries that have stabilized fertility at close-to-replacement levels have developed a range of policies designed to help families balance the competing demands of paid employment and child care while also providing a secure social safety net: universal child care, health care, paid family leaves, and lower penalties on part-time work.[39] Reduction of economic insecurity and youth unemployment also plays a role.[40]

Along with public support and workplace flexibility, fathers' willingness to shoulder some of the direct burdens of child care and housework also encourages motherhood.[41] The high incidence of childlessness among women even in countries with strong traditional family and religious values, such as Italy and Spain, is sometimes described as a "birth strike." Gender equity may be a necessary prerequisite of the institutional framework required to maintain fertility at replacement levels.[42] A number of specific policies have been designed to encourage sharing of paid work and family responsibilities.[43]

Standard economic accounting shows that European social democracies such as France, Sweden, and the Netherlands have lower per capita income than the United States, which would suggest that their standards of living are lower. A closer look shows that citizens of these countries typically devote less time to paid employment and more time to leisure and family work. Their income per hour of paid employment is higher than ours.[44] Similarly, standard accounting shows that they pay higher taxes than we do. But the government programs financed by these taxes reduce the amount of spending necessary to meet their families' needs for care, education, and health services. In those countries, families with children are far less vulnerable to poverty than they are in the United States.[45]

These successes, however, do not nullify the mounting costs of support for the elderly. Publicly funded pension systems are often resistant to change, and their lack of flexibility imposes both costs and risks. Family policies cannot be defined merely as those that affect the younger generation. They must be reinterpreted in terms that encompass fairness and adequacy over the life cycle as a whole.

Political Redesign

The democratic welfare state may not be able to develop intergenerational reciprocity without significant, even radical redesign. The burden of taxes individuals pay weighs less heavily than the difficulty of seeing what is delivered in return. Most children receive significant transfers from the U.S. government, become adults who pay a significant share of their income in taxes, then receive more transfers after they retire. Yet there is virtually no way of assessing what one has received from the government relative to what one has paid in.

The structure of political representation is also flawed. In the United States, as in most democracies, individuals are not given the right to vote until they reach age eighteen. By the time children are allowed to participate, many of the decisions influencing the strength of their future political voice have already been made. Parents may cast votes with their children's present and future interests in mind, but they still have only one vote apiece. In a world in which most people become parents and most adults live with children, this difference in political representation might not matter. But in a world in which many individuals choose not to rear children or to contribute to their support, generational conflict intensifies.[46]

Recognizing this problem, German politicians have developed a proposal to give children the right to vote in national elections. Parents of children under the age of twelve would have the right to vote on behalf of their children in national elections. Children ages twelve and above would hold the right to vote on their own behalf. In the United States, persons living in low-income households are politically disempowered in part because many are too young to vote. In 2000 about 40 percent of all persons in the lowest household income group (those with per capita income less than 50 percent of the median) were under eighteen, compared to only about 15 percent of the highest income group.[47] Giving children the right to vote would likely alter both political alignments and public policies.

However their accounting and voting systems evolve, democratic welfare states will likely face problems governing their own social reproduction. The increased mobility of capital and information is eroding the influence of political rules on economic transactions. International competition creates incentives for corporations to seek the lowest-cost environments. Why pay the taxes necessary to rear and educate U.S. workers when highly skilled labor is increasingly available elsewhere? As is true for environmental assets, the ability to utilize resources without paying for their replenishment provides short-run gain at the expense of long-run sustainability. Like global climate change, global family change will have international effects.

Toward a New Social Family Contract

Public policies in the United States have socialized the benefits of children more successfully than the costs, redistributing resources from parents to nonparents and from mothers (who devote the most time and money to the next generation) to everyone else. Age-based redistribution through the state is embedded not only in retirement and health programs, but also in the very structure of an economic system that endows the younger generation with knowledge, technology, and capital and retains the right to tax their earnings to repay public debt. Commitments to raising the next generation may be intrinsically satisfying. Economically, however, they go largely unrewarded.

The gender- and age-based transfer of resources among the family, the state, and the more visible, dollar-denominated realm of immediate exchange reveals the extent to which our economy relies on a nonmarket system that is being transformed by the expansion of the market itself. This underlying problem is one that even the most powerful groups within society will be forced to confront and that modern welfare states will be impelled to resolve. In theory, political democracy provides the opportunity to renegotiate the social family contract. Such renegotiation will require a clear picture of resource transfers from adults to children and back again. It will also require the design of political strategies that can align the incentives of competing groups and foster their cooperation.

Notes

1. Children and the Economy

1. For an earlier effort to describe the distribution of the costs of social reproduction see my *Who Pays for the Kids: Gender and the Structures of Constraint* (New York: Routledge, 1994).
2. Duncan Ironmonger, "Counting Outputs, Capital Inputs and Caring Labor: Estimating Gross Household Product," *Feminist Economics* 2 (1996): 37–64.
3. Herbert A. Simon, "Organizations and Markets," *Journal of Economic Perspectives* 5 (1991): 25, 27.
4. Duncan Ironmonger, "Time Use," in S. Blume and S. Durlauf, eds. *The New Palgrave Dictionary of Economics*, 2nd Ed. (Basingstoke, U.K.: Palgrave MacMillan, 2007).
5. U.S. Bureau of Labor Statistics, American Time Use Survey, 2003, at www .bls.gov/tus/home.htm (accessed March 14, 2007).
6. Katharine G. Abraham and Christopher Mackie, eds., *Beyond the Market: Designing Nonmarket Accounts for the United States* (Washington, D.C.: National Academies Press, 2005), Chap. 4.
7. Jonathan Grant, Stijn Hoorens, Suja Sivadsan, Mirjam van het Loo, Julie DaVanzo, Lauren Hale, Shawna Gibson, and William Butz, *Low Fertility and Population Aging: Causes, Consequences, and Policy Options*. Rand Europe Report prepared for the European Commission (Santa Monica, Calif.: Rand Corporation, 2004), xiii.
8. Amara Bachu and Martin O'Connell, "Fertility of American Women" (Current Population Report P20–526, June 1998, U.S. Census Bureau Washington, D.C., 2000).
9. Phillip Longman, *The Empty Cradle: How Falling Birthrates Threaten*

World Prosperity and What to Do about It (New York: Basic Books, 2004); Ben Wattenberg, *The Birth Dearth* (New York: Pharos, 1987).

10. Few textbooks explore this issue. For instance, consider Dennis C. Mueller, *Public Choice III* (New York: Cambridge University Press, 2003). The words *family, children,* and *dependents* seldom appear and are not included in the index.

11. Ronald Lee and Tim Miller, "Population Policy and Externalities to Child-bearing," *Annals of the American Academy of Political and Social Science* 510 (1990): 17–32; Nancy Folbre, "Children as Public Goods," *American Economic Review* 84, 2 (1994): 86–90.

12. Congressional Budget Office, *Who Pays and When? An Assessment of Generational Accounting* (Washington, D.C.: Congressional Budget Office, 1995).

13. Rishab Aiyer Ghosh, "Cooking-Pot Markets and Balanced Value Flows," 153–168 in Ghosh, ed., *Code: Collaborative Ownership and the Digital Economy* (Cambridge: MIT Press, 2005).

14. Ulla Grapard, "Robinson Crusoe: The Quintessential Economic Man?" *Feminist Economics* 1 (1995): 33–52.

15. Hillard Kaplan, "Evolutionary and Wealth Flows Theories of Fertility: Empirical Tests and New Models," *Population and Development Review* 20 (1994): 753–791; Arthur J. Robson and Hillard Kaplan, "The Evolution of Human Life Expectancy and Intelligence in Hunter-Gatherer Economies," *American Economic Review* (2003): 150–169; see the summary in Ronald Lee, "Demographic Change, Welfare, and Intergenerational Transfers: A Global Overview," *Center for the Economics and Demography of Aging, CEDA Papers:* Paper 2003–0004CL, March 13, 2003, at http://repositories.cdlib.org/iber/ceda/papers/2003=0004Cl (accessed March 10, 2007).

16. John C. Caldwell "Towards a Restatement of Demographic Transition Theory," *Population and Development Review* 3 (1976): 321–366; Caldwell, *Theory of Fertility Decline* (London: Academic Press, 1982); Donald O. Parsons, "On the Economics of Intergenerational Control," *Population and Development Review* 10 (1984): 41–54.

17. Gary Becker and Kevin Murphy, "The Family and the State, *Journal of Law and Economics* 31 (1988): 1–18. See also Ron Lee, "Demographic Change."

18. T. T. Dang, P. Antolin, and H. Oxley, "The Fiscal Implications of Aging: Projections of Age-Related Spending" (OECD Economics Department Working Papers, No. 305, Organization for Economic Cooperation and Development, 2001), 13.

19. Folbre, *Who Pays for the Kids?*

20. Caldwell, *Theory of Fertility Decline;* Nancy Folbre, "Of Patriarchy Born: The Political Economy of Fertility Decisions," *Feminist Studies* 9 (1983): 261–284; Elissa Braunstein and Nancy Folbre, "To Honor or Obey: The Patriarch as a Residual Claimant," *Feminist Economics* 7 (2001): 25–54.

21. Folbre, *Who Pays for the Kids?*

22. Douglas Wolf, "The Family as Provider of Long-Term Care: Efficiency, Equity, and Externalities," *Journal of Aging and Health* 11 (1999): 360–382.

2. Commitments and Capabilities

1. Gary S. Becker, *A Treatise on the Family*, enlarged ed. (Cambridge: Harvard University Press, 1991).
2. Sue Himmelweit, "Economic Theory, Norms, and the Care Gap, or Why Do Economists Become Parents?" 231–250 in A. Carling, S. Duncan, and R. Wedwards, eds., *Analyzing Families* (London: Routledge, 2002).
3. Audre Lorde, "To my daughter the junkie on the train," in her *Poems of New York* (New York: Alfred A. Knopf, 2002), 157.
4. Thomas Lewis, Fari Amini, and Richard Lannon, *A General Theory of Love* (New York: Vintage, 2000).
5. Robert Frank, *Passions within Reason: The Strategic Role of the Emotions* (New York: Norton, 1988); Ted O'Donoghue and Matthew Rabin, "Risky Behavior Among Youths: Some Issues from Behavioral Economics," 29–67 in Jon Gruber, ed., *Risky Behavior among Youths: An Economic Analysis* (Berkeley: University of California Press, 2001).
6. Alan Guttmacher Institute, "Get in the Know about Pregnancy, Childbirth, and Abortion," at www.guttmacher.org (accessed August 2006).
7. Robert J. Willis and John G. Haaga, "Economic Approaches to Understanding Nonmarital Fertility," *Population and Development Review* 22, Supplement (1996): 67–86.
8. Oded Stark, *Altruism and Beyond* (New York: Cambridge University Press, 1995); Casey B. Mulligan, *Parental Priorities and Economic Inequality* (Chicago: University of Chicago Press, 1997).
9. Rhona Mahoney, *Kidding Ourselves: Breadwinning, Babies, and Bargaining Power* (New York: Basic Books, 1995); Notburga Ott, *Intrafamily Bargaining and Household Decisions* (New York: Springer-Verlag, 1992).
10. Robert Pollak, "Gary Becker's Contributions to Family and Household Economics," *Journal of Household Economics* 1 (2003): 111–141.
11. Richard A. Easterlin, *Birth and Fortune: The Impact of Numbers on Personal Welfare* (Chicago: University of Chicago Press, 1987).
12. James Andreoni, "Impure Altruism and Donations to Public Goods: A Theory of Warm-Glow Giving," *Economic Journal* 100 (1989): 1447–1458.
13. Carolyn Pape Cowan and Philip A. Cowan, *When Partners Become Parents: The Big Life Change for Couples* (New York: Basic Books, 1992), 36.
14. Sarah Blaffer Hrdy, *Mother Nature: A History of Mothers, Infants, and Natural Selection* (New York: Pantheon, 1999).
15. George A. Akerlof, "Men Without Children," *Economic Journal* 108 (1998): 287–309.
16. Samuel Bowles, *Microeconomics: Behavior, Institutions, and Evolution* (Princeton: Princeton University Press, 2004).

17. Amartya Sen, "Rational Fools: A Critique of the Behavioral Foundations of Economic Theory," *Philosophy and Public Affairs* 6 (1977): 317–344.
18. Julie A. Nelson, *Feminism, Objectivity and Economics* (New York: Routledge, 1996), 70.
19. Louis Genevie and Eva Margolies, *The Motherhood Report: How Women Feel about Being Mothers* (New York: Macmillan, 1987), 408.
20. Terry Lugaila, "A Child's Day: 2000. Selected Indicators of Child Well-Being" (Current Population Reports P70–89, U.S. Census Bureau, Washington, D.C., August 2003), 15.
21. Hrdy, *Mother Nature.*
22. Ibid., 174.
23. Irwin Garfinkel, Sara S. McLanahan, Daniel R. Meyer, and Judith A. Seltzer, eds., *Fathers under Fire: The Revolution in Child Support Enforcement* (New York: Russell Sage, 1998); Frank Furstenberg Jr., Christine Windquist Nord, James L. Peterson, and Nicholas Zill, "The Life Course of Children of Divorce: Marital Disruption and Parental Conflict," *American Sociological Review* 48 (1983): 656–668.
24. Scott Coltrane, *Family Man: Fatherhood, Housework, and Gender Equity* (New York: Oxford University Press, 1996); David Popenoe, *Life without Father* (New York: Free Press, 1996); Allison Munch, J. Miller McPherson, and Lynn Smith-Lovin, "Gender, Children, and Social Contact: The Effects of Childrearing for Men and Women," *American Sociological Review* 62 (1997): 509–520.
25. Robert Axelrod, *The Evolution of Cooperation* (New York: Basic Books, 1984).
26. John Stuart Mill, *Principles of Political Economy: And Chapters on Socialism* (1848; rept., New York: Oxford Classics, 1999), 350.
27. David A. Karp, *The Burden of Sympathy: How Families Cope with Mental Illness* (New York: Oxford University Press, 2001), 261; Nicholas Eberstadt, "Demographic Disaster," *National Interest* 36 (Summer 1994): 53–57.
28. Marianne Bitler, Jonah Gelbach, and Hilary Hoynes, "Welfare Reform and Children's Living Arrangements," *Journal of Human Resources* 41 (2006): 1–27.
29. Richard Easterlin, "Toward a Socio-Economic Theory of Fertility," 127–150 in S. J. Behrman, Leslie Corsa, and Ronald Freedman, eds., *Fertility and Family Planning* (Ann Arbor: University of Michigan Press, 1969).
30. Francesco C. Billari and Hans-Peter Kohler, "Patterns of Low and Lowest-Low Fertility in Europe," *Population Studies* 58(2004): 161–176.
31. Amara Bachu and Martin O'Connell, U.S. Census Bureau, *Fertility of American Women: June 2000* (Washington, D.C.: Government Printing Office, 2001), 4, table 2.
32. David T. Ellwood and Christopher Jencks, "The Spread of Single Parent Families in the United States since 1960," in Daniel P. Moynihan, Timothy Smeeding, and Lee Rainwater, eds., *The Future of the American Family* (New York: Russell Sage, 2004).

33. A. Leibowitz, "Home Investments in Children," *Journal of Political Economy* 82 (1974): 111–131; C. R. Hill and F. P. Stafford, "Parental Care of Children: Time Diary Estimates of Quantity, Predictability, and Variety," *Journal of Human Resources* 15 (1980): 219–239; Suzanne Bianchi, "Maternal Employment and Time with Children: Dramatic Change or Surprising Continuity?" *Demography* 37 (2000): 401–414.

34. Liana C. Sayer, Nathan Wright, and Kathryn Edin, "Class Differences in Family Attitudes" (manuscript, Department of Sociology, Ohio State University, Columbus, Ohio, 2007).

35. John Gottman, *Why Marriages Succeed or Fail and How You Can Make Yours Last* (New York: Simon and Schuster, 1995).

36. Shelly Lundberg and Robert A. Pollak, "Separate Spheres Bargaining and the Marriage Market," *Journal of Political Economy* 101 (1993): 988–1010.

37. Susan Walzer, *Thinking about the Baby* (Philadelphia: Temple University Press, 1998), 180.

38. Julie Brines, "Economic Dependency, Gender, and the Division of Labor at Home," *American Journal of Sociology* 100 (1994): 652–688; Michael Bittman, Paula England, Liana Sayer, Nancy Folbre, and George Matheson, "When Does Gender Trump Money? Bargaining and Time in Household Work," *American Journal of Sociology* 109 (2003): 186–214.

39. William Lord, *Household Dynamics: Economic Growth and Policy* (New York: Oxford University Press, 2002), 163–164.

40. George Akerlof, Michael Katz, and Janet Yellen, "An Analysis of Out-of-Wedlock Births in the U.S.," *Quarterly Journal of Economics* 111 (1996): 277–317.

41. Gerald Mackie, "Ending Footbinding and Infibulation: A Convention Account," *American Sociological Review* 61 (1996): 999–1017.

42. Amartya Sen, "Human Capital and Human Capability," *World Development* 25 (1997): 22.

43. For a summary that comments on the inadequacy of such a narrow definition of human capital, see Robert H. Haveman, Andrew Bershadker, and Jonathan A. Schwabish, *Human Capital in the United States from 1975 to 2000* (Kalamazoo, Mich.: W. E. Upjohn Institute for Employment Research, Alcorn, 2003).

44. For examples of willingness to pay applied to health, see W. Kip Viscusi, "The Value of Risks to Life and Health," *Journal of Economic Literature* 31 (1993): 1912–1946. For a thoughtful critique of this approach, see Frank Ackerman and Lisa Heinzerling, *Priceless* (New York: New Press, 2004).

45. Adam Smith, *The Theory of Moral Sentiments*, ed. D. D. Raphael and A. L. Macfie, vol. 4 (Oxford: Clarendon, 1975), 24.

46. Amartya Sen, *The Standard of Living* (Cambridge: Cambridge University Press, 1987); Sen, *Development as Freedom* (New York: Alfred A. Knopf, 1999); Martha Nussbaum, *Women and Human Development* (New York: Cambridge University Press, 2001).

47. Diane Elson, "Male Bias in Macro-economics: The Case of Structural Ad-

justment," in D. Elson, ed., *Male Bias in the Development Process* (Manchester: Manchester University Press, 1991), 7.

3. Defining the Costs of Children

1. Daniel T. Slesnick, *Consumption and Social Welfare: Living Standards and Their Distribution in the United States* (New York: Cambridge University Press, 2001).
2. Paul Streeten, *First Things First: Meeting Basic Needs* (New York: Oxford University Press, 1982).
3. Amartya Sen, *The Standard of Living* (New York: Cambridge University Press, 1987); Martha Nussbaum, *Women and Human Development* (New York: Cambridge University Press, 2001).
4. Kenneth C. Land, Vicki L. Lamb, and Sarah Kahler Mustillo, "Child and Youth Well-Being in the United States, 1975–1998: Some Findings from a New Index," *Social Indicators Research* 56 (2001): 241–320.
5. As Slesnick concisely puts it in *Consumption and Social Welfare*, 18, "If fertility is perfectly controllable and family size is a 'choice' rather than a 'constraint,' the increase in utility associated with a larger family exactly compensates for the increase in consumption requirements." For a classic discussion of this issue, see Robert A. Pollak and Terence J. Wales, "Welfare Comparisons and Equivalence Scales," *American Economic Review* 69 (1979): 216–221.
6. Henry Simons, *Personal Income Taxation: The Definition of Income as a Problem of Fiscal Policy* (Chicago: University of Chicago Press, 1938), 140.
7. Edward J. McCaffery, *Taxing Women* (Chicago: University of Chicago Press, 1997), 111.
8. Elinor Burkett, *The Baby Boon: How Family-Friendly America Cheats the Childless* (New York: Free Press, 2000).
9. Victor Fuchs, *Women's Quest for Economic Equality* (Cambridge: Harvard University Press, 1988).
10. M. Luisa Ferreira, Reuben C. Buse, and Jean-Paul Chavas, "Is There a Bias in Computing Household Equivalence Scales?" *Review of Income and Wealth* 44 (1998): 183–198. For a detailed critique, see Hilde Bojer and Julie Nelson, "Equivalence Scales and the Welfare of Children: A Comment on "Is There Bias in the Economic Literature on Equivalence Scales," *Review of Income and Wealth* 45 (1999): 531–534.
11. William Vickrey, *Agenda for Progressive Taxation* (New York: Ronald Press, 1947), 292.
12. James Surowiecki, "Leave No Parent Behind" *New Yorker,* August 18 and 25, 2003, 48.
13. Other relevant factors include the irreversibility of parental decisions and the credit constraints that make it difficult for parents to smooth consumption over the life cycle. See Bruce Bradbury, "The Welfare Interpretation of Consumer Equivalence Scales," *International Journal of Social Economics* 30 (2003): 770–787.

14. Julie Nelson, "Household Equivalence Scales: Theory versus Policy," 78–96 in her *Feminism, Objectivity, and Economics* (New York: Routledge, 1996). See also Slesnick, *Consumption and Social Welfare*, 22.

15. Charles Blackorby and David Donaldson, "Measuring the Cost of Children: A Theoretical Framework," 247–264 in Richard Blundell, Ian Preston, and Ian Walker, eds., *The Measure of Household Welfare* (New York: Cambridge University Press, 1994).

16. Kathryn Edin and Christopher Jencks, "Do Poor Women Have a Right to Bear Children?" *American Prospect* (Winter 1995): 43–52.

17. For a clear exposition of the superiority of consumption over income as a measure of social welfare, see Slesnick, *Consumption and Social Welfare*. His book focuses on household welfare defined in terms of individual or joint utility, rather than on material standards of living; it largely ignores the consumption of non-market services.

18. M. L. Oliver and T. M. Shapiro, *Black Wealth, White Wealth: A New Perspective on Racial Inequality* (New York: Routledge, 1995).

19. U.S. Census Bureau, U.S. Summary, 2000 (Washington, D.C.: Government Printing Office, 2002), table DP1.

20. Angus Deaton and John Muellbauer, "On Measuring Child Costs: With Applications to Poor Countries," *Journal of Political Economy* 94 (1986): 720–744; Nelson, "Household Equivalence Scales."

21. Julie Nelson, "Household Equivalence Scales," and "Methods of Estimating Household Equivalence Scales: An Empirical Investigation," *Review of Income and Wealth* 38 (1992): 295–310; David M. Betson, "Poverty Equivalence Scales: Adjustment for Demographic Differences across Families" (manuscript, Department of Economics and Policy Studies, University of Notre Dame, 2004).

22. Erwin Rothbarth, "Note on a Method of Determining Equivalent Income for Families of Different Composition," in C. Madge, ed., *War-Time Patterns of Saving and Spending* (Cambridge: Cambridge University Press, 1943); Edward P. Lazear and Robert T. Michael, *Allocation of Income within the Household* (Chicago: University of Chicago Press, 1988).

23. Deaton and Muellbauer, "On Measuring Child Costs."

24. Eva Jacobs, Stephanie Shipp, and Gregory Brown, "Families of Working Wives Spending More on Services and Nondurables," *Monthly Labor Review* 112 (1989): 15–23; Rose M. Rubin and Bobye J. Riney, *Working Wives and Dual-Earner Families* (Westport, Conn.: Praeger, 1994); Martin Browning and Costas Meghir, "The Effects of Male and Female Labor Supply on Commodity Demands," *Econometrica* 59 (1991): 925–951.

25. Shelley A. Phipps and Peter S. Burton, "What's Mine Is Yours? The Influence of Male and Female Incomes on Patterns of Household Expenditure," *Economica* 65 (1998): 599–613.

26. Mark Lino, "Factors Affecting Expenditures of Single-Parent Households," *Home Economics Research Journal* (1990): 191–201.

27. Shelly Lundberg and Elaina Rose, "Investments in Sons and Daughters: Evidence from the Consumer Expenditure Survey," 163–180 in Ariel Kalil and

Thomas DeLeire, eds., *Family Investments in Children: Resources and Behaviors That Promote Success* (Mahwah, N. J.: Erlbaum, 2004).

28. Lee Rainwater and Timothy M. Smeeding offer an alternative interpretation in *Poor Kids in a Rich Country: America's Children in Comparative Perspective* (New York: Russell Sage, 2003), writing, "An equivalence scale should represent the net of additional consumption required by an additional family member and the gain to the family's lifecycle contributed by that additional member" (169). This interpretation seems to violate the principle of a conditional equivalence scale by including consideration of the happiness or "gain" that parents may enjoy from children. A similar tendency to include the "consumption value" of children themselves in consideration of equivalence scales sometimes appears in explanations of why noncustodial parents should not be required to pay the same percentage of their income in child support as custodial parents. See, for instance, Irwin Garfinkel and Marygold S. Melli, "The Use of Normative Standards in Family Law Decisions: Developing Mathematical Standards for Child Support," *Family Law Quarterly* 24 (1990): 167.

29. Constance Citro and Robert T. Michael, eds., *Measuring Poverty: A New Approach* (Washington, D.C.: National Academy Press, 1995).

30. Economies of scale arise from an underlying production function describing the efficiency with which households convert income into a material standard of living, not the underlying utility function that is at issue in comparisons of happiness. From a traditional neoclassical perspective, individuals who choose to live alone do so because they get sufficient subjective happiness from doing so to compensate them fully for the additional costs. But it is difficult to ascertain whether they choose to live alone or lack another option. Hence, utility comparisons are seldom brought into play in comparing households with different numbers of adults.

31. This exponential function can be combined with age- and gender-specific weights. For instance, Constance Citro and Robert Michael use a scale parameter or elasticity of .65 and a child-adult parameter of .7. They divide income by $[A + .7C]^{.65}$, where A is the number of adults in the household and C is the number of children. Citro and Michael, eds., *Measuring Poverty*, 161-162 (Washington, D.C.: National Academy Press, 1995).

32. Patricia Ruggles, *Drawing the Line: Alternative Poverty Measures and Their Implications for Public Policy* (Washington, D.C.: Urban Institute Press, 1990), 87.

33. Ibid.; Citro and Michael, *Measuring Poverty.*

34. As Ruggles puts it in *Drawing the Line,* "There is no justification for the continued use of the existing detailed family size by family composition cells, because the basis for the distinctions they embody appears extremely tenuous," (67).

35. Official poverty thresholds by size of family and number of children are available on the U.S. Census Bureau Website at www.census.gov/hhes/www/poverty/Threshld.html

36. Citro and Michael, *Measuring Poverty*; Kathleen Short and Thesia I. Garner, "A Decade of Experimental Poverty Thresholds, 1990 to 2000" (Current Population Reports, Consumer Income, P60–205 U.S. Census Bureau, Washington, D.C., 1999).

37. The experimental measures also include various ways of taking into account both housing subsidies and the value of home ownership, which reduce the amount families must pay for shelter.

38. Jared Bernstein, "Let the War on the Poverty Line Commence" (working paper, Foundation for Child Development New York, June 2001).

39. Lynn A. Karoly, Peter W. Greenwood, Susan S. Everingham, Jill Houbé, W. Rebecca Kilburn, C. Peter Rydell, Matthew Sanders, andJames Chiesa, *Investing in Our Children: What We Know and Don't Know about the Costs and Benefits of Early Childhood Interventions* (Santa Monica, Calif.: Rand, 1998); Janet Currie, "Early Childhood Education Programs," *Journal of Economic Perspectives* 15 (2001): 213–238; J. P. Shonkoff and D. A. Phillips, eds., *From Neurons to Neighborhoods: The Science of Early Childhood Development* (Washington, D.C.: National Academy Press, 2000).

40. The NAS also applies weights and scale-economy parameters that seem outdated for the reasons discussed above. They recommend a two-parameter equivalence scale that weights children at .7 of an adult and applies an economy-of-scale parameter of between .65 and .75. These weights imply that the addition of a child to a single-adult household requires additional income of from 41 to 48 percent to achieve the same standard of living, compared to 57 to 68 percent for an additional adult. More recent research suggests an alternative, three-parameter scale that would treat the first child in a household much the same as a second adult but otherwise uses the same parameters. Though this three-parameter scale is preferable, the general approach, like that in the other equivalence scales described above, makes children seem cheap relative to adults. The three-parameter scale is formulated as follows: $S(A,K) = (1 + \alpha(A-1) + \beta K)^f$, where A = number of adults, K = number of children, and α, β, and f are equal to .8, .5, and .7, respectively. Betson, "Poverty Equivalence Scales," 17.

41. Robert Pollin and Stephanie Luce, *The Living Wage: Building a Fair Economy* (New York: New Press, 1998); Living Wage Resource Center, http://livingwagecampaign.org (accessed March 28, 2007).

42. In countries with a political legacy of minimum wage regulation, research on this topic is more extensive. Australian researchers, for instance, have developed detailed estimates of the expenditures that the addition of a child to a household is likely to entail. Peter Saunders, "Budget Standards and the Cost of Children," *Family Matters* 53 (Winter 1999): 62–70.

43. Trudi Renwick and Barbara Bergmann, "A Budget-Based Definition of Poverty," *Journal of Human Resources* 28 (1993): 1–24.

44. Heather Boushey, Chauna Brocht, Bethney Gunderson, and Jared Bernstein, *Hardships in America: The Real Story of Working Families* (Washington, D.C.: Economic Policy Institute, 2001); see also Jared Bernstein, Chauna

Brocht, and Maggie Space-Aguilar, *How Much Is Enough? Basic Family Budgets for Working Families* (Washington, D.C.: Economic Policy Institute, 2000). Their budget standards are based on estimates of "fair market rents" for one-, two-, and three-bedroom apartments that are slightly lower than typical, Department of Agriculture estimates of "low-cost" food requirements, and other official sources for health and transportation costs. EPI researchers do not compare expenses for families with no children and those with one child.

45. The family budgets published by the Economic Policy Institute include the average cost per state at child-care centers for four-year-olds (for one-child families), for one four-year-old and one school-age child for two-child families, and for a four-year-old and two school-age children for three-child families. The cost they apply is the average cost per state at child-care centers for four-year-olds and school-age children. Based on these assumptions, their calculation of the cost of child care ranges from $11,700 a year in New York City to about $5,508 in Hattiesburg, Mississippi. This amount represents between about 28 and 32 percent of the family budget standard they estimate.

46. See www.sixstrategies.org (accessed June 2004).

47. These figures omit consideration of taxes or tax credits and are based on calculations for the following communities: Oakland, California; San Diego, California; Miami-Dade County, Florida, Bronx, New York; Austin, Texas; and Chicago–Cook Country, Illinois.

48. Linda Giannarelli and James Barsimantov, "Child Care Expenses of America's Families" (Occasional Paper Number 40, Urban Institute, Washington, D.C., 2000), 6.

49. National Center for Education Statistics, Special Analysis 2001, "Students Whose Parents Did Not Go to College," at http://nces.ed.gov (accessed March 26, 2007).

50. Students themselves paid about another 24 percent, and public subsidies accounted for the remainder. Congressional Budget Office, *Private and Public Contributions to Financing College Education* (Washington, D.C.: Congressional Budget Office, 2004), 19, table 8.

51. For a prescient discussion of this problem see Citro and Michael, *Measuring Poverty*, app. C.

52. Claire Vickery, "The Time-Poor: A New Look at Poverty," *Journal of Human Resources* 7 (1977): 27–48.

53. Statistics Canada, *Households' Unpaid Work: Measurement and Valuation: Studies in National Accounting* (Ottawa: Canada, 1995); Sue Holloway, Sandra Short, Sarah Tamplin, *Household Satellite Account Experimental Methodology* (London: Office of National Statistics, 2007); Australian Bureau of Statistics, *Unpaid Work and the Australian Economy, 1997* (Canberra: Australia, 2000).

54. Bureau of Labor Statistics, American Time Use Survey (ATUS), Preliminary Results, table 3, at www.bls.gov/tus/home.htm (accessed March 14, 2007).

55. Nancy Folbre and Julie Nelson, "For Love or Money, or Both?" *Journal of Economic Perspectives* 14 (2000): 123–140.

56. Ibid., 125.

57. Philip N. Cohen, "The Gender Division of Labor: 'Keeping House' and Occupational Segregation in the United States," *Gender and Society* 18 (2004): 239–252.

58. Anne Chadeau, "What Is Households' Non-Market Production Worth?" OECD Economics Studies 18 (1992): 85–103; United Nations International Research and Training Institute for the Advancement of Women (INSTRAW), *Valuation of Household Production and the Satellite Accounts* (Santo Domingo, Dominican Republic: United Nations INSTRAW, 1996). Katharine G. Abraham and Christopher Mackie, eds., *Beyond the Market: Designing Nonmarket Accounts for the United States* (Washington, D.C.: National Academy Press, 2005).

59. Reuben Gronau, "Household Production: A Forgotten Industry," *Review of Economics and Statistics* 62 (1980): 408–415.

60. Inge O'Connor, Peter Saunders, and Timothy Smeeding, "The Distribution of Welfare: Inequality, Earnings Capacity and Household Production in a Comparative Perspective," 75–110 in S. P. Jenkins, A. Kapteyn, and B. M. S. van Praag, eds., *The Distribution of Welfare and Household Production: International Perspectives* (Cambridge: Cambridge University Press, 1998); Peter Gottschalk and Susan E. Mayer, "Changes in Home Production and Trends in Economic Inequality," in Daniel Cohen, Thomas Piketty, and Gilles Saint-Paul, eds., *The Economics of Rising Inequalities* (New York: Oxford University Press, 2002).

61. BLS, ATUS, Preliminary Results, table 6.

62. See Rainwater and Smeeding, *Poor Kids in a Rich Country,* 173; see also Lee Rainwater, *What Money Buys: Inequality and the Social Meanings of Income* (New York: Basic Books, 1974); Steven Dubnoff, "How Much Income Is Enough? Measuring Public Judgments," *Public Opinion Quarterly* 49 (1985): 285–299.

63. Sandra L. Hanson and Theodora Ooms, "The Economic Costs and Rewards of Two-Earner, Two-Parent Families," *Journal of Marriage and the Family* 53 (1991): 622–634; see also Jacobs et al., "Families of Working Wives."

64. Philip N. Cohen, "Replacing Housework in the Service Economy: Gender, Class, and Race-Ethnicity in Service Spending," *Gender and Society* 12 (1998): 219–231.

65. Suzanne Bianchi, Melissa Milkie, Liana Sayer, and John Robinson, "Is Anyone Doing the Housework? Trends in the Gender Division of Household Labor," *Social Forces* 79 (2000): 191–228.

66. Peter D. Brandon, "An Analysis of Kin-Provided Child Care in the Context of Intrafamily Exchanges," *American Journal of Economics and Sociology* 59 (2000): 191–216.

67. Daniel Kahneman, Alan B. Krueger, David A. Schkade, Norbert Schwarz,

and Arthur A. Stone, "A Survey Method for Characterizing Daily Life Experience: The Day Reconstruction Method," *Science* 306 (2004): 1776–1780.

4. *Children and Family Budgets*

1. Mark Lino, "Expenditures on Children by Families" (2000 Annual Report, U.S. Department of Agriculture, Center for Nutrition Policy and Promotion. Miscellaneous Publication No. 1528-2000, 2001), ii. This figure represents cumulative expenditures, without any discounting of the value of expenditures in different years.
2. This estimate assumes continuous compounding of expenditures as estimated by the USDA.
3. Gary S. Becker, *A Treatise on the Family,* enlarged ed. (Cambridge: Harvard University Press, 1991).
4. Gary Becker and Nigel Tomes, "Human Capital and the Rise and Fall of Families," *Journal of Labor Economics* 4, 3 (1986): S1–S39; Pedro Carneiro and James Heckman, "Human Capital Policy," 77–239 in James J. Heckman and Alan B. Krueger, *Inequality in America: What Role for Human Capital Policies?* (Cambridge: MIT Press, 2003).
5. Gary Becker discusses endogenous preferences in *Accounting for Tastes* (Cambridge: Harvard University Press, 1996). See also the discussions in Oded Stark, *Altruism and Beyond* (New York: Cambridge University Press, 1995), and Casey B. Mulligan, *Parental Priorities and Economic Inequality* (Chicago: University of Chicago Press, 1997). These discussions do not consider the possibility that parental income affects parental influence over children's preferences.
6. Greg Duncan, Aletha C. Huston, and Thomas S. Weisner, *Higher Ground: New Hope for the Working Poor and Their Children* (New York: Russell Sage, 2007).
7. Nancy Folbre and Robert Goodin, "Revealing Altruism," *Review of Social Economy* 62, 1 (2004): 1–25.
8. Martha Minow, "How Should We Think about Child Support Obligations?" 302–330 in Irwin Garfinkel, Sara S. McLanahan, Daniel R. Meyer, and Judith A. Seltzer, *Fathers under Fire: The Revolution in Child Support Enforcement* (New York: Russell Sage, 1998).
9. For a discussion of the historical evolution and significance of patriarchal property rights, see Elissa Braunstein and Nancy Folbre, "To Honor and Obey: Efficiency, Inequality, and Patriarchal Property Rights," *Feminist Economics* 7, 1 (2001): 25–44.
10. See www.supreme.state.az.us/casa/prepare/neglect.html (accessed March 27, 2007).
11. "Child Maltreatment 2002: Summary of Key Findings" (National Clearinghouse on Child Abuse and Neglect Information, Washington, D.C., 2004).
12. These estimates imply that if one episode of maltreatment occurred per child,

about 20 percent of children, on average would experience maltreatment before they reached the age of nineteen.

13. Dorothy Roberts, *Shattered Bonds: The Color of Child Welfare* (New York: Basic Books, 2001).

14. Marcia Meyers and Janet Gornick, "Public or Private Responsibility? Inequality and Early Childhood Education and Care in the Welfare State," *Journal of Comparative Family Studies* 34, 3 (2003): 379–411.

15. "The Cost of Children," *U.S. News and World Report*, March 30, 1998, 51–53, 56–58; Mark Lino, "USDA's Expenditures on Children by Families Project: Uses and Changes over Time," *Family Economics and Nutrition Review* 13, 1 (2001): 81–86.

16. John Ryan, *A Living Wage* (New York: Macmillan, 1920); Alice Kessler-Harris, *A Woman's Wage: Historical Meanings and Social Consequences* (Lexington,: University Press of Kentucky, 1990); David Johnson, John M. Rogers, and Lucilla Tan, "A Century of Family Budgets in the United States," *Monthly Labor Review* (May 2001): 28–45.

17. Louis I. Dublin and Alfred J. Lotka, *The Money Value of a Man* (New York: Ronald Press, 1946).

18. The same source of data informed estimates made in the 1970s, as well as the Engel and Rothbarth equivalence scales described in Chapter 3. Thomas J. Espenshade, *The Cost of Children in Urban United States*, Population Monograph Series, no. 14. (Berkeley: Institute of International Studies, University of California, Berkeley, 1973); Espenshade, *Investing in Children: New Estimates of Parental Expenditures* (Washington, D.C.: Urban Institute Press, 1984).

19. A consumer unit includes all members of the household when they are related by blood or legal arrangement. Other individuals and groups that share living expenses, whether alone or in households with others, are considered separate consumer units.

20. The income reported by respondents is lower than that reported in other surveys such as the Current Population Survey. Reported expenditures are lower than those that emerge from macroeconomic estimates of consumer spending. The quarterly design of the survey leads to some attrition bias that may result in underrepresentation of low-income households. Money expenditures do not capture the value of in-kind benefits such as food stamps or employer-provided health insurance.

21. Ingrid Rothe, Judith Cassety, and Elizabeth Boehnen, "Estimates of Family Expenditures for Children: A Review of the Literature" (Institute for Research on Poverty, University of Wisconsin–Madison, 2001). For more detailed comparisons regarding specific categories of spending, see Mark Lino and David S. Johnson, "Housing, Transportation, and Miscellaneous Expenditures on Children: A Comparison of Methodologies," *Family Economics Review* 8, 1 (1995): 2–12.

22. The analysis is restricted to households with no members other than parents

and children (those with coresident grandparents or adult cohabitors are excluded) that are complete income reporters. Estimates are based on pooled CE data for 1990–1993, updated to 2000 dollars using the Consumer Price Index. The definition of expenditures excludes investments, such as payments of principal on a loan for house or car.

23. Lino, "Expenditures on Children by Families," 10.

24. Center for Surrogate Parenting Inc., at www.creating families.com (accessed March 27, 2007).

25. Rachel Connelly, "The Effect of Child Care Costs on Married Women's Labor Force Participation," *Review of Economics and Statistics* 74, 1 (February 1992): 83–90.

26. Linda Giannarelli, Sarah Adelman, Stefanie Schmidt, "Getting Help with Child Care Expenses" (Urban Institute Occasional Paper No. 62. (Washington, D.C., 2003).

27. Shelley A. Phipps and Peter S. Burton, "What's Mine Is Yours? The Influence of Male and Female Incomes on Patterns of Household Expenditures," *Economica* 65 (1998): 599–613. As I emphasized in earlier chapters, it is difficult to ascertain the extent to which income is pooled and expenses are allocated within families.

28. Sue Shellenbarger, "Child-Care Poor: More Families Find Babysitting Costs Rival Mortgage, Tuition," *Wall Street Journal,* September 12, 2002, D1.

29. Sue Shellenbarger, "As Cost of Child Care Rises Sharply, Here's How Some Families Are Coping," *Wall Street Journal,* October 21, 2004, D1.

30. Linda Giannarelli and James Barsimantov, "Child Care Expenses of America's Families" (Urban Institute Occasional Paper No. 40, Washington, D.C., 2000).

31. Thomas DeLeire and Ariel Kalil, "How Do Cohabiting Couples with Children Spend Their Money?" *Journal of Marriage and Family* 67, 2(2005): 286–294.

32. Shelly Lundberg and Robert Pollak, "Separate Spheres Bargaining and the Marriage Market," *Journal of Political Economy* 101, 6 (December 1993): 988–1010; Phipps and Burton, "What's Mine is Yours?; Geoffrey D. Paulin and Yoon G. Lee, "Expenditures of Single Parents: How Does Gender Figure In?" *Monthly Labor Review* (July 2002): 16–37; Shelly Lundberg and Elaina Rose, "Investments in Sons and Daughters: Evidence from the Consumer Expenditures Survey," 163–180 in Ariel Kalil and Thomas DeLeire, eds., *Family Investments in Children: Resources and Behaviors That Promote Success* (Mahwah, N. J.: Erlbaum, 2004).

33. The Keynesian consumption function treating consumption as a function of income was inspired in part by earlier studies of the components of consumption as a function of total consumption. See, for instance, R. G. D. Allen and A. L. Bowley, *Family Expenditure: A Study of Its Variation* (London: P. S. King and Son, 1935).

34. Jacques van der Gaag, "On Measuring the Cost of Children," in Irwin Gar-

finkel and M. S. Melli, eds., "Child Support: Weaknesses of the Old and Features of a Proposed New System" (Institute for Research on Poverty, Special Report No. 32 C, University of Wisconsin–Madison, 1982). See also Rothe, Cassetty, and Boehnen, "Estimates of Family Expenditures for Children."

5. Children outside the Household

1. William G. Gale and John Karl Scholz, "Intergenerational Transfers and the Accumulation of Wealth," *Journal of Economic Perspectives* 8 (1994): 145–160.
2. C. J. Wolf, "A Theory of Non-Market Failures," *Public Interest* 55 (1974): 114–133.
3. James Andreoni, "Cooperation in Public Goods Experiments: Kindness or Confusion?" *American Economic Review* 85 (1995): 891–904.
4. H. Elizabeth Peters, Jeremy Clark, A. Sinan Unur, and William D. Schulze, "Free-Riding and the Provision of Public Goods in the Family: An Experimental Test of the Rotten Kid Theorem," *International Economic Review* 45 (2004): 283–299.
5. Betsey Stevenson and Justin Wolfers, "Bargaining in the Shadow of the Law: Divorce Laws and Economic Distress," *Quarterly Journal of Economics* 121, 1 (2006): 267–288.
6. Paula England and Nancy Folbre, "Involving Dads: Parental Bargaining and Family Well Being," 387–408 in Catherine S. Tamis-LeMonda and Natasha Cabrera, eds., *Handbook of Father Involvement: Multidisciplinary Perspectives* (Mahwah, N.J.: Erlbaum, 2002).
7. James M. Buchanan, "The Samaritan's Dilemma," in Edmund Phelps, ed., *Altruism, Morality, and Economic Theory* (New York: Russell Sage, 1975), 71–85. For an application to the family, see Neil Bruce and Michael Waldman, "The Rotten-Kid Theorem Meets the Samaritan's Dilemma," *Quarterly Journal of Economics* 105 (1990): 155–165.
8. For a summary of criticisms of inherited wealth, see Jim Grote, "Is Unlimited Inheritance Un-American?" at Responsible Wealth: A Project of United for a Fair Economy, www.responsiblewealth.org (accessed March 27, 2007).
9. Timothy S. Grall, "Custodial Mothers and Fathers and Their Child Support: 2001" (Current Population Report P60–225, U.S. Census Bureau, Washington, D.C., October 2003).
10. Ibid., 7. Note that this does not imply that custodial parents considered these transfers adequate. The low reliability of formal agreements makes informal ones seem more attractive.
11. Yoram Weiss and Robert Willis, "Children as Collective Goods and Divorce Settlements," *Journal of Labor Economics* 3, 3 (1985): 268–292.
12. Grall, "Custodial Mothers and Fathers," 7.
13. E. Peters, L. Argys, E. E. Maccoby, and R. H. Mnookin, "Enforcing Divorce Settlements: Evidence from Child Support Compliance and Award Modi-

fications," *Demography* 30 (1993): 719–735; G. Greif, "When Divorced Fathers Want No Contact with Their Children," *Journal of Divorce and Remarriage* 23 (1995): 75–84.

14. Robert I. Lerman and Elaine Sorensen, "Child Support: Interactions between Private and Public Transfers" (National Bureau of Economic Research Working Paper 8199, Cambridge, Mass., April 2001).

15. E. Sorensen and C. Zibman, "To What Extent Do Children Benefit from Child Support?" (Assessing the New Federalism Discussion Paper No. 19, Urban Institute, Washington, D.C., 2000).

16. Vicki Turetsky, *You Get What You Pay For: How Federal and State Investment Decisions Affect Child Support Performance* (Washington, D.C.: Center for Law and Social Policy, 1998).

17. Andrea H. Beller and John W. Graham, *The Economics of Child Support* (New Haven: Yale University Press, 1993), 200.

18. Robert G. Williams, "Guidelines for Setting Levels of Child Support Orders," *Family Law Quarterly* 21 (1987): 282–350.

19. Irwin Garfinkel and Marygold S. Melli, "The Use of Normative Standards in Family Law Decisions: Developing Mathematical Standards for Child Support," *Family Law Quarterly* 24 (1990): 157–178.

20. Ingrid Rothe, Judith Cassety, and Elizabeth Boehnen, "Estimates of Family Expenditures for Children: A Review of the Literature" (Institute for Research on Poverty, University of Wisconsin–Madison, 2001), 34.

21. Jane Venohr and Robert Williams, "The Implementation and Periodic Review of State Child Support Guidelines," *Family Law Quarterly* 33, 1 (1999): 7–39; William M. Rodgers III and Yana van der Meulen Rodgers, "The Pitfalls of Using a Child Support Schedule Based on Outdated Data" (manuscript, Bloustein School of Public Policy, Rutgers University, September 2004).

22. Jessica Pearson and Nancy Thoennes, "Programs to Increase Fathers' Access to Their Children," 220–250 in Irwin Garfinkel, Sara S. McLanahan, Daniel R. Meyer, and Judith A. Seltzer, *Fathers under Fire: The Revolution in Child Support Enforcement* (New York: Russell Sage, 1998).

23. William V. Fabricius and Sanford L. Braver, "Non-Child Support Expenditures on Children by Nonresidential Divorced Fathers," *Family Court Review* 41 (2003): 321–336.

24. Terri Cullen, "How Parents Can Help Children Pay for College," *Wall Street Journal, College Journal* at www.collegejournal.com/aidadmissions/financialissues/20040303-cullen.html, (accessed March 28, 2007).

25. As of 1998, about twenty one states authorized courts to bring consideration of college expenses into mandatory child support awards. See William V. Fabricius, Sanford L. Braver, and Kindra Deneau, "Divorced Parents' Financial Support of Their Children's College Expenses," *Family Court Review* 41 (2003): 224–241.

26. Qualifying conditions include being an orphan or ward of the court until age eighteen or being a U.S. military veteran.

27. See www.finaid.org (accessed March 30,2007).

28. Charlene M. Kalenkoski, "Parent-Child Bargaining, Parental Transfers, and the Postsecondary Education Decision," *Applied Economics*, forthcoming.

29. Judith S. Wallerstein, Julia M. Lewis, and Sandra Blakeslee, *The Unexpected Legacy of Divorce: A 25 Year Landmark Study* (New York: Hyperion, 2000).

30. Based on the calculator at http://apps.collegeboard.com (accessed March 12, 2007).

31. Jane Bryant Quinn, "Helping Grandchildren Pay Their Tuition," *Washington Post*, May 28, 1995, H2.

32. Investment Company Institute, *Profile of Households Saving for College* (Fall 2003), 19 at www.ici.org/statements/res/rpt_03_college_saving.pdf (accessed March 27, 2007).

33. T. Mortenson, "Educational Opportunity by Family Income, 1970 to 1997," *Postsecondary Education Opportunity* 86 (1999): 1–8.

34. Congressional Budget Office, *Private and Public Contributions to Financing College Education* (Washington, D.C.: Congressional Budget Office, 2004).

35. L. C. Steelman and B. Powell, "Acquiring Capital for College: The Constraints of Family Configuration," *American Sociological Review* 54 (1989): 844–855; L. C. Steelman and B. Powell, "Sponsoring the Next Generation: Parental Willingness to Pay for Higher Education," *American Journal of Sociology* 96 (1991): 1505–1529; F. K. Goldscheider and C. Goldscheider, "The Intergenerational Flow of Income: Family Structure and the Status of Black Americans," *Journal of Marriage and the Family* 53 (1991): 499–508.

36. Congressional Budget Office, *Private and Public Contributions*.

37. Investment Company Institute, *Profile of Households*, 3.

38. P. Carneiro and J. Heckman, "The Evidence on Credit Constraints in Post-Secondary Schooling," *Economic Journal* 112 (2002): 705–734.

39. T. Kane, The *Price of Admission: Rethinking How Americans Pay for College* (Washington, D.C.: Brookings Institution Press, 1999); D. Ellwood and T. Kane, "Who Is Getting a College Education? Family Background and the Growing Gaps in Enrollment," 264–282 in S. Danziger and J. Waldfogel, eds., *Securing the Future: Investing in Children from Birth to College* (New York: Russell Sage, 2000).

40. S. Dynarski, "Hope for Whom? Financial Aid for the Middle Class and Its Impact on College Attendance," *National Tax Journal* 53 (2000): 629–662; S. Cameron and J. Heckman, "Can Tuition Policy Combat Rising Wage Inequality?" 76–124 in M. Kosters, ed., *Financing College Tuition: Government Policies and Educational Priorities* (Washington, D.C.: American Enterprise Institute Press, 1999).

41. M. McPherson and M. Shapiro, *Keeping College Affordable: Government and Educational Opportunity* (Washington, D.C.: Brookings Institution Press, 1991).

42. Tracey King and Ivan Frishberg, "Big Loans, Bigger Problems: A Report on the Sticker Shock of Student Loans." U.S. PIRG, the Federation of State

PIRGs, Washington, D.C., 2001, at www.pirg.org.highered/studentdebt (accessed March 30, 2007).

43. Lawrence Mishel, Jared Bernstein, and Sylvia Allegretto, *State of Working America 2004/2005* (Ithaca: Cornell University Press, 2005), fig. 2-K.

44. William G. Bowen and Derek Bok, *The Shape of the River: Long-Term Consequences of Considering Race in College and University Admissions* (Princeton: Princeton University Press, 2000).

45. William G. Bowen, Martina A. Kurzweil, and Eugene M. Tobin, "From 'Bastions of Privilege' to 'Engines of Opportunity,'" *Chronicle of Higher Education*, February 25, 2005, B18.

46. D. J. Eggebeen and D. P. Hogan. "Giving between Generations in American Families," *Human Nature* 1 (1990): 1–32.

47. D. P. Hogan and D. J. Eggebeen. "Sources of Emergency Help and Routine Assistance in Old Age," *Social Forces* 73 (1995): 917–936.

48. Douglas Wolf, "The Family as Provider of Long-Term Care: Efficiency, Equity, and Externalities," *Journal of Aging and Health* 11 (1999): 360–382.

49. Dennis P. Hogan, David J. Eggebeen, and Clifford C. Clogg, "The Structure of Intergenerational Exchanges in American Families," *American Journal of Sociology* 98 (1993): 1428–1458.

50. Frank F. Furstenberg, Saul D. Hoffman, and Laura Shrestha, "The Effect of Divorce on Intergenerational Transfers: New Evidence," *Demography* 32 (1995): 319–333.

51. Joseph Altonji, Fumio Hayashi, and Laurence J. Kotlikoff, "Is the Family Altruistically Linked? Direct Tests Using Micro Data," *American Economic Review* 82 (1992): 117–198; Joseph Altonji, Fumio Hayashi, and Laurence J. Kotlikoff, "Parental Altruism and Inter Vivos Transfers: Theory and Evidence," *Journal of Political Economy* 105 (1997): 1121–1166.

52. Donald Cox and George Jakubson, "The Connection between Public Transfers and Private Interfamily Transfers," *Journal of Public Economics* 55 (1995): 129–167.

53. Kathleen McGarry, "Inter Vivos Transfers and Intended Bequests," *Journal of Public Economics* 73 (1999): 321–351; Kathleen McGarry and Robert F. Schoeni, "Transfer Behavior within the Family: Results from the Asset and Health Dynamics Survey" (National Bureau of Economic Research Working Paper 7593, March 2000, at www.nber.org, accessed August 2005).

54. Douglas Bernheim, Andrei Shleifer, and Lawrence H. Summers, "The Strategic Bequest Motive," *Journal of Political Economy* 93 (1985): 1045–1076.

55. Kathleen McGarry, "Inter Vivos Transfers and Intended Bequests"; Mark Wilhelm, "Bequest Behavior and the Effect of Heirs' Earnings: Testing the Altruistic Model of Bequests," *American Economic Review* 86 (1996): 874–892.

56. Jere R. Behrman, Robert A. Pollak, and Paul Taubman, "Parental Preferences and Provision for Progeny," *Journal of Political Economy* 90 (1982): 52–73; Wilhelm, "Bequest Behavior."

57. Wilhelm, "Bequest Behavior."

58. Douglas B. Bernheim and Serge Severinov, "Bequests as Signals: An Explanation for the Equal Division Puzzle" (National Bureau of Economic Research Working Paper 7791, at www.nber.org, accessed August 2005).
59. Donald Cox and Beth J. Soldo, "Motivation for Money and Care That Adult Children Provide for Parents: "Evidence from 'Point-Blank' Survey Questions" (Working Paper 2004–17, Center for Retirement Research at Boston College, Chestnut Hill, Mass., May 2004).
60. Diane N. Lye, "Adult Child–Parent Relationships," *Annual Review of Sociology* 22 (1996): 79–102; D. P. Hogan et al., "The Structure of Intergenerational Exchange in American Families"; D. P. Hogan, L. Hao, W. L. Parish, "Race, Kin Networks, and Assistance to Mother Headed Families," *Social Forces* 68 (1990): 797–798.
61. Altonji, Hayashi, and Kotlikoff, "Parental Altruism and Inter Vivos Transfers: Theory and Evidence." See also McGarry and Schoeni, "Transfer Behavior within the Family."
62. Robert F. Schoeni and Karen E. Ross, "Material Assistance from Families during the Transition to Adulthood," 396–416 in Richard A. Settersten Jr., Frank F. Furstenberg Jr., and Ruben G. Rumbaut, eds., *On the Frontiers of Adulthood* (Chicago: University of Chicago Press, 2005).
63. Larry Bumpass, "What's Happening to the Family? Interactions between Demographic and Institutional Change," *Demography* 27 (1990): 483–498.
64. Mitja Ng-Baumhackl, John Gist, and Carlos Figueiredo, "Pennies from Heaven: Will Inheritances Bail out the Boomers?" AARP Public Policy Institute, October 2003, at www.aarp.org/research/family/charitable/aresearch=import=348=DD90.html (accessed March 27, 2007).
65. Melvin Oliver and Thomas Shapiro, *Black Wealth, White Wealth: A New Perspective on Racial Inequality* (New York: Routledge, 1997).
66. William G. Gale and Joel B. Slemrod, "Rethinking the Estate and Gift Tax: An Overview" 1–64 in William G. Gale, James R. Hines Jr., and Joel B. Slemrod, eds., *Rethinking Estate and Gift Taxation* (Washington, D.C.: Brookings Institution Press, 2000).

6. Accounting for Family Time

1. For more discussion of this issue, see Nancy Folbre and Michael Bittman, eds., *Family Time: The Social Organization of Care* (New York: Routledge, 2004).
2. W. Keith Bryant and Catherine D. Zick, "Are We Investing Less in the Next Generation? Historical Trends in Time Spent Caring for Children," *Journal of Family and Economic Issues* 17 (1996): 385–392; John Robinson and Geoffrey Godbey, *Time for Life: The Surprising Ways Americans Use Their Time* (University Park: Pennsylvania State University Press, 1997); Suzanne Bianchi, "Maternal Employment and Time with Children: Dramatic Change or Surprising Continuity?" *Demography* 37 (2000): 405.
3. For a qualitative study of the way parents think about time with their chil-

dren (as well as the specific quote from the mother cited here) see Susan Walzer, *Thinking about the Baby: Gender and Transitions into Parenthood* (Philadelphia: Temple University Press, 1998), 23.

4. Elizabeth Cady Stanton, *The Revolution*, December 24, 1868, 393.

5. William Leach, *True Love and Perfect Union* (New York: Basic Books, 1980), 193.

6. Nancy Folbre, "The Unproductive Housewife: Her Evolution in Nineteenth-Century Thought," *Signs* 16 (1991): 42–63.

7. Many of these studies were summarized in Hazel Kyrk, *Economic Problems of the Family* (New York: Harper and Brothers, 1929). For a more modern summary, see Joanne Vanek, "Time Spent in Housework," *Scientific American* 231 (1974): 116–120.

8. Louis Dublin and Alfred Lotka, *The Money Value of a Man* (New York: Ronald Press, 1946), 40.

9. Margaret Reid, *Economics of Household Production* (New York: John Wiley and Sons, 1934).

10. Gail Warshofsky Lapidus, *Women in Soviet Society: Equality, Development, and Social Change* (Berkeley: University of California Press, 1978).

11. Alexander Szalai, *The Use of Time* (The Hague: Mouton, 1973).

12. F. Thomas Juster and Frank P. Stafford, eds., *Time, Goods, and Well-Being*, (Ann Arbor: Survey Research Center, Institute for Social Research, University of Michigan, 1985); Robinson, and Godbey, *Time for Life*.

13. Marilyn Waring, *If Women Counted: A New Feminist Economics* (New York: Harper and Row, 1988).

14. Sara Berk, *The Gender Factory: The Apportionment of Work in American Households* (New York: Plenum, 1985); Michael Bittman and Jocelyn Pixley, *The Double Life of the Family: Myth, Hope and Experience* (Sydney: Allen and Unwin, 1997); Suzanne Bianchi, Melissa Milkie, Liana Sayer, and John Robinson, "Is Anyone Doing the Housework? Trends in the Gender Division of Household Labor," *Social Forces* 79 (2000): 191–228.

15. Michele Budig and Nancy Folbre, "Activity, Proximity, or Responsibility? Measuring Parental Child Care Time," 51–68 in Folbre and Bittman, *Family Time*.

16. Gary Becker, "A Theory of the Allocation of Time," *Economic Journal* 75 (1965): 493–517.

17. Mihaly Csikszentmihalyi, *Flow: The Psychology of Optimal Experience* (New York: Harper and Row, 1990); Thomas F. Juster, "Preferences for Work and Leisure," 333–351, and Gregory K. Dow and F. Thomas Juster, "Goods, Time, and Well-being: The Joint Dependence Problem," 397–413, both in Juster and Stafford, *Time, Goods, and Well-Being*.

18. Robinson and Godbey, *Time for Life*, 245.

19. Katherine S. Newman, *No Shame in My Game: The Working Poor in the Inner City* (New York: Alfred A. Knopf, 1999).

20. Arlie Hochschild, *The Time Bind: When Work Becomes Home and Home Becomes Work* (New York: Metropolitan Books, 1997).

21. This does not imply that they are fully compensated. See Michelle Budig, Paula England, and Nancy Folbre, "Wages of Virtue: The Relative Pay of Care Work," *Social Problems* 49 (2002): 455–473.

22. Reid, *Economics of Household Production*, 11.

23. Duncan Ironmonger, "Counting Outputs, Capital Inputs and Caring Labor: Estimating Gross Household Product," *Feminist Economics* 2 (1996): 37–64.

24. Jeff E. Biddle and Daniel S. Hamermesh, "Sleep and the Allocation of Time," *Journal of Political Economy* 98 (1990): 922–943.

25. Yoshinori Kamo, "He Said, She Said: Assessing Discrepancies in Husbands' and Wives' Reports on the Division of Household Labor," *Social Science Research* 29 (2000): 459–476.

26. Michael Bittman, Lyn Craig, and Nancy Folbre, "Packaging Care: What Happens When Children Receive Non-Parental Care?" 133–151 in Folbre and Bittman, *Family Time*.

27. Australian Bureau of Statistics, *How Australians Use Their Time*, Cat. no. 4153.0 (Canberra: Australian Bureau of Statistics, 1994): 8, 15.

28. A. H. Gauthier, T. M. Smeeding, and F. F. Furstenberg Jr., "Are Parents Investing Less Time in Children? Trends in Selected Industrialized Countries," *Population and Development Review* 30 (2004): 647–671.

29. Robinson and Godbey found that adding secondary-activity child-care time increased the total amount of time devoted to child care by 50 percent, which implies that it represented about a third of the total. Similarly, in their analysis of an eleven-state survey of two-parent, two-child families, Keith Bryant and Kathleen Zick found that secondary child-care time accounted to about 44 percent of primary child-care time. On the other hand, Suzanne Bianchi found that total time spent with children was about three times the amount of time spent in direct care, results similar to those Gauthier et al. reported for Canada. See Robinson and Godbey, *Time for Life*, 107; Keith W. Bryant and Cathleen D. Zick, "An Examination of Parent-Child Shared Time," *Journal of Marriage and the Family*, 58 (1996): 227–237. See also their "Are We Investing Less in the Next Generation?"; and Bianchi, "Maternal Employment and Time with Children," 401–414. The relative proportion of primary and secondary time devoted to children varies considerably with the age of the child, but most U.S. studies are based on small sample sizes that make this difficult to disaggregate. For a detailed consideration of this issue in the Australian context, see Duncan Ironmonger, "Bringing Up Bobby and Betty: The Inputs and Outputs of Child Care Time," 93–109 in Folbre and Bittman, *Family Time*.

30. Boone Turchi, *The Demand for Children: The Economics of Fertility in the United States* (Cambridge, Mass.: Ballinger, 1975); Peter Lindert, *Fertility and Scarcity in America* (Princeton: Princeton University Press, 1978); Warren Robinson, "The Time Cost of Children and Other Household Production," *Population Studies* 41 (1987): 313–323.

31. Nancy Folbre, Kade Finnoff, Jayoung Yoon, and Alison Fuligni, "By What

Measure? Family Time Devoted to Children in the U.S.," *Demography* 42 (2005):56–61.

32. Reid, *Economics of Household Production*, 319.

33. Nina Bernstein, "Daily Choice Turned Deadly: Children Left on Their Own," *New York Times*, October 19, 2003, N1.

34. Budig and Folbre, "Activity, Proximity, or Responsibility?"

35. In recent cognitive pretesting for the American Time Use Survey, the Bureau of Labor Statistics found that participants "strongly suggested that the concept of secondary child care is not intuitively meaningful, because most parents would consider those activities, 'just part of being a parent,'"; Lisa K. Schwartz, "The American Time Use Survey: Cognitive Pretesting," *Monthly Labor Review* 125 (February 2002): 35.

36. *Time Use Survey, Australia, Users' Guide 1997* (Canberra: Australian Bureau of Statistics, 1998).

37. Schwartz, "American Time Use Survey," 34–44.

38. Shelley E. Taylor, *The Tending Instinct: Women, Men, and the Biology of Our Relationships* (New York: Henry Holt, 2002), 85.

39. Nancy Folbre and Marjorie Abel, "Women's Work and Women's Households: Gender Bias in the U.S. Census," *Social Research* 56 (1989): 545–570.

40. Philip N. Cohen and Suzanne M. Bianchi, "Marriage, Children, and Women's Employment: What Do We Know?" *Monthly Labor Review* 122 (1999): 22–31.

41. Laura Sanchez and Elizabeth Thomson, "Becoming Mothers and Fathers: Parenthood, Gender, and the Division of Labor," *Gender and Society* 11 (1997): 757.

42. Jerry A. Jacobs and Janet C. Gornick, "Hours of Paid Work in Dual-Earner Couples: The United States in Cross-National Perspective," *Sociological Focus* 35 (2002): 169–187.

43. Janet Gornick and Marcia Meyers, *Families That Work: Policies for Reconciling Parenthood and Employment* (New York: Russell Sage, 2003); Michael Bittman, "Parenthood without Penalty: Time Use and Public Policy in Australia and Finland" 224–237 in Folbre and Bittman, *Family Time*.

44. Gauthier et al., "Are Parents Investing Less Time in Children?"; Michael Bittman, "Parenting and Employment: What Time Use Surveys Show" 152–170 in Folbre and Bittman, *Family Time*.

45. Bianchi, "Maternal Employment and Time with Children."

46. Office of the Assistant Secretary for Planning and Evaluation, U.S. Department of Health and Human Services, *Indicators of Child, Family, and Community Connections* (Washington, D.C.: U.S. Department of Health and Human Services, 2004), 25, table 10.

47. Harriet Presser, *Working in a 24/7 Economy. Challenges for American Families* (New York, Russell Sage, 2003), 77.

48. Ellen Galinsky, *Ask the Children* (New York: Quill, 2000).

49. Jody Heymann, *The Widening Gap* (New York: Basic Books, 2000); Randy Albelda, "Fallacies of Welfare-to-Work Policies," 79–94 in Randy Albelda

and Ann Withorn, eds., *Lost Ground: Welfare Reform, Poverty, and Beyond* (Boston: South End Press, 2002).

50. Steven J. Haider, Alison Jacknowitz, and Robert F. Schoeni, "Welfare Work Requirements and Child Well-being: Evidence from the Effects on Breast-feeding," *Demography* 40 (2003): 479–498.

51. Joan Williams, *Unbending Gender: Why Family and Work Conflict and What to Do about It* (New York: Oxford University Press, 2000).

52. Robert Frank and P. J. Cook, *The Winner-Take-All Society* (New York: Free Press, 1995).

53. Heidi I. Hartmann, "The Family as a Locus of Gender, Class, and Political Struggle: The Example of Housework," *Signs* 6 (1981): 366–394.

54. Bianchi et al., "Is Anyone Doing the Housework?

55. American Time Use Survey, at www.bls.org.gov/tus/home.htm (accessed March 14, 2007); see Table 6, Average hours per day spent in primary activities for the population eighteen years and over by sex, labor force status, and presence and age of children, 2003 annual averages.

56. Joni Hersch and Leslie S. Stratton, "Housework, Wages and the Division of Housework Time for Employed Spouses," *American Economic Review* 84 (1994): 120–125.

57. Sanchez and Thomson, "Becoming Mothers and Fathers," 757.

58. Marybeth J. Mattingly and Suzanne Bianchi, "Gender Differences in the Quantity and Quality of Free Time: The U.S. Experience," *Social Forces* 81 (2003): 999–1030. The presence of children under the age of three tends to reduce mothers' sleep significantly, while leaving fathers' time, on average, unaffected. See Biddle and Hamermesh, "Sleep and the Allocation of Time," 928.

59. Sanchez and Thompson, "Becoming Mothers and Fathers"; Carolyn Pape Cowan and Philip A. Cowan, *When Partners Become Parents: The Big Life Change for Couples* (New York: Basic Books, 1992).

60. Rhona Mahony, *Kidding Ourselves. Breadwinning, Babies, and Bargaining Power* (New York: Basic Books, 1995).

61. The PSID is a longitudinal survey of a representative sample of U.S. men, women, and children, and the families in which they live. In 1997 the Child Development Supplement collected information on one or two randomly selected children under twelve of PSID respondents, both from the primary caregiver and from the children themselves. About 3,563 children were included.

62. This number would be lower but for the fact that 13 percent of children living with a single parent are living with a father.

63. Another parent is participating 26 percent of the time. Coparticipation of a relative accounts for an additional 6 percent and coparticipation of a non-relative an additional 3 percent. The overlap is small in the latter case because nonrelatives are generally paid care providers or teachers substituting for parents. See Folbre et al., "By What Measure?"

64. Ibid.

65. Sufficient information is presented in Table 6.3 to allow readers to make different calculations of parental-care work time suspending any or all of these assumptions.
66. Note that this comparison takes overlaps with siblings into account, but it ignores the extra benefit of time with two parents at once.
67. Taylor, *The Tending Instinct*, 32–33.
68. This is consistent with the assumption, made in calculations of average parental-care time, that an hour in which two parents engage in an activity with a child is effectively thirty minutes contribution from each, rather than two hours in total.
69. Sandra Hofferth, "Race/Ethnic Differences in Father Involvement in Two-Parent Families," *Journal of Family Issues* 24 (2003): 185–216.

7. Valuing Family Work

1. Gary S. Becker, *A Treatise on the Family,* enlarged ed. (Cambridge: Harvard University Press, 1991).
2. Patricia Apps and Ray Rees, "Household Production, Full Consumption, and the Costs of Children," *Labour Economics* 8 (2002): 621–648.
3. Charles A. Calhoun and Thomas J. Espenshade, "Childbearing and Wives' Foregone Earnings," *Population Studies* 42 (1988): 5–37.
4. Robert Haveman and Barbara Wolfe, "The Determinants of Children's Attainments: A Review of Methods and Findings," *Journal of Economic Literature* 33 (1995): 1829.
5. Heather Joshi, "The Cash Opportunity Costs of Childbearing: An Approach to Estimation Using British Data," *Population Studies* 44 (1990): 41–60; Joshi, "The Opportunity Costs of Childbearing: More than Mothers' Business," *Journal of Population Economics* 11 (1998): 161–183; Jane Waldfogel, "The Effect of Children on Women's Wages," *American Sociological Review* 62 (1997): 209–217; Michelle Budig and Paula England, "The Wage Penalty for Motherhood," *American Sociological Review* 66 (2001): 204–225; Shelley Phipps, Peter Burton, and Lynn Lethbridge, "In and Out of the Labour Market: Long-Term Income Consequences of Child-related Interruptions to Women's Paid Work," *Canadian Journal of Economics* 34 (2001): 411–429.
6. Jane Waldfogel, "Understanding the 'Family Gap' in Pay for Women with Children," *Journal of Economic Perspectives* 12 (1998): 137–156.
7. Wendy Sigle-Rushton and Jane Waldfogel, "Family Gaps in Income: A Cross-National Comparison," and Matthew Gray and Bruce Chapman, "Child Rearing, Relationship Breakdown and the Economic Welfare of Australian Mothers and Their Children" (papers presented at the conference "Supporting Children: English-Speaking Countries in International Context," Princeton University, Princeton, N.J., January 8–9, 2004).
8. Heather Joshi, Pierella Paci, and Jane Waldfogel, "The Wages of Mother-

hood: Better or Worse," *Cambridge Journal of Economics* 23 (1999): 543–564.

9. Janet Gornick and Marcia Meyer, *Families That Work* (New York: Russell Sage, 2003).

10. Katharine G. Abraham and Christopher Mackie, eds., *Beyond the Market: Designing Nonmarket Accounts for the United States* (Washington, D.C.: National Academy Press, 2005); Luisella Goldschmidt-Clermont, "Monetary Valuation of Non-Market Productive Time: Methodological Considerations," *Review of Income and Wealth* 39 (1993): 419–433.

11. Thomas R. Ireland, "Compensable Nonmarket Services in Wrongful Death Litigation: Legal Definitions and Measurement Standards," *Journal of Legal Economics* 7 (1997): 15–34.

12. Willford I. King, Wesley G. Mitchell, Frederick Macaulay, and Oswald W. Knauth, *Income in the United States, Its Amount and Distribution 1909–1919*, National Bureau of Economic Research (New York: Harcourt, Brace, 1921); Nancy Folbre and Barnet Wagman, "Counting Housework: New Estimates of Real Product in the U.S., 1800–1860," *Journal of Economic History* 53 (1993): 275–288; Barnet Wagman and Nancy Folbre, "Household Services and Economic Growth in the U.S., 1870–1930," *Feminist Economics* 2 (1996): 43–66.

13. Robert Eisner, *The Total Incomes System of Accounts* (Chicago: University of Chicago Press, 1989).

14. Australian Bureau of Statistics, *Unpaid Work and the Australian Economy* (Canberra: Australian Bureau of Statistics, 2000); Statistics Canada, *Household's Unpaid Work: Measurement and Valuation: Studies in National Accounting* (Ottawa: Statistics Canada, 1995).

15. For a summary, see Abraham and Mackie, *Beyond the Market*.

16. Sue Holloway and Sarah Tamplin, "Valuing Informal Childcare in the U.K." (Office for National Statistics, London, September 2001); Sue Holloway, Sandra Short, Sarah Tamplin, "Household Satellite Account (Experimental) Methodology" (Office for National Statistics, London, April 2002).

17. Jack P. Shonkoff and Deborah A. Phillips, eds., *From Neurons to Neighborhoods: The Science of Early Childhood Development* (Washington, D.C.: National Academy Press, 2000).

18. Tabulated from Child Welfare League's National Data Analysis System, at http://ndas.cwla.org (accessed March 31, 2007).

19. Sandra Bass, Margie K. Shields, and Richard E. Behrman, "Children, Families, and Foster Care: Analysis and Recommendations," *Future of Children* 14 (2004): 5–29.

20. Specifically, the hours that both parents are actively caring for a child, as shown in Table 7.1, are calculated twice rather than once, since they represents a "double" input.

21. Though the USDA estimates were presented for three separate household income groups, the sample size of the PSID-CD is too small to allow

such disaggregation. Hence, for purposes of comparison, we use the middle-income group for two-parent families (with before-tax income between $38,000 and $64,000) and the lower-income group for single-parent families (with before-tax income under $38,000).

22. Calhoun and Espenshade, "Childbearing and Wives' Foregone Earnings"; Robert Haveman and Barbara Wolfe, "The Determinants of Children's Attainments: A Review of Methods and Findings," *Journal of Economic Literature* 33 (1995): 1829–1878. Haveman and Wolfe explore the implications of different assumptions regarding quantity of time devoted to children in this article (1831n2), and they arrive at a much higher upper-bound estimate.

8. Subsidizing Parents

1. Anne Gauthier, *The State and the Family: A Comparative Analysis of Family Policies in Industrialized Countries* (Oxford: Clarendon Press, 1996); Sheila B. Kamerman and Alfred J. Kahn, "Child and Family Policies in an Era of Social Policy Retrenchment and Restructuring," in Timothy M. Smeeding and Koen Vleminckx, eds., *Child Well-Being, Child Poverty and Child Policy in Modern Nations* (Bristol, Eng.: Policy Press, 2001); Janet Gornick and Marcia Meyer, *Families That Work* (New York: Russell Sage, 2003).

2. J. Caldwell, P. Caldwell, and P. McDonald, "Policy Responses to Low Fertility and Its Consequences: A Global Survey," *Journal of Population Research* 19 (2002): 1–24.

3. Joya Misra, "Mothers or Workers? The Value of Women's Labor: Women and the Emergence of Family Allowance Policy," *Gender and Society* 12 (1998): 376–398.

4. Gauthier, *The State and the Family*, 74.

5. Anne H. Gauthier, "Family Policies in Industrialized Countries: Is There Convergence?" *Population* 57 (2002): 447–474.

6. Ingallil Montanari, "From Family Wage to Marriage Subsidy and Child Benefits: Controversy and Consensus in the Development of Family Support," *Journal of European Social Policy* 10 (2000): 307–333.

7. Paul H. Douglas, *Wages and the Family* (Chicago: University of Chicago Press, 1925).

8. Eugene Steuerle, "The Tax Treatment of Households of Different Size," 73–79 in Rudolph G. Penner, ed., *Taxing the Family* (Washington, D.C.: American Enterprise Institute for Public Policy Research, 1983); Leslie A. Whittington, "Taxes and the Family: The Impact of the Tax Exemption for Dependents on Marital Fertility," *Demography* 29 (1992): 215–226.

9. Montanari, "From Family Wage to Marriage Subsidy."

10. Laura Wheaton, "Low-Income Families and the Marriage Tax" (Strengthening Families Research Report no. 1, Urban Institute Washington, D.C., 2001); Jane G. Gravelle, "The Marriage Penalty and Other Family Tax Issues" (Congressional Research Service Report for Congress, September 29, 1998); Eugene Steuerle, "Valuing Marital Commitment in Our Transfer and

Tax System" (testimony before the U.S. House of Representatives Subcommittee on Human Resources, Committee on Ways and Means, May 2001).

11. Edward J. McCaffery, *Taxing Women* (Chicago: University of Chicago Press, 1997).
12. Adam Carasso, Jeffrey Rohaly, and C. Eugene Steuerle, "Tax Reform for Families: An Earned Income Child Credit" (Brookings Institution WR and B Brief no. 26, Washington, D.C., 2003).
13. U.S. Social Security Administration, "Social Security Programs Through the World: Europe, 2002" at www.ssa.gov/policy/docs (accessed March 2007).
14. Gornick and Meyers, *Families That Work*, 124, table 5.1; Christopher J. Ruhm and Jacqueline L. Teague, "Parental Leave Policies in Europe and North America," 133–165 in Francine D. Blau and Ronald G. Ehrenberg, eds., *Gender and Family Issues in the Workplace* (New York: Russell Sage, 1997); Linda Haas, *Equal Parenthood and Social Policy: A Study of Parental Leave in Sweden* (Albany: State University of New York Press, 1992).
15. Social Security Administration, *Social Security Programs*.
16. Gornick and Meyers, *Families That Work*, 124–127, table 5.1.
17. Gornick and Meyers, *Families That Work*.
18. Jody Heymann, *The Widening Gap: Why America's Working Families Are in Jeopardy, and What Can Be Done about It* (New York: Basic Books, 2000); Kristen Smith, Barbara Downs, and Martin O'Connell, "Maternity Leave and Employment Patterns: 1961–1995" (Household Economic Studies report P70–79, U.S. Bureau of the Census, Washington, D.C., 2001).
19. M. V. Lee Badgett, *Money, Myths, and Change: The Economic Lives of Lesbians and Gay Men* (Chicago: University of Chicago Press, 2001).
20. Congressman Charles Stenholm, quoted in "Social Security and the Family: Highlights from Session 1," Urban Institute, June 19, 2000, at www.urban.org (accessed April 6, 2007).
21. Melissa M. Favreault, Frank J. Sammartino, and E. Eugene Steuerle, "Introduction: Perspectives on the Structure and Role of Family Benefits," 1–18 in Melissa M. Favreault, Frank J. Sammartino, and E. Eugene Steuerle, eds., *Social Security and the Family* (Washington, D.C.: Urban Institute Press, 2002).
22. Lawrence H. Thompson and Adam Carasso, "Social Security and the Treatment of Families," 123–176 in *Social Security and the Family*.
23. Lee Rainwater and Timothy M. Smeeding, *Poor Kids in a Rich Country* (New York: Russell Sage, 2003).
24. Diana Pearce, "The Feminization of Poverty: Women, Work and Welfare," *Urban and Social Change Review* (1978); 28–36.
25. *Green Book 2004*. U.S. House of Representatives, Committee on Ways and Means, 106th Cong.
26. Sandra Bass, Margie K. Shields, and Richard E. Behrman, "Children, Families, and Foster Care: Analysis and Recommendations," *Future of Children*, 14 (2004): 5–29.
27. R. Cook, *A National Evaluation of Title IV-E Foster Care Independent Living Programs for Youth, Phase 1* (Rockville, Md.: Westat, 1990); M. E.

Courtney and I. Piliavin, *Foster Youth Transitions to Adulthood: Outcomes 12 to 18 Months after Leaving Out-of-Home Care* (Madison: University of Wisconsin, 1998).

28. Dorothy Roberts, *Shattered Bonds: The Color of Child Welfare* (Basic Books, 2002).

29. Shelley Waters Boots and Rob Geen, *Family Care or Foster Care? How State Policies Affect Kinship Caregivers* (Washington, D.C.: Urban Institute Press, 2000).

30. McCaffrey, *Taxing Women*, 110–119.

31. Jacqueline E. King, *2003 Status Report on the Pell Grant Program* (Washington, D.C.: American Council on Education, Center for Policy Analysis, 2003).

32. College Board, "Trends in College Pricing 2003," at www.collegeboard.com (accessed April 7, 2007).

33. College Board, *Trends*, p. 4.

34. General Accounting Office, *Student Aid and Tax Benefits*, GAO-02–751 (Washington, D.C.: General Accounting Office, September 2002), 7.

35. College Board, "Trends in Student Aid 2004," at www.collegeboard.com (accessed August 2005); see also *Losing Ground: A National Status Report on the Affordability of American Higher Education* (San Jose, Calif.: National Center for Public Policy and Higher Education 2002), at www.highereducation.org (accessed March 25, 2007).

36. For a clear summary of these programs, see *Losing Ground,* Chapter 6.

37. General Accounting Office, *Student Aid and Tax Benefits*, 10.

38. Susan Dynarski, "Who Benefits from the Education Savings Incentives: Income, Educational Expectation, and the Value of the 529 and Coverdell" (National Bureau of Economic Research Working Paper 10470, www.nber.org, accessed August 2006).

39. General Accounting Office, *Student Aid and Tax Benefits*, 3.

40. David T. Ellwood and Jeffrey B. Liebman, "The Middle Class Parent Penalty: Child Benefits in the U.S. Tax Code" (National Bureau of Economic Research Working Paper no. W8031, December 2000); Paula England and Nancy Folbre, "Reforming the Social Family Contract: Public Support for Child Rearing in the U.S,"290–323 in Greg Duncan and Lindsay Chase-Lansdale, eds., *For Better or Worse: The Effects of Welfare Reform on Children* (New York: Russell Sage, 2002).

41. Catherine Hill and Virginia Reno, "Children's Stake in Social Security" (Social Security Brief no. 14, National Academy of Social Insurance, Washington, D.C., February 2003), 2.

42. Of all single-parent families with children maintained by mothers, fewer than 5 percent are maintained by widows (figures for the percentage of families maintained by fathers alone who are widowers are not available, but this is a relatively small number); *Green Book 2004,* table G-5. The number of children living with a disabled parent receiving Social Security is about the same

as the number living with a survivor of a deceased parent. Assuming that the average number of children in families with a deceased parent, a disabled parent, and a parent absent for another reason is about the same, the number of children living with a widowed or disabled parent is unlikely to exceed about 10 percent of all children living with a single mother.

43. *Social Security Survivors' Benefits,* Publication no. 05–10084, July 1999, at www.ssa.gov (accessed August 2005).

44. Ibid., 4.

45. The average benefit for nondisabled children under age eighteen was $538.30 per month, and for a widowed mother or father, $595.00 per month. Thus, the average monthly benefit for a widowed mother or father and two children amounted to $1,671.60. See "OASDI Current-Pay Benefits: Dependents and Survivors," Social Security Administration, *Annual Statistical Supplement 2001,* 216, table 5.F.

46. Hill and Reno, "Children's Stake," 2.

47. In 2000 the maximum benefit for a parent with two children ranged from a low of $1,968 per year in Alabama to $11,076 in Alaska. *Green Book 2004,* 7-38–7-39, table 7-10.

48. This calculation is based on average monthly benefits by state for TANF families in 2000 (*Green Book 2004,* 7-36, table 7-9, weighted by the number of recipients per state, calculated from total cash expenditures in 2001 (*Green Book 2004,* 7-69, table 7-21), and adjusted to reflect a family size of 3 rather than the average family size of 2.6.

49. Ibid., 7-12.

50. Ibid., 7-89.

51. Chris L. Jenkins, "Mental Illness Sends Many to Foster Care," *Washington Post,* November 29, 2004, B1.

52. This is based on estimates of average monthly payments for two-year-olds, nine-year-olds, and sixteen-year-olds in forty-four states, reported in the U.S. House Ways and Means Committee *Green Book 2003,* 11-28, table 11-9. It represents a lower bound because many states provided supplementary payments for specific expenditures.

53. Boots and Geen, *Family Care or Foster Care?*

54. Sandra Stukes Chipungu and Tricia B. Bent-Goodley, "Meeting the Challenges of Contemporary Foster Care," *Future of Children,* Special Issue on Children, Families, and Foster Care, 14 (2004): 74–93; A. C. Baum, S. J. Crase, and K. L. Crase, "Influences on the Decision to Become or Not Become a Foster Parent," *Families in Society* 82 (2001): 202–213; B. S. Fees, D. F. Stockdale, and S. J. Crase, "Satisfaction with Foster Parenting: Assessment One Year after Training, *Children and Youth Services Review* 20 (1998): 347–363.

55. The child-care tax credit was increased slightly in 2001, to $3,000 per child up to a maximum of $6,000 for two or more children.

56. William Gentry and Alison Hagy, "The Distributional Effects of the Tax

Treatment of Child Care Expenses," 99–134 in Martin Feldstein and James M. Poterba, eds., *Empirical Foundations of Household Taxation* (Chicago: University of Chicago Press, 1996).

57. Eligibility requires adjusted gross income of no more than $50,000 for a single filer or $100,000 for jointly filed returns.

58. GAO, *Student Aid and Tax Benefits*, 3.

59. Ibid., 4, 11–14.

60. Ken Battle and Michael Mendelson, eds., *Benefits for Children: A Four Country Study* (Ottawa: Caledon Institute of Social Policy, 2001), 19.

61. Holly Sutherland, "Can Child Poverty Be Abolished? Promises and Policy in the UK," *Economic and Labour Relations Review* 17 (2006): 7–32; Peter McDonald, "Reforming Family Support in Australia" *People and Place* 11 (2003): 1–15.

62. U.S. Social Security Administration, "Social Security Programs Throughout the World: Europe 2004" at www.ssa.gov/policy (accessed July 2005).

63. Institute on Taxation and Economic Policy, *Who Pays? A Distributional Analysis of the Tax Systems in All 50 STates,* 2nd ed. (Washington, D.C.: Institute on Taxation and Economic Policy, 2003).

64. Michael J. Graetz and Jerry L. Mashaw, *True Security: Rethinking American Social Insurance* (New Haven: Yale University Press, 1999).

65. *Effective Tax Rates, 1997 to 2000* (Washington, D.C.: Congressional Budget Office, 2003), 2.

9. *Public Spending on Children's Education and Health*

1. Samuel Preston, "Children and the Elderly: Divergent Paths for America's Dependents," *Demography* 21 (1984): 437.

2. *Statistical Abstract of the United States, 2001* (Washington, D.C.: Government Printing Office, 2001) table 49, 54.

3. Ibid., Table 51, 58.

4. Author's estimates, from 2001 Current Population Survey.

5. Christopher Ugen and Jeff Manza, "Democratic Contraction? The Political Consequences of Felon Disenfranchisement in the United States," *American Sociological Review* 67 (2002): 777–803.

6. Richard B. Freeman, "Fighting Turnout Burnout," *American Prospect* 15 (June 2004): 16.

7. C. Eugene Steuerle, "The Incredible Shrinking Budget for Working Families and Children" (National Budget Issues Report no. 1, Urban Institute, Washington, D.C., 2003).

8. Calculations based on Congressional Budget Office, *Federal Spending on the Elderly and Children* (Washington, D.C., 2000) 3, table 1.

9. This calculation is based on the value of the dependent exemption and child credit for a family in the 15 percent tax bracket, amounting to $2,288 (as described in Chapter 8), to their estimate of federal spending (excluding health) per child of $1,295.

10. Carmen DeNavas-Walt, Bernadette D. Proctor, and Cheryl Hill Lee, "Income, Poverty, and Health Insurance Coverage in the United States: 2005" (U.S. Census Bureau Current Population Report P60-231), 10–11, available at www.census.gov/prod/2006pubs/p60-231.pdf (accessed April 18, 2007); Rebecca L. Clark, Rosalind Berkowitz King, Christopher Spiro, and C. Eugene Steuerle, "Federal Expenditures on Children: 1960–1997, Assessing the New Federalism" (Occasional Paper 45, Urban Institute Press, Washington, D.C., 2001); Pati et al., "Generational Differences in U.S. Public Spending."

11. William Nordhaus, "The Health of Nations: The Contribution of Improved Health to Living Standards," 9–40 in K. Murphy and R. Topen, eds., *Measuring the Gains from Medical Research* (Chicago: University of Chicago Press, 2003); Katharine G. Abraham and Christopher Mackie, eds., *Beyond the Market: Designing Nonmarket Accounts for the United States* (Washington, D.C.: National Academies Press, 2005), chap. 12.

12. James Heintz, Nancy Folbre, and the Center for Popular Economics, *The Ultimate Field Guide to the U.S. Economy* (New York: New Press, 2000), 38.

13. Congressional Budget Office, *Federal Spending on the Elderly and Children, 2000,* 3, table 1, and 5, table 2.

14. General Accounting Office, Report 02–431R "Nursing Homes: Quality of Care More Related to Staffing than Spending," June 13, 2002; Report 02–312, "Nursing Homes: More Can be Done to Protect Residents," March 2002.

15. Peter Cunningham and James Kirby, "Children's Health Coverage: A Quarter-Century of Change," *Health Affairs* 23 (September–October 2004): 27–38; Genevieve Kenney and Debbie Chang, "The State Children's Health Insurance Program: Successes, Shortcomings, and Challenges," *Health Affairs* 23 (September–October 2004): 51–63.

16. Thomas M. Selden, Julie L. Hudson, and Jessica S. Banthin, "Tracking Changes in Eligibility and Coverage among Children, 1996–2002," *Health Affairs* 23 (September–October 2004): 39–41. This estimate is slightly higher than that offered in Cunningham and Kirby, "Children's Health Coverage," but it is based on a more accurate source, the Medical Expenditure Panel Survey.

17. P. W. Newacheck et al., "Access to Health Care for Children with Special Health Care Needs," *Pediatrics* 105, Part 1 (April 2000): 760–766; and Institute of Medicine, *Health Insurance Is a Family Matter* (Washington: National Academies Press, 2002).

18. Anne C. Beal, "Policies to Reduce Racial and Ethnic Disparities in Child Health and Health Care," *Health Affairs* 23 (September–October 2004): 171–180.

19. Susmita Pati, Ron Keren, Evaline A. Alessandrini, and Donald F. Schwarz, "Generational Differences in U.S. Public Spending, 1980–2000," *Health Affairs* 23 (September–October 2004): 131–142; Paul W. Newacheck and A. E. Benjamin, "Intergenerational Equity and Public Spending," *Health Affairs* 23 (September–October 2004): 142–147.

20. Clark et al., "Federal Expenditures on Children," 3.
21. The Congressional Budget Office estimates of spending on the elderly and children in 2000 show that the average spending on children, not counting either medical or educational spending categories, came to about $1,010 in 2000. Adding in the value of the dependent exemption and child tax credit in the 15 percent tax bracket in that year, $2,288, yields $3,298. Adding in the value of primary and secondary educational expenditures per capita of $8,212 yields $11,510. This is higher than the estimate of federal nonmedical spending on the elderly from the CBO of $10,900, even without inclusion of spending on child care or higher education. Most state and local spending on the elderly falls in the category of medical expenses.
22. National Center for Education Statistics, 2003, Digest of Education Statistics 2003, table 166, at http://nces.ed/gov/programs/digest (accessed March 27, 2007).
23. *Statistical Abstract of the U.S., 2004–2005*, table 221.
24. David Card and Abigail Payne, "School Finance Reform, the Distribution of School Spending, and the Distribution of SAT Scores" (National Bureau of Economic Research Working Paper 6766, 1998, www.nber.org, accessed August 2005).
25. Elizabeth Warren and Amelia Warren Tyagi, *The Two-Income Trap: Why Middle-Class Mothers and Fathers Are Going Broke* (New York: Basic Books, 2003).
26. Michael A. Rebell, "Why Adequacy Lawsuits Matter," *Education Week*, August 11, 2004, at www.edweek.org (accessed August 2005).
27. Tomas A. Downes and David N. Figlio, "Economic Inequality and the Provision of Schooling," *Economic Policy Review* (September 1999): 99–110.
28. *Statistical Abstract of the U.S., 2001*, table 242.
29. Jack P. Shonkoff and Deborah Phillips, eds., *From Neurons to Neighborhoods: The Science of Early Childhood Development* (Washington, D.C.: National Academy Press, 2000); Jay Bainbridge, Marcia Meyers, Sakiko Tanaka, and Jane Waldfogel, "Who Gets an Early Education? Family Income and the Enrollment of Three- to Five-Year-Olds from 1968 to 2000," *Social Science Quarterly* 86 (September 2005): 724–745.
30. *Statistical Abstract of the United States: 2004–2005*, table 222.
31. Hyon B. Shin, "School Enrollment—Social and Economic Characteristics of Students: October 2003" (Current Population Reports P20–554, U.S. Census Bureau, 2005), 3.
32. Bainbridge et al., "Who Gets an Early Education?"
33. Jennifer Mezey, Rachel Schumacher, Mark Greenberg, Joan Lombardi, and John Hutchins, "Unfinished Agenda: Child Care for Low-Income Families since 1996" (Center for Law and Social Policy, Washington, D.C., March 2002), 2.
34. Jennifer Mezey and Brooke Richie, "Welfare Dollars No Longer an Increasing Source of Child Care Funding," (Center for Law and Social Policy, Washington, D.C., August 6, 2003).
35. Mezey et al., "Unfinished Agenda"; see also Jennifer Mezey, "Threatened

Progress: U.S. in Danger of Losing Ground on Child Care for Low-Income Working Families" (Center for Law and Social Policy, Brief no. 2, Washington, D.C., June, 2003).

36. Kevin Dougherty, "Financing Higher Education in the United States: Structure, Trends, and Issues" (manuscript, Teacher's College, Columbia University, May 25, 2004), 9.

37. College Board, *Trends in Student Aid 2004,* at www.collegeboard.com (accessed August 2005); see also "Losing Ground: A National Status Report on the Affordability of American Higher Education" (National Center for Public Policy and Higher Education, San Jose, Calif., May 2002, at www.highereducation.org, accessed August 2005).

38. Pell Institute, "Indicators of Opportunity in Higher Education" (Fall 2004), at www.pellinstitute.org (accessed April 3, 2007), 7.

39. See National Center for Education Statistics, "International Education Indicators," at http://nces.ed.gov/surveys (accessed August 2005).

40. John Palmer, Timothy Smeeding, and Barbara Torrey, eds., *The Vulnerable* (Washington, D.C.: Urban Institute Press, 1988); Timothy Smeeding, Sheldon Danziger, and Lee Rainwater, "Making Social Policy Work for Children," 368–389 in Giovanni Andrea Cornea and Sheldon Danziger, eds., *Child Poverty and Deprivation in the Industrialized Countries, l945–1995* (Florence, Italy: UNICEF International Child Development Centre, 1997); Sheila B. Kamerman and Alfred J. Kahn, *Starting Right: How America Neglects Its Youngest Children and What We Can Do about It* (New York: Oxford University Press, 1995); Sheila B. Kamerman and Alfred J. Kahn, eds., *Family Change and Family Policies in Great Britain, Canada, New Zealand, and the United States* (New York: Oxford University Press, 1997).

41. Karen Christopher, Paula England, Katherin Ross, Timothy Smeeding, and Sara McLanahan, "Women's Poverty Relative to Men's in Affluent Nations: Single Motherhood and the State," 199–220 in Koen Vleminckx and Timothy Smeeding, eds., *Child Well-being, Child Poverty, and Child Policy in Modern Nations* (London: Policy Press, 2001).

42. Children's Defense Fund, *Children in the States, 2001* (Washington, D.C.: Children's Defense Fund, 2001), v. Differences in state efforts to promote family economic security as well as child poverty rates for 2000 are available from the National Center for Children in Poverty at Columbia University, "Map and Track 2000," at www.nccp.org/pub_mat00.html (accessed March 2007) See also Marcia K. Meyers, Janet C. Gornick, and Laura Peck, "Packaging Support for Low-Income Families: Policy Variation across the United States," *Journal of Policy Analysis and Management* 20 (Summer 2001): 457–483.

43. Children's Defense Fund, *Children in the States, 2000,* at www.childrensdefense.org/states/2000_data_introduction.htm (accessed July 4, 2001).

44. Meyers et al., "Packaging Support for Low-Income Families."

45. *UNICEF Report Card 6, Child Poverty in Rich Countries, 2005* (Florence, Italy: UNICEF Innocenti Research Centre, 2005).

46. Irwin Garfinkel, Lee Rainwater, and Timothy Smeeding, "A Reexamination of Welfare States and Inequality in Rich Nations: How In-Kind Transfers and Indirect Taxes Change the Story," *Journal of Policy Analysis and Management* 25 (Fall 2006): 897–919.

47. Barbara Starfield, "U.S. Child Health: What's Amiss, and What Should Be Done About It?" *Health Affairs* 23 (September–October 2004): 165–170.

48. Steven Haider, Alison Jacknowitz, and Robert F. Schoeni, "Welfare Work Requirements and Child Well-being: Evidence from the Effects on Breast-feeding," *Demography* 40 (August 2003): 479–497.

49. Christopher Ruhm, "Parental Leave and Child Health," *Journal of Health Economics* 19 (2000): 931–960.

50. Shelly Phipps, "Health Outcomes for Children in Canada, England, Norway and the United States," *Social Indicators Research* 80 (January 2007): 179–221.

51. Centers for Disease Control and Prevention. "Healthy People 2010" 2003, Chapter 15 (National Center for Health Statistics, at www.healthypeople.gov, accessed August 2006).

52. Preston, "Children and the Elderly."

53. In an important early study Robert Haveman and Barbara Wolfe defined public investments in children as the sum of means-tested programs targeted to them and educational expenditures. See Haveman and Wolfe, "The Determinants of Children's Attainments: A Review of Methods and Findings," *Journal of Economic Literature* 33 (1995): 1830.

54. Congressional Budget Office, *Federal Spending on the Elderly and Children, 2000,* at www.cbo.gov (accessed April 4, 2007); Clark et al., "Federal Expenditures on Children"; Pati et al., "Generational Differences in U.S. Public Spending."

55. Christopher Howard, *The Hidden Welfare State: Tax Expenditures and Social Policy in the United States* (Princeton: Princeton University Press, 1999); Jacob Hacker, *The Battle over Public and Private Social Benefits in the United States* (New York: Cambridge University Press, 2002).

56. Miles Corak, Christine Lietz, and Holly Sutherland, "The Impact of Tax and Transfer Systems on Children in the European Union" (Innocenti Working Paper 2005-4, UNICEF), and Horatio Levy, Christine Lietz, and Holly Sutherland, "Strategies to Support Children in the European Union: Recent Alternative Tax-Benefit Reforms in Austria, Spain, and the United Kingdom, EUROMOD Working Paper EM1/0/05, 2005).

57. Laurence J. Kotlikoff, *Generational Accounting* (New York: Free Press, 1992).

58. Jay Bainbridge, "Who Supports Children in the U.S.?" (Ph.D. dissertation, School of Social Work, Columbia University, 2002). See also Irwin Garfinkel, "Economic Security for Children: From Means Testing and Bifurcation to Universality," 33–82 in I. Garfinkel, J. Hochschild, and S. McLanahan, eds., *Social Policies for Children* (Washington, D.C.: Brookings Institution Press, 1996).

59. Samuel Preston, "Children and the Elderly," 451.

60. Ester Duflo, "Grandmothers and Granddaughters: Old Age Pension and Intrahousehold Allocation in South Africa," *World Bank Economic Review* 17 (2003): 1–26.

61. Robert Barro, "Are Government Bonds Net Wealth?" *Journal of Political Economy* 82 (1974): 1095–1117.

10. Who Should Pay for the Kids?

1. Fred R. Harris, ed., *The Baby Bust: Who Will Do the Work? Who Will Pay the Taxes?* (New York: Rowman and Littlefield, 2006); Phillip Longman, *The Empty Cradle: How Falling Birthrates Threaten World Prosperity and What to Do about It* (New York: Basic Books, 2004).

2. For an earlier version of some of the arguments presented here, see Paula England and Nancy Folbre, "Who Should Pay for the Kids?" *Annals of the American Academy of Political and Social Science* 563 (1999): 194–207.

3. Thomas C. Schelling, *Choice and Consequence: Perspectives of an Errant Economist* (Cambridge: Harvard University Press, 1984), 120.

4. Katharine G. Abraham and Christopher Mackie, eds., *Beyond the Market: Designing Nonmarket Accounts for the United States* (Washington, D.C.: National Academies Press, 2005), 80.

5. Dale Jorgenson and Barbara Fraumeni, "The Accumulation of Human and Non-Human Capital, 1948–1984," 227–282 in R. E. Lipsey and H. S. Tice, eds., *The Measurement of Savings, Investment, and Wealth* (Chicago: University of Chicago Press, 1989).

6. Michael Grossman, "Education and Nonmarket Outcomes" 577–633 in Eric Hanushek and Finis Welch, eds., *Handbook of the Economics of Education*, vol. 1 (Amsterdam: Elsevier Science, 2006); Janet Currie and Enrico Moretti, "Mother's Education and the Intergenerational Transmission of Human Capital: Evidence from College Openings," *Quarterly Journal of Economics* 118 (2003): 1495–1532; Kevin Milligan, Enrico Moretti, and Philip Orepoulos, "Does Education Improve Citizenship? Evidence from the U.S. and the U.K.," *Journal of Public Economics* 88 (2004): 1667–1695.

7. Michelle Budig, Paula England, and Nancy Folbre, "Wages of Virtue: The Relative Pay of Care Work," *Social Problems* 49 (2000): 455–473.

8. Jim Hightower, "Going Down the Road: The Wellstone Way," *Nation*, January 27, 2003, 8.

9. James Heckman, "Skill Formation and the Economics of Investing in Disadvantaged Children," *Science* 312 (2006): 1900–1902; Robert G. Lynch, "Exceptional Returns: Economic, Fiscal, and Social Benefits of Investment in Early Childhood Development" (Economic Policy Institute, Washington, D.C., 2004).

10. Lawrence Schweinhart, *Significant Benefits: The High/Scope Perry Preschool Study through Age 27* (Ypsilanti, Mich.: High/Scope Press, 1993).

11. Art Rolnick and Rob Grunewald, "Early Childhood Development: Eco-

nomic Development with a High Public Return" (Federal Reserve Bank of Minneapolis, March 2003, at http://minneapolisfed.org/, accessed April 4, 2007).

12. Christopher B. Forrest and Anne W. Riley, "Childhood Origins of Adult Health: A Basis for Life-Course Health Policy," *Health Affairs* 23 (September–October 2004): 155–164.

13. Paul H. Wise, "The Transformation of Child Health in the United States," *Health Affairs*, 23 (September–October 2004): 9–25.

14. Richard Rothstein, *Class and Schools: Using Social, Economic, and Educational Reform to Close the Black-White Achievement Gap* (New York: Teachers College Press, 2004); Valerie E. Lee, *Inequality at the Starting Gate: Social Background Differences in Achievement as Children Begin School* (Washington, D.C.: Economic Policy Institute, 2002).

15. Greg J. Duncan and Jeanne Brooks-Gunn, eds., *Consequences of Growing Up Poor* (New York: Russell Sage, 1999).

16. Susan Eaton, *What Money Can't Buy: Family Income and Children's Life Chances* (Cambridge: Harvard University Press, 1998).

17. Greg J. Duncan, Aletha C. Huston, and Thomas S. Weisner, *Higher Ground: New Hope for the Working Poor and Their Children* (New York: Russell Sage Foundation, 2007).

18. Kingsley Davis, "Reproductive Institutions and the Pressure for Population," *Sociological Review* 29, 3 (1937): 289–306; Andrew J. Cherlin, "The Deinstitutionalization of American Marriage," *Journal of Marriage and Family* 66 (2004): 848–861.

19. Gary Becker and Kevin Murphy, "The Family and the State, *Journal of Law and Economics* 31 (1988): 1–18; Ronald Lee, "Demographic Change, Welfare and Intergenerational Transfers: A Global Overview" (Center for the Economics and Demography of Aging Working Paper, University of California at Berkeley, 2003).

20. Robert Shiller, *The New Financial Order: Risk in the 21st Century* (Princeton: Princeton University Press, 2003).

21. Richard Musgrave, *Public Finance in a Democratic Society,* Vol. 2, *Fiscal Doctrine, Growth and Institutions* (New York: New York University Press, 1986).

22. John Myles, "A New Social Contract for the Elderly," 130–172 in Gøsta Esping-Andersen, with Duncan Gallie, Anton Hemerijck, and John Myles, *Why We Need a New Welfare State* (New York: Oxford University Press, 2002).

23. Ron Lee, "Demographic Change."

24. Estimate based on *Statistical Abstract of the U.S., 2002,* 13, table 11.

25. Ibid., 424, table 641.

26. Robert Eisner, *The Total Incomes System of Accounts* (Chicago: University of Chicago Press, 1989).

27. Ronald D. Lee and Timothy W. Miller, "The Current Fiscal Impact of Immigrants and Their Descendants: Beyond the Immigrant Household," 183–205 in James P. Smith and Barry Edmonston, eds., *The Immigration Debate:*

Studies on the Economic, Demographic, and Fiscal Effects of Immigration (Washington, D.C.: National Research Council, 1998).

28. Devesh Kapur and John McHale, *Give Us Your Best and Brightest: The Global Hunt for Talent and Its Impact on the Developing World* (Washington, D.C.: Center for Global Development, 2005).

29. Laurence J. Kotlikoff, *Generational Accounting: Knowing Who Pays, and When, for What We Spend* (New York: Free Press, 1992); Laurence J. Kotlikoff and Scott Burns, *The Coming Generational Storm: What You Need to Know about America's Economic Future* (Cambridge: MIT Press, 2004).

30. David Collard, "Generational Accounting and Generational Transfers," *Ageing Horizons* 1 (2004): 1–10; Robert Haveman, "Should Generational Accounts Replace Public Budgets and Deficits?" *Journal of Economic Perspectives*, 8(1994): 95–111.

31. Adam Carasso and C. Eugene Steuerle, "The Hefty Penalty on Marriage Facing Many Households with Children," *Future of Children* 15 (2005): 157–175.

32. Gary S. Becker, *A Treatise on the Family*, enlarged ed. (Cambridge: Harvard University Press, 1991).

33. Elissa Braunstein and Nancy Folbre, "To Honor or Obey: The Patriarch as Residual Claimant," *Feminist Economics* 7, 1 (2001): 25–54.

34. Sara McLanahan, "Diverging Destinies: How Children Are Faring under the Second Demographic Transition," *Demography* 41 (2004): 607–627.

35. Paul Demeny, "Re-Linking Fertility Behavior and Economic Security in Old Age: A Pronatalist Reform," *Population and Development Review* 13 (1987): 128–132; Shirley P. Burggraf, *The Feminine Economy and Economic Man* (Reading, Mass.: Addison-Wesley, 1997); Julian L. Simon, "Re-Linking Fertility Behavior and Economic Security in Old Age: Comment on Demeny," *Population and Development Review* 14 (1988): 327–331.

36. Longman, *The Empty Cradle*.

37. Anne Alstott, *No Exit: What Parents Owe Their Children and What Societies Owe Parents* (New York: Oxford University Press, 2004).

38. J. Caldwell, P. Caldwell, and P. McDonald, "Policy Responses to Low Fertility and Its Consequences: A Global Survey," *Journal of Population Research* 19 (2002): 1–24.

39. Francesca Bettio and Paola Villa, "A Mediterranean Perspective on the Breakdown of the Relationship between Participation and Fertility," *Cambridge Journal of Economics* 22 (March 1998): 137–171; Peter McDonald, "Gender Equity in Theories of Fertility Transition," *Population and Development Review* 26 (2000): 427–439.

40. Hans-Peter Kohler, Francesco C. Billari, and Jose Antonio Ortega, "Low Fertility in Europe: Causes, Implications and Policy Options," 48–109 in F. R. Harris, ed., *The Baby Bust: Who Will Do the Work? Who Will Pay the Taxes?* (Lanham, Md.: Rowman and Littlefield, 2005).

41. Berna Miller Torr and Susan E. Short, "Second Births and the Second Shift," *Population and Development Review* 38 (2004): 109–130.

42. Peter McDonald, "Gender Equity."

43. Janet Gornick and Marcia Meyers, *Families That Work* (New York: Russell Sage, 2003); Eileen Appelbaum, Thomas Bailey, Peter Berg, and Arne L. Kalleberg, *Shared Work, Valued Care: New Norms for Organizing Market Work and Unpaid Care Work* (Washington, D.C.: Economic Policy Institute, 2002).

44. Olivier J. Blanchard, "Is Europe Falling Behind," *The Globalist*, June 8, 2004, www.theglobalist.com (accessed August 18, 2006).

45. For comparative data on market income of families with children, see Luxembourg Income Study, Key Figures, "Distribution of Children Living in Different Income Households," at www.lisproject.org/keyfigures.htm (accessed March, 2007).

46. Philippe Van Parijs, "The Disfranchisement of the Elderly, and Other Attempts to Secure Intergenerational Justice," *Philosophy and Public Affairs* 27 (1998): 292–333.

47. Author's calculations from the 2001 Current Population Survey.

Index